Applied Ecological Psychology for Schools Within Communities

Assessment and Intervention

Applied Ecological Psychology for Schools Within Communities

Assessment and Intervention

Edited by

Jody L. Swartz
Northern Arizona University
University of Wisconsin–Superior

William E. Martin, Jr.
Northern Arizona University

 LAWRENCE ERLBAUM ASSOCIATES, PUBLISHERS
1997   Mahwah, New Jersey   London

Lawrence Erlbaum Associates, Inc., Publishers
10 Industrial Avenue
Mahwah, New Jersey 07430

Library of Congress Cataloging-in-Publication Data

Applied ecological psychology for schools within communities : assessment and
    intervention / edited by Jody L. Swartz, William E. Martin, Jr.
        p. cm.
Includes bibliographical references and index.
ISBN 0-8058-1990-8 (alk. paper)
    1. School psychology.   2. Environmental psychology.   I.
Swartz, Jody L. II. Martin, William E., Jr.
LB1027.55.A66   1997
371.7'13—dc21   97–10287
                                                              CIP

Books published by Lawrence Erlbaum Associates are printed on acid-free paper,
and their bindings are chosen for strength and durability.

Printed in the United States of America
10 9 8 7 6 5 4 3 2 1

Contents

Foreword
Edison J. Trickett   ix

PART I: INTRODUCTION

1   Ecological Psychology Theory: Historical Over-
        view and Application to Educational Ecosystems
        Jody L. Swartz and William E. Martin, Jr.   3

PART II: ASSESSMENT AND INTERVENTION WITH STUDENTS

2   Characteristics of the Learning Environment:
        Students, Teachers, and Their Interactions
        Lena R. Gaddis and Leilani Hatfield   31

3   Ecological Interventions With Students
        Jane Close Conoley and Pamela Carrington Rotto   55

PART III: ASSESSMENT AND INTERVENTION WITH TEACHERS
        IN CLASSROOMS

4   Principles and Application of Ecological
        Assessment for Teachers
        Mary J. McLellan and Irene Sanchez   77

5   Ecosystemic Intervention With Teachers:
       A Collaborative Approach
       Julia S. Shaftel and Marvin J. Fine   **95**

PART IV: ASSESSMENT AND INTERVENTION WITH SCHOOLS

6   Assessment and Interventions With Schools
       Eugene R. Moan and Ramona N. Mellott   **117**

7   Developing an Ecological Mind-Set
       on School–Community Collaboration
       Edison J. Trickett   **139**

PART V: ASSESSMENT AND INTERVENTION WITH COMMUNITIES

8   School-to-Work Transition: Ecological
       Considerations for Career Development
       Edna Mora Szymanski   **167**

9   Reconnecting Schools With Families
       of Juvenile Offenders
       Sonja K. Schoenwald, Scott W. Henggeler,
       Michael J. Brondino, and John C. Donkervoet   **187**

PART VI: CONCLUSION

10 Integrated Application of Applied Ecological
       Psychology in Schools Within Communities
       William E. Martin, Jr. and Jody L. Swartz   **209**

       Future Directions: Specification, Validation,
       and Funding of Ecologically Based Interventions
       for Schools Within Communities
       Scott W. Henggeler   **221**

Author Index 225

Subject Index 235

Foreword

Edison J. Trickett
University of Maryland, College Park

Thomas Kuhn, in the *Structure of Scientific Revolutions* (1970) discusses the difference in the evolution of new paradigms between persuasion and conversion, the former referring to a translation of a theory or worldview into one's own language and the latter to the incorporation of its tenets into a lived worldview which permeates one's scientific endeavors. Through living and breathing the new paradigm, one's world is literally changed, a process well articulated by Roger Barker (1978) in describing the evolution of his eco-behavioral perspective:

> The towns I observed from the Illinois Central train in 1940 are still there and easily recognized despite some changes. ... But the changes in the towns are less dramatic than the changes in my comprehension of them. In 1940 I only asked "what do people do in these towns?" In 1977 I ask in addition "what do these towns do to people?" (p. 285). In 1940 I looked on the towns as collections of people, each person a dynamic entity freely carrying out his plans within the environment the town provided, ... an environment that, although frustrating and constraining to some extent, was a relatively stable, reliable ground for action. In 1977, I see the towns as assemblies of dynamic, homeostatic entities where people are components. These are behavior settings, and within them people do not act in relation to a relatively fixed, dependable environment of benefits, deficiencies, and constraints because stores, meetings, classes, and all other behavior settings have plans for their human components and armories of alternative ways of reinforcing their plans (p. 286). In 1940, I looked on the towns as a psychologist; in 1977 I also see them as an eco-behavioral scientist. (p. 285)

The chapters in this book provide an important step in the conversation among applied social scientists relating to the persuasiveness of an ecological perspective and the conversion of adherents to living, thinking, and acting ecologically. To do so means the dismissal of the idea that behavior can be interpreted and understood without reference to context and how context affects the meaning of behavior to individuals; that the oft-heard phrase "it all depends on the individual" be taken to include an appreciation of the individual's sociocultural history and perception of current contextual constraints and options for achieving goals; that intervention no longer be viewed as the task of developing technologies that can be easily transported across varying social contexts.

This book emerges in the context of varying changes in American society that propel the idea of context to the forefront of our collective consciousness. The changing demographics of the school-age population; the shrinking economic resources available to school systems; the increasing disparity in wealth in the United States between the rich and the poor, which differentially affect the school-age populations in urban and suburban areas; and policy initiatives such as the recent welfare legislation, which impacts adversely not only on many children and adolescents born in the United States, but on particular segments of immigrant and refugee children and adolescents as well, all provide a cultural and contextual framework within which teachers must teach, students must learn, administrators must innovate and generate hope, and parents must find ways to support their children's education in often violent and drug-available neighborhoods. Interventions carried out in these varied ecological contexts can ignore the power of local ecology only at their own peril. Indeed, if there is one consistent intervention message in this book's chapters, it is that the day of the context-free intervention is long past. The ecology of schooling and the ecology of the lives of students must take center stage if schools are to serve their social mission adequately.

Although it is unlikely that any single volume could scratch all the itches implied in the foregoing, the current work makes giant strides in focusing on classroom interaction, intervention in schools, school–community interdependence, school-to-work transitions, and the relations among juvenile offenders and their schools. Together, they make the case for the importance of different levels of analysis of the ecological environment as it affects individuals, that problems in the school setting are multiply determined and can thus be approached in terms of intervention from a variety of leverage points, and that thinking and acting ecologically, whether one is a teacher, administrator, consultant, or researcher, can provide an appreciation of the diversity and variety of real life lived in real contexts that are really different from one another.

While sensitizing the reader to the importance of culture and context as it involves the lives of individual children and adolescents in schools, the current volume also whets the appetite for the next step in ecological thinking applied to schools, a focus on schools as the level of ecological analysis and the development of interventions designed to alter their structure, function, social and educational climate, and relations to parents. Such an emphasis would focus less on an ecological perspective on individual student problems and more on promoting systemic competence to generate and sustain resources for both individual problem solving and the development of the school as a competent community. One way of peeling the ecological onion is to keep thinking at the next higher level of analysis. The editors have made that task considerably easier by their thoughtful construction of this book.

REFERENCES

Barker, R. G., & Associates. (1978). *Habitats, environments, and human behavior.* San Francisco: Jossey-Bass.

Kuhn, T. S. (1970). *The structure of scientific revolutions.* Chicago: University of Chicago Press.

I

INTRODUCTION

1

Ecological Psychology Theory: Historical Overview and Application to Educational Ecosystems

Jody L. Swartz
Northern Arizona University
University of Wisconsin–Superior
William E. Martin, Jr.
Northern Arizona University

The conception that an individual's developmental and adaptational processes are influenced by his or her interaction with the environment has long been discussed in the psychological and educational literature. Although there is an abundance of theoretical applications and research supporting this concept, the predominant trend has been to emphasize the properties of the person. As a result, one is left to assume that the genesis of difficulties in adaptation lies in internal or personal states and traits of the individual. According to Bronfenbrenner (1979), "There has been a hypertrophy of research focusing on the properties of the person and only the most rudimentary conception and characterization of the environment in which the person is found" (p. 16). Although the growth of the field of ecological psychology is evidenced by an increase in research, there still exists little information on how to conceptualize concerns and apply interventions from an ecological perspective (Hewett, 1987; Johnson, Johnson, & DeMatta, 1991). Indeed, it continues to be true that "It … is not much clearer how one creates an ecological classroom, an ecological curriculum, or trains an ecological teacher" (Hewett, 1987, p. 62).

The importance of using an ecological approach to understanding and effecting positive change for problems in ecosystems such as schools and communities must be underscored, particularly when considering the multiple and multifaceted environments in which the individual functions.

Communities, the families and schools located within them, and the individuals comprising these systems are integral parts of ecological networks. Consequently, positive intervention outcomes rely on understanding these networks. This is particularly true for school-aged youth who are influenced not only by the school, family, peer, and community systems in which they function, but also by the complex interrelationships among these systems (Christenson, 1993; Hobbs, 1966). However, this is an often difficult and cumbersome task for educators, parents, and school systems to undertake (Hendrickson, Gable, & Shores, 1987). To this end, the following eight chapters provide a brief review of the foundations of ecological psychology and focus on the functional application of ecological psychology for schools within communities. To provide a more comprehensive understanding of the development and current status of ecological psychology, we discuss the theoretical undergirdings of ecological psychology, review past research using the ecological approach, and suggest the role and function of an applied ecological approach to working with individuals who experience difficulties in adaptation in their schools and, consequently, lack "fit" with their environment.

PHILOSOPHICAL UNDERPINNINGS
OF ECOLOGICAL PSYCHOLOGY

Collectively, ecological psychology theories endeavor to compensate for the paucity of research on the characteristics and impact of the environment (Johnson, Swartz, & Martin, 1995). Ecological psychology theories, in the broadest sense, strive to explain the natural patterns of stimuli, both social and physical, which exist in the individual's immediate environment and subsequently impact the individual's behavior and experience (LeCompte, 1972). When considering that the relationship between the individual and the environment is continuous, reciprocal, and interdependent (Bijou & Baer, 1978; Evans, Gable, & Evans, 1993), it is clear that as individuals and environments interact, new stimuli emerge that require constant adaptation for both the individual and the environment to maintain a balance, or a good match. As such, ecological approaches are concerned with how to optimize this adaptation process and, in doing so, examine both the match and/or mismatch between an individual and the reciprocal nature of the person–environment association (Conoley & Haynes, 1992; Fine, 1985).

When an individual experiences difficulties in adaptation, it is explained in terms of the lack of fit between the existing properties of the individual and the environment—a discordance in the system (Hewett, 1987). It is important to keep in mind, however, that this discordance is sometimes specific to certain settings and the variables within those settings rather than pervasive behavioral deficits seen across settings (Evans et al., 1993; Hendrickson et al., 1987). Regardless of whether the difficulties are situation specific or cross-situational, an ecological understanding of the student is of paramount importance. For students, who are at the same time participants and observers in several distinct and overlapping settings, it is essential to explore this person–environment interaction. More specifically, to adequately understand individuals requires the simultaneous examination of both the situational influences and the adaptive processes employed by individuals to select and create environments (Moos, 1980; Smead, 1982) and then to work with the knowledge gained to help individuals and their environment achieve a successful adaptation or adjustment process.

DEVELOPMENT OF ECOLOGICAL PSYCHOLOGY AS AN APPLIED PSYCHOLOGY

When reviewing the development of applied ecological psychology, one limitation lies in its sometimes confusing and complex theoretical history. Perhaps it is this confusion that has led some educational researchers, such as Hilton (1987), to presume that an ecological orientation is not grounded in theory. Contrary to this supposition, ecological psychology has a long history tracing back to the early 1900s. In 1909, counseling psychologist Frank Parsons[1] proposed that satisfaction can be achieved through knowledge of both individuals and environments, not merely one or the other. This premise of person–environment psychology was later expanded in the interactionist framework under which ecological psychology is subsumed. Specifically, as early as 1924, Kantor suggested that, as the person is a function of the environment and the environment is a function of the person, the unit of study in psychology should be the individual as that individual interacts with the contexts which produce behavior. In other words, behavior is a function of the interaction between the person and the environment, B = $f(P,E)$. A decade later, Koffka (1935), a gestalt psychologist, further delineated the environmental components of the interactionist model into the geographical environment that is shared by individuals (i.e., all individuals in a classroom are in the same geographical environment) and the

---

[1]Dawis (1992) provided an excellent analysis of the development of the individual differences tradition and its relationship to person–environment psychology.

behavioral (psychological) environment that is a result of the interaction between the geographical environment and the individual (i.e., how an individual perceives the geographical environment). According to Koffka's framework, understanding an individual's behavior cannot be gleaned from examining either the person or the environment in isolation, but is dependent upon simultaneous consideration of both.

Although the roots of the ecological model appear to have a long history (see Ekehammer, 1974; Schmid, 1987; Walsh & Betz, 1995), it was not until the 1930s that ecological psychology as a separate domain began to emerge through the work of Kurt Lewin (1935, 1951) and later Roger Barker and his colleagues (Barker, 1965, 1968, 1978; Barker & Gump, 1964; Barker & Schoggen, 1973; Barker & Wright, 1954; Gump, 1975; Wicker, 1973, 1983, 1992). Through these and other theorists, the primary assumption undergirding ecological psychology emerged: Behavior is a function of the person and the environment, and the unit of study is the natural environment. Although the underlying premise of ecological psychology retained its original intent, theorists approached the ecological "problem" from different perspectives, placed along a continuum from a focus on the more subjective or the psychological features of the environment to the more objective or the social and physical features of the environment. According to Allport (cited in Fuhrer, 1990), this difference is referred to as the inside–outside problem or the ecological–psychological gap between the actual and perceived environment. Within this gap, and similarly important, is that different theorists and researchers tend to organize their definitions and constructs according to individual or group explanatory models, that is, whether the unit of study should be the individual or the group. Taken together, the actual environment versus perceived environment and the individual versus the group, both historical and contemporary psychologists who have impacted our understanding of the person–environment relationships can be conceived of as conceptualizing behavior in terms of an integration of the following four dimensions: perceived environment, actual environment, individual, and group. Figure 1.1 presents a two-dimensional graphic depicting this relationship between the historical and contemporary theorists and researchers in ecological psychology.

Actual or Perceived? Individual or Group?

Historical Theorists

$B = f(Perceived[Environment] \times Individual[Person])$. Theorists more interested in the psychological features of the environment, such as Lewin

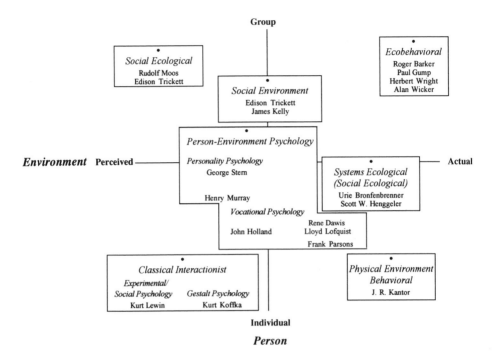

Group

Social Ecological
Rudolf Moos
Edison Trickett

Ecobehavioral
Roger Barker
Paul Gump
Herbert Wright
Alan Wicker

Social Environment
Edison Trickett
James Kelly

Person-Environment Psychology

Environment Perceived —— Personality Psychology
George Stern

Henry Murray

—— Actual

Systems Ecological
(Social Ecological)
Urie Bronfenbrenner
Scott W. Henggeler

Vocational Psychology
John Holland

Rene Dawis
Lloyd Lofquist
Frank Parsons

Classical Interactionist
Experimental/
Social Psychology   Gestalt Psychology
Kurt Lewin   Kurt Koffka

Physical Environment
Behavioral
J. R. Kantor

Individual
Person

FIG. 1.1.   Matrix of influential ecological psychology theorists by subspecialty.

(1935, 1951), emphasized the people's phenomenological experience of their environmental situation in understanding individuals. Although Lewin is considered an ecological psychologist and an experimental social psychologist, his training and primary orientation in gestalt psychology is evident in his emphasis on consideration of the whole situation rather than either the person or the environment piecemeal. Lewin (1935) posited that behavior is a function of the whole environment, including the mutually dependent interaction between the person and the environment, from which individuals generate subjective observations about the environment, themselves, and their behavior. Lewin termed this psychological environment the life space, which is defined as all aspects of individuals and their subjective environments that impact behavior. According to Lewin, the life space is interdependent with the nonpsychological (objective) environment. Although Lewin accepted that the nonpsychological environment impacts behavior, his focus remained primarily on the psychological environment. Specifically, he maintained that individuals' behavioral environments are the result of their subjective experience of the objective physical environment at any given time and that it is this experience that generates patterns of action and subsequently interaction between the individual and the environment. Changes in behavior, then, rely on modifications in how the individual perceives the environment.

$B = f(Actual[Environment] \times Group[Person])$. On the other end of the continuum are those researchers, such as Barker and his colleagues (Barker, 1965, 1968, 1978; Barker & Gump, 1964; Barker & Schoggen, 1973; Barker & Wright, 1954; Gump, 1975; Wicker, 1973, 1983, 1992), who focused their attention on the more objective characteristics of the environment. Although Barker (1968) concurred with Lewin's assertion that people's momentary behavior is determined by their life space, he further stated that "if we wish to understand more than the immediate ... behavior, ... knowledge of the ecological environment is essential ... Development is not a momentary phenomenon, and the course of the life space can only be known within the ecological environment in which it is embedded" (p. 9). According to Barker (1968), because a person's behavior changes from setting to setting, and individuals within a setting tend to behave in a similar manner, it is not necessarily the people in the settings, but the setting itself, that is the unit of study. Accordingly, Barker posited that the focus of analysis should be on the functioning environment or nonpsychological environment that is comprised of multiple behavior settings or small ecosystems that call forth particular behavior. Behavior settings are persistent patterns of behavior that occur within a specific period of time and in a specific place (Carlson, Scott, & Eklund, 1980; Wicker, 1983). In addition to physical attributes (e.g., arrangement of furniture, size, accessories), behavior settings have social characteristics such as rules and norms that dictate a routinized pattern of action carried out by the people inhabiting the setting (Wandersman, Murday, & Wadsworth, 1979). Thus, it is the setting itself, rather than the person's perception of the setting, that calls forth certain types of behavior from the individuals who inhabit them (Barker, 1968; Trickett & Moos, 1974) such that, when in school, students "behave school" and, when at home, they "behave home." Despite his obvious partiality toward the environment, Barker did concede that an individual's satisfaction with the environment and goals within the environment will affect the degree to which the rules of the setting influence the individual's behavior (Walsh & Betz, 1995). Barker's student, Alan Wicker, explored this area more fully in his work on cause maps and major life pursuits (see Wicker, 1992).[2]

---

[2]For the interested reader, Cantrell and Cantrell (1985) provided a thorough description of assessment with children modeled after Barker's ecological psychology.

Although the approaches come from different foci, both delineate a means of understanding how environments determine an individual's adaptation or adjustment (Wandersman et al., 1979). Specifically, when individuals either adapt or adjust their behavior, they are striving to retain concordance (or fit) with their environment. In this manner, understanding the individual's interdependent relationship with the environment draws on delineating both how the individual is impacted by changes in the environment (e.g., changes in norms or rules; Barker, 1968) and how the environment is impacted by changes in the individual (e.g., shifts in perception; Lewin, 1951). Consequently, this interplay between individuals and their environment is a continuous process whereby individuals seek to maintain homeostasis within their system and subsystems.

Contemporary Ecological Psychology

Drawing upon the notion of the importance of the individual's perception of the environment (Lewin, 1951) and the necessity of understanding the environment to discern the individual's pattern of behavior (Barker, 1968), are logical outgrowths of Lewin's and Barker's work in ecological psychology. Although contemporary interactionists are aligned with different fields of psychology, their work continues to fall under the auspices of ecological psychology and integrates the four dimensions of ecological psychology mentioned previously. Discussed here are the social environment researchers such as Kelly and his colleagues (Kelly, 1967, 1970, 1971, 1979, 1986; Trickett, Kelly, & Todd, 1972; Trickett, Kelly, & Vincent, 1985; Trickett & Todd, 1972; Watts, 1992), Moos and his colleagues (Moos, 1970, 1976; Trickett & Moos, 1973, 1974), and the systems ecological perspective (SEP) researchers (Fine, 1985, 1990, 1995; Henggeler & Borduin, 1990; Henggeler, Schoenwald, & Pickrel, 1995; Schoenwald, Henggeler, Pickrel, & Cunningham, 1996) most closely aligned to the work of Bronfenbrenner in his social ecological and person–process–context–time model (1979, 1980, 1986, 1995).

$B = f(Perceived[Environment] \times Group[Person])$.   Like Barker, Moos and his colleagues (Moos, 1970, 1976; Moos & Trickett, 1987; Trickett & Moos, 1973, 1974) focused their work on delineating the environmental impact on behavior. However, using a social ecological perspective, Moos examined a more person-oriented environment than did Barker. Specifically, whereas Barker's primary intent was to describe behavior settings in terms of physical characteristics and social patterns, Moos' approach was to describe not necessarily the settings, but the social environment of the settings in psychological terms, hence, considering the subjective perceptions of individuals as emphasized by Lewin. This integration of physical and subjective features has been referred to as the "'perceived environment,' in which the environment of a particular setting is defined by the shared perceptions of members of that setting along a number of environmental 'dimensions'" (Trickett & Moos, 1974, p. 2). It follows, then, that how individuals perceive the environment will affect their subsequent behavior; "one cannot overemphasize the extent to which environments may shape their inhabitants ... Information about social and physical environments is of utility precisely because people vary their behavior substantially in accordance with the characteristics of their social and physical settings" (Moos, 1976, p. 397). As such, Moos' (1984, 1987) approach is premised on three primary assumptions: Environmental dimensions can be delineated, these dimensions shape the individual's behavior in that environment, and the perception of these dimensions will differ between individuals. Whereas Moos and his colleagues focused on group perceptions as the unit of study, a similar but opposite perspective can be found in Schneider's (Schneider & Bartlett, 1970) work on the definition of the environment as an individual perception (similar to Lewin).

$B = f(Actual[Environment] + Perceived[Environment] \times Individual[Person] + Group[Person])$. In his emphasis on the social environment, Kelly's (1967, 1970, 1971, 1979, 1986; Trickett, Kelly, & Todd, 1972; Trickett, Kelly, & Vincent, 1985; Trickett & Todd, 1972; Watts, 1992) work in community psychology is similar to Moos'; however, Kelly went beyond describing environments, either through physical or social boundaries or individual perceptions, to identify key considerations in intervention planning. Kelly's approach to ecological psychology draws from the principles of field biology to examine the structure and function of environments (Trickett & Moos, 1973). Trickett and Todd (1972) likened this approach to an ecological metaphor of a pond where "behavior ... is determined by a network of living and non-living elements that interact and evolve as a community" (p. 28). Trickett and Todd further stated that the metaphor "suggests that the behavior of individuals or groups has important implications both for the survival and development of the individual and for the evolution of the habitat" (pp. 28–29). With this in mind, Trickett proposed the following four principles based on the work of Kelly and his colleagues that provide the necessary framework for understanding the individual as embedded in context and the context itself: interdependence, adaptation cycling of resources, and succession (see Trickett, chapter 7, this volume).

$B = f(Actual[Environment] + Perceived[Environment] \times Individual[Person] + Group[Person])$. Conceptually similar to the foundational theories, social/systems ecological theorists, as a whole, perceive behavior to be determined by both internal and external characteristics of the interaction between the individual and the environment. They also perceive that this process occurs in seemingly boundaried settings. Rather than looking at individuals in isolation from their relationships with others or the objective components of boundaried settings in isolation from its relationship to other settings, they emphasize the study of the total of interacting systems in which the individual functions. Moreover, while recognizing both the internal and external forces which impact individuals' behavior, they underscore the importance of acknowledging the reciprocal relationship between individuals and the various systems in which they participate to ascertain both the direct and indirect factors that impact individuals' functioning. What the social ecological approach adds, then, is a focus on the multiple settings within which the individual exists and how these different settings impact the individual's functioning within that setting and within the other settings.

Bronfenbrenner's theory of human ecology (1979) and, later, his person–process–context–time (PPCT) model (1995) provide the necessary structure for gaining a theoretical understanding the person–environment process. According to Cairns and Cairns (1995), "Bronfenbrenner brought Lewinian life-space into the real world. ... There was a pragmatic need to go beyond the person's phenomenology to confront the real world of interactions, relationships, and contexts. Actions then lie at the adaptive interaction between the person and the environment." (p. 403). Bronfenbrenner (1979, 1980, 1995) sought to explain how the larger context in which individuals function impacts the reciprocal relationship of the individuals and the dynamic properties of the immediate settings in which they live. Within this is the concept of proximal processes: enduring reciprocal interactions between individuals and persons, objects, and symbols in their immediate environment (Ceci & Hembroke, 1995). Further, Bronfenbrenner maintained that to understand an individual requires examination of two primary constructs: ecological structures and ecological transitions. Within this is the reminder that process, or the concept of the chronosystem, underlies both (Elder, 1995).

Similar to Lewin's concept of existence (1951) and based on Barker's ecological environment (1968), Bronfenbrenner (1979) posited that the individual's environment can be divided into four embedded structures that act reciprocally to influence the individual:

Microsystem is comprised of the intimate aspects of the individual's development in the family and workplace including goal directed behavior, interpersonal relationships, and system-defined roles and experience. For example, for a child, the school, the home, and peers are all microsystems. According to Bronfenbrenner (1980), within each microsystem setting, three dimensions need to be considered: (a) design of physical space and materials, (b) the people in differing roles and relationships with the child (including others besides parents and teachers), and (c) the activities in which the individual and others interact.

Mesosystem consists of the link between and among the individual's multiple microsystems. For example, this would include the interrelationship of the work and home environments such that events at work would impact home functioning.

Exosystem is comprised of events that do not directly affect, or are not directly affected by, the individual. For example, these may include governmental agencies, institutions, and media.

Macrosystem consists of the cultural and societal belief systems and underlying ideologies that may be present at the other levels but inherently influence individuals' functioning within their microsystem.

Understanding an individual, then, requires both a knowledge of how each of the ecological structures impacts the individual and an awareness of how the different levels of the ecology interact to produce both the perceived and actual environment in which the individual functions. When considering that individuals exist within several different microsystems and transition between microsystems throughout their day, understanding how the different microsystems interact and impact the individual is of additional importance.

As part of this, one must consider the impact of ecological transitions. Specifically, as individuals move through their ecological space, they are both a product of and a producer of change, referred to as *mutual accommodation*. Bronfenbrenner (1979) characterized the process of mutual accommodation as replete with ecological transitions such that a transition occurs whenever there is a change in the individual's position (i.e., roles, setting, or both) within the ecological environment. As such, the transition from one role or setting to another can be characterized as individuals' attempts to both accommodate and adjust to the changing environmental situation, and thus can be further conceived of as individuals' attempts to maintain homeostasis within their environment. Moreover, these periods of transition, of adaptation and adjustment, occur each time an individual encounters a new environment (Diamond, Spiegel-McGill, & Hanrahan, 1988).

Indeed, it is true that when individuals change roles or alter their *social niche* (Elder, 1995) within their microsystem, or when they develop new microsystemic relationships, they must adapt to these environmental changes; however, according to Elder, the concept of ecological transitions does not encompass those developmental changes or proximal processes that naturally occur as individuals and environments interact across time. In light of the interconnectedness and evolving nature of multifaceted and multidimensional person–environment relationships, Bronfenbrenner (1989) proposed the concept of the *chronosystem*. "The ecological concept of a chronosystem was devised to capture all of these interacting elements over time—the developing person, the nature of the environment, and their proximal processes of interaction" (Elder, 1995, p. 123).

Influences Outside the Field of Ecological Psychology

As an individual does not develop or exist within a vacuum, neither does ecological psychology. The development of ecological psychology has historically been influenced by several domains of psychology including gestalt psychology, personality psychology, counseling psychology, community psychology, and developmental psychology. Similarly, the development of ecological psychology has, in turn, impacted on these same domains. Indeed, many theorists and researchers have discussed the importance of examining the interaction between the person and the environment as a means for understanding behavior.

The influence of Koffka's and Lewin's conception of the environment can be seen in Murray's (1938) and Stern's (1970) work in personality psychology. Specifically, Murray (1938) posited that the problem of understanding and predicting behavior can be resolved by working with each person as an individual, examining the match between each person's needs and environmental presses. In his interpretation of Murray's theory of personality, Stern (1970) stated that an individual's needs are essentially "objectives individuals characteristically strive to achieve for themselves … that are revealed in the modes of behavior employed by the individual. … They may lend themselves to different explanations, in accordance with the specific context in which they occur" (p. 6). Presses, on the other hand, can refer to both the real (alpha) and the perceived (beta) environment. The difference between the alpha press and the beta press is akin to the difference between an observer's and an individual's interpretation of a specific behavioral act (1970). Specifically, the alpha press represents the explicit objectives of an environment. The beta press is more complex in that it is comprised of the phenomenological world of both the individual (private beta) and the group (consensual beta). Stern (1970) later extended and added to Murray's needs/press model by operationally defining the major constructs and, for the most part, using the consensual beta to evaluate person–environment congruence.

Similar to Murray and Stern, Lofquist and Dawis (1969, 1972, 1991; Dawis & Lofquist, 1984) conceptualized the work environment as replete with needs and presses (although not necessarily using those terms). In the work setting, the individual has needs which, when met, lead to a sense of satisfaction, and the environment has requirements (presses) from which evaluations of the individual's satisfactoriness are derived. When individuals do not get their needs met, or the requirements of the environment are not met, there is a lack of fit. John Holland, like Dawis and Lofquist, proposed that environments where there is a congruency (i.e., a good fit) between an individual's personality orientation and the personality orientation of the work environment lead to job satisfaction. More specifically, Holland (1973, 1985, 1996) categorized both individuals and environments as belonging to one of six primary personality types (i.e., realistic, investigative, artistic, social, enterprising, and conventional) with each type having its own specific needs, values, preferences, and requirements. Holland (1973, 1985) posited that people search for environments that will enable them to express their personality style; that is, they actively seek environments where there will be a good fit. In a recent review of research on the congruency construct, Holland (1996) concluded that this person–environment congruence is conducive to satisfaction and stability in both interpersonal and vocational relations.

Summary

Ecological psychology has a long theoretical history with a relatively recent use in applied settings. One concern has been the seemingly vast difference between theories that are subsumed under the umbrella of ecological psychology. Indeed, when ecological psychology is identified as the theory guiding research, assessment, or intervention, one is left to wonder which theory? Ecological theories range from focus on the individual's subjective experience of the environment to the near exclusion of physical properties of the environment to a focus on the physical and social attributes of the environment to the near exclusion of the individual's subjective experience. Along the middle of the continuum lie theories that, to differing degrees, integrate the perceptual and actual characteristics of the environment into an ecological understanding of the individual, the environment, and their interaction. Contributions from outside the specific domain of ecological psychology clarified and augmented existing ecological principles. Keeping in mind that the unifying assumption of ecological psychology is that behavior is a function of the person and the environment, three common themes emerge: a) organisms do not act or exist in isolation but are embedded within a complex network of interrelated systems, b) all organisms are affected by internal and external drives, and c) individuals adapt in that they actively shape and are shaped by their environment in attempts to attain and maintain homeostasis. Given this, Toro, Trickett, Wall, and Salem (1991) proposed that the following features define ecological orientations, both historical and current:

- a focus on describing the contexts in which people are embedded and in which behavior occurs
- conceptualization of the ecological environment through multiple levels of analysis
- recognition that there can be vast differences between seemingly similar type environments
- acceptance that individual behavior is transactional, and cannot be understood separate from the context in which it occurs
- the belief that interventions must be tailored to the specific ecologies in which they are implemented. (p. 1209)

Culture, Psychosocial Adaptation, and the Ecological Environment

Subsumed within ecological approaches is the assumption of homeostasis. Culture can be viewed as an individual's medium of adaptation to the demands of the environment such that an individual must simultaneously incorporate information based on what is occurring in their immediate context and those environments that surround it (Cole, 1991). Where culture is concerned, the environment may call upon the individual to possess, to some degree, certain attributes that will alleviate or ease the psychosocial adjustment and adaptation process. These attributes, whether biological, psychological, or cultural in origin, may or may not be part of the individual's repertoire of behaviors, and as such, may result in a mismatch between the individual and the environment. In this same vein, there are cultural and contextual factors that result in positive psychosocial adaptation. Like any other setting, the school and work environments possess cultural contexts comprised of an aggregate of cultural characteristics brought into the setting by the inhabitants. This aggregate, however, is based on the predominant cultural characteristics. As such, there will be individuals whose cultural background is not represented in the environment, and this may, through creation of a lack of fit, lead to poor psychosocial adaptation.

The Ecological Model in School Settings

Students exist within several different systems including the school, family, peer, and community settings (Hobbs, 1966), and they are active and sometimes passive participants in different systems within those settings (Christenson, 1993). The result is that students are embedded within a multiplicity of multifaceted environments in which they hold specific roles, that within each are expectations of and for the individual, and that sometimes these roles and subsequent expectations are in conflict with one another. This conflict can lead to a discrepancy in the individual's ability to meet the requirements of the environment or the environment's ability to meet the needs of the individual. The lack of fit, then, is not simply located within the person or the environment, but in the interaction between the two (Apter, 1982). As such, it is essential with school-aged youth experiencing difficulties to examine this person–environment interaction. Conoley and Haynes (1992) noted that this lack of fit is considered a discordance in the system or a failure of match. Indeed, according to Hewett (1987) and Evans and Evans (1987), this failure of match is evident when the individual's characteristics such as abilities, needs, and perceptions differ from that of key agents in the ecological environment such that there is a greater potential for maladjustment. As such, to fully understand this process, and to intervene when a lack of fit exists, the use of an ecological approach is of paramount importance.

It must be underscored, however, that, in contrast to traditional models of disturbance, the ecological model "attempts to shift the locus of the disturbance from the child to an encounter point between the child and the microcommunity or communities which surround him" (Rhodes, 1970, p. 310). Although not denying that some children do have biological, educational, or social deficiencies, and that these will require intervention, the importance of going beyond the child to consider contextual and environmental deficits is underscored. The goal of ecological approaches, then, is not to fix the child but to make the system work (Hobbs, 1975). To this end, researchers have proposed that the unifocused assessments and interventions predominantly employed in academic and mental health settings are no longer viewed as the most beneficial (Carlson et al., 1980; Schmid, 1987).

Ecological Assessment

Ecological assessment is premised on the notion that behavior must be examined with regard to how it fits the surrounding environmental conditions and expectations (Evans & Evans, 1987, 1990). In this, ecological assessment offers a more comprehensive and accurate view of the problem (1990). As standard assessment is bound by time, and therefore measures only a narrow segment of the "cycle of behavior," it lacks the sensitivity to the environmental context afforded by an ecological approach (Evans et al., 1993). Moreover, when considering that attempts to predict future behavior without information about the environmental conditions is more a process of hoping than predicting (Mischel, 1968), it is clear that an ecological approach is necessary. Ecological approaches do not deny the importance of traditional assessment (Christenson, 1993), instead they maximize the knowledge obtained in traditional standardized assessment by integrating this information with what can be known about the total of interacting systems in which the individual functions (Conoley, 1988).

The primary goal of ecological assessment is to determine how well the child's behavior and expectations match environmental requirements and expectation, and identify behaviors, settings, and conditions with which to intervene (Evans & Evans, 1990). As such, it calls for a "thorough contextual analysis of all possible sources of discordance. ... Elements of a student's physical, social, academic, and behavioral environment are combined to create a holistic view of the problem situation (not just the problem itself)" (Evans et al., 1993, p. 183). The factors that can influence a child's situation are numerous and codetermine concrete expression of behavior; these factors can be located within the child, the environment, or most importantly the interaction of the two (Kaser, 1993). Factors such as child temperament; pupil personality development; student teachability; classroom environment; teacher tolerance, beliefs, and expectancies (Johnson et al., 1991); inter- and intrapersonal, biophysical, social, and environmental variables (Evans & Evans, 1987; Evans et al., 1993); physical milieu (e.g., classroom setting, size and density, spatial arrangement), personal interactions (e.g., teacher role, student role, peer interaction), learner styles and academic deficits, and expectancies (student's, teacher's, parent's, peer's; Bulgren & Knackendoffel, 1986); and school environment (e.g., adminis-

trative leadership style, expectations related to effective student characteristics and cognitive abilities; Felsenthal, 1982) can all contribute to a poor
person–environment fit. Several authors proposed models and instruments
for assessing ecological factors (e.g., instructional variables, Welch, 1994;
natural environment, Cantrell & Cantrell, 1985; social environments [e.g.,
classroom, Moos & Trickett, 1987; family, Moos & Moos, 1987]). For
example, using the Classroom Environment Scale, Trickett and Moos
(Barrett & Trickett, 1979; Moos & Trickett, 1987; Trickett, Leone, Fink, &
Braaten, 1993; Trickett & Moos, 1973, 1974) identified three general
dimensions along which classrooms differ: relationship (e.g., support), goal
orientation (e.g., task orientation), and system maintenance/change (e.g.,
rule clarity). The positive effects of ecological assessment were shown by
Linehan, Brady, and Hwang (1991) in their study of ecological versus
developmental assessment with severely disturbed students. Specifically,
they found that teacher expectations are linked to assessment results such
that ecological assessment information for a student tended to lead to higher
expectations for academic performance than developmental assessment
results and that this translates into effects on instructional planning.

Similarly, models for assessment have been proposed for special populations
as well (e.g., early childhood special education, Lowenthal, Landerholm, &
Augustyn, 1994; learning disabilities, Szymanski, Dunn, & Parker, 1989;
preschoolers, Lowenthal, 1991). Among them is Lowenthal's (1991) model for
preschool assessment. Lowenthal suggested the following steps for assessment: (a) Identify the major environmental settings for the child, (b) determine
the behavioral expectations in each setting, and (c) assess the child's ability to
meet these expectations. Similar to Lowenthal, Carlson et al. (1980) proposed
that because behavior that does not adapt to changes in the environment is
considered maladaptive, assessment should identify the behavior settings the
child functions within, identify the pattern of behavior attached to the settings,
and evaluate the child's behavior in comparison to the requirements of the
setting. What this means, then, is that assessment may need to encompass
characteristics not only of the student (see Gaddis & Hatfield, chapter 2, this
volume), but also of the classroom (see McLellan & Sanchez, chapter 4, this
volume), the school (see Moan & Mellott, chapter 6, this volume), and the
community (see Trickett, chapter 7, this volume), as well as the dynamic
interrelationships that exist among and between these systems.

Ecological Intervention

Results from ecological assessments can be used in multiple ways. As
mentioned previously, the information is helpful in working with individual

children (see Conoley & Rotto, chapter 3, this volume), families (see Schoenwald, Henggeler, Brondino, & Donkervoet, chapter 9, this volume), and teachers (see Shaftel & Fine, chapter 5, this volume). It can also be used to adapt curriculum and instruction (Welch, 1994), facilitate collaborative consultation and intervention (see Shaftel & Fine, chapter 5, this volume), plan for prevention activities (see Moan & Mellott, chapter 6, this volume), and help reconnect families with schools (see Schoenwald et al., chapter 9, this volume). Of concern, however, is that, despite acknowledgment of the impact of the environment and the person–environment interaction, "interventions frequently become one-dimensional and are centered almost wholly on changing the child's behavior to fit the demands of a teacher or parent" (Evans & Evans, 1987, p. 12).

Similar to assessment, traditional approaches to intervention focus on changing the child. According to Schmid (1987), when systems are out of balance, four processes can occur: adaptation by one component of the system, assimilation of the component by creating a niche for it, expelling the component, or change in the total system. As Siegel (1981) found in his study of school personnel (i.e., educators, school psychologists), the greater the disparity between a child's behavior and the expectations of the environment, the more likely it was that the student would be referred out for services and possible removal from a least-restricted setting. However, to take children out of their natural environment, "fix" the children, and return them to the same unchanged environment would be impractical (Muscott, 1987; Rhodes, 1970). According to Henggeler (1994), more emphasis needs to be placed on working with youth in their natural ecologies (i.e., home, school, community). As such, ecological interventions attempt to change the total system, thereby affecting adaptation and assimilation in all concerned. More specifically, Conoley and Haynes (1992) and Fine (1985) noted that, because disturbance is viewed as a discordance in the system rather than a disease of individuals, ecologically based interventions focus on increasing concordance between individuals and the multiple contexts in which they exist, not simply changing one to benefit the other.

Intervention from an ecological perspective takes into account the inherent uniqueness of the individual and does not assume that one strategy is appropriate for all individuals across all settings (Reynolds, Gutkin, Elliott, & Witt, 1984). As such, the nature and structure of the intervention will differ with each child. Indeed, according to Henggeler (1994), "therapeutic interventions should be dictated by the strengths, weaknesses, and needs of the child and family" (p. 5). However, one thing that remains consistent across individuals and settings is the necessity of cooperation and participation by teachers, school personnel (e.g., school psychologist, administrator), family, peers, and community members (e.g., clinicians, members from religious organizations, community elders; Conoley, 1988; Henggeler, 1994; Lowenthal, 1991; Paget & Nagle, 1986; Schoenwald et al., 1996). According to Paget and Nagle (1986), early involvement of the child's parents in the assessment process can facilitate collaboration and cooperation during the intervention process. Despite this reality, seemingly few educational programs provide direct training in working with members in the home environment (e.g., parents, family; Conoley, 1988; Fine, 1990; Young, Gable, & Hendrickson, 1989).

According to Conoley (1988), creating supportive classroom ecologies that value individual differences and, correspondingly, school environments, requires the "adults to 'get their acts together' prior to assuming the children will" (p. 44). Optimally, interrelationships between teachers and other school personnel (e.g., other teachers, administrators, counselors), and between the school and the family are based on coordinated services, cooperation, exchange of feedback, and flexibility (1988). Conoley (1987) proposed that ecological interventions linking schools and families are comprised of four levels: level one—sharing information with parents related to their child's school performance; level two—collaborating with the family to provide information such as instructions for tutoring, behavior modification programs, and social skills training; level three—engaging parents in activities at the school such as serving as room parent or becoming active in volunteer programs; and level four—exchanging information between parents and educators in a reciprocal and continuous manner. Such interventions have shown promise in affecting positive change in school, home, and community settings. For example, using a "Parents-as-Teachers Model" for parents of children with learning and/or behavior disorders, Polirstok (1987) found that engaging parents in educational and collaborative training led to increases in positive perceptions of the teacher, self-esteem in the child, effective use of behavior modification strategies by parents, and involvement by the community. It appears, then, that ecological intervention is not focused solely on making changes in one environment, but there is also an emphasis on promoting consistency between settings such as home and school (Conoley, 1988). To achieve optimal consistency, however, relies on consideration of ecological transitions.

Ecological Transitions

Similar to assessment and intervention, conceptualizing and undertaking transitions from one ecosystem to another benefit from using an ecological approach (see Szymanski, chapter 8, this volume). "As individuals grow older, their environments expand to include peers, community, and school" (Diamond et al., 1988, p. 245). For students, the educational experience is rife with ecological transitions, from home to school, elementary to junior to senior high school, from high school to the work place, and sometimes from detention centers or jails into the school or community (Diamond et al., 1988; Putnam, 1987). Differences between the philosophies and expectations of the settings and the needs of the student may lead to school failure and withdrawal (Azar, 1996). According to Bronfenbrenner (1986), stress and other psychological discomfort inherent in the transition process can be ameliorated through careful planning and preparation. First, the intersetting relationship must be examined for indications of expectations, information, and attitudes regarding what will occur in the new environment. This requires an accurate assessment of both the individual as well as the new environment. As the individual enters the new environment, changes in his or her existing microsystems will occur. As such, after the individual has begun the transition process and is in the new setting and functioning in the new role, the individual, other individuals in the relevant microsystems, and individuals in the new microsystem must reexamine their expectations and attitudes about the individual's new role and current behavior. Once the transition has occurred and the systems have had time to adjust to the individual's new role, there will still be changes over time that will affect the individual's functioning. As a result, the impact of the ecological transition process is ongoing; continued interaction and communication among individuals in the affected systems is encouraged. Diamond et al. (1988) maintained that planning and ongoing communication throughout the transition process can circumvent the potential for breakdowns in the interrelationships between the individual's microsystems and can, subsequently, facilitate healthy adaptation. Indeed, planning for transitions and continued monitoring of the transition process serve as preventative efforts which can circumvent the need for intervention efforts.

Summary

As individuals structure, change, and organize their environments (Moos, 1980), their environments work to do the same. Adding to the reality that environmental or contextual and individual variables act reciprocally to shape an individual's behavior, is the idea that the various systems in which the individual functions impacts the acquisition and maintenance of unique behavioral repertoires. As discussed in the following chapters, for school-aged youth, this reality necessitates an ecological approach to assessment, intervention, and prevention. To this end, Gaddis and Hatfield (chapter 2), McLellan and Sanchez (chapter 4), and Moan and Mellott (chapter 6) discuss foundations and applications of ecological psychology to the assessment of individuals, individuals within classrooms, and schools within communities, respectively. Close Conoley and Rotto (chapter 3), Shaftel and Fine (chapter 5), and Trickett (chapter 7) explore the fundamentals of and effective strategies for ecological intervention with individuals, individuals within classrooms, schools within communities, and families within communities, respectively. Szymanski (chapter 8) examines preventative planning for the ecological transition from school to work. Finally, Schoenwald et al. (chapter 9) provide a comprehensive picture of school–family collaboration as a means of effecting change in the ecological environment of juvenile delinquents.

SUMMARY AND CONCLUSIONS

Given that aspects of the environment that influence behavior are determined by how the individual interacts with the environment, each individual's unique constellation of traits serves to create different environments such that no two people experience the environment in the same way (Bandura, 1985). According to Kendler (1986), understanding an individual's actions relies on knowledge of the context in which the behavior occurs. In the same way, understanding the process of psychosocial adaptation for any individual relies on knowledge of how and whether an individual's competencies and characteristics meet the requirements of the different contexts in which people exist. In contrast to psychology theories that focus primarily on the individual, incorporation of ecological psychology concepts allows for a more comprehensive and in-depth analysis of sources contributing to the individual's ability to adapt to the psychosocial environment. Ecological theories that drive assessment, intervention, and prevention efforts provide the necessary framework for assisting school-aged youth and their associated ecological networks to cope with and overcome the multidetermined, multifaceted concerns that arise during the school years. Concurrently, more efficacy studies are needed to show the utility of applied ecological psychology approaches in educational ecosystems. In light of this, it is clear that ecological researchers, including teachers, school mental health professionals, and community mental health professionals need to undertake research that can provide rich information about the effectiveness of ecological approaches to assessment, intervention, and preventative planning with individuals within families within schools within communities.

REFERENCES

Apter, S. J. (1982). *Troubled children/Troubled systems*. New York: Pergamon.

Azar, B. (1996, June). Schools the source of rough transitions. *The Monitor*, p. 14.

Bandura, A. (1985). Model causality in social learning theory. In M. J. Mahoney, & A. Freeman (Eds.), *Cognition and psychotherapy* (pp. 81–99). New York: Plenum.

Barker, R. G. (1965). Explorations in ecological psychology. *American Psychologist, 20*, 1–14.

Barker, R. G. (1968). *Ecological psychology: Concepts and methods for studying human behavior*. Stanford, CA: Stanford University Press.

Barker, R. G. (1978). *Habitats, environments, and human behavior*. San Francisco, CA: Jossey-Bass.

Barker, R. G., & Gump, H. F. (1964). *Big school, small school: High school size and student behavior*. Stanford, CA: Stanford University Press.

Barker, R. G., & Schoggen, P. (1973). *Qualities of community life*. San Francisco, CA: Jossey-Bass.

Barker, R. G., & Wright, H. F. (1954). *Midwest and its children: The psychological ecology of an American town*. Evanston, IL: Row, Peterson.

Barrett, D. M., & Trickett, E. J. (1979). Change strategies and perceived environment data: Two conceptual models and their applications. *Journal of Community Psychology, 7*, 305–312.

Bijou, S. W., & Baer, D. W. (1978). *Behavior analysis of child development*. Englewood Cliffs, NJ: Prentice Hall.

Bronfenbrenner, U. (1979). *The ecology of human development*. Cambridge, MA: Harvard University Press.

Bronfenbrenner, U. (1980). Ecology of childhood. *School Psychology Review, 9*, 294–297.

Bronfenbrenner, U. (1986). Ecology of the family as a context for human development: Research perspectives. *Developmental Psychology, 22*, 723–742.

Bronfenbrenner, U. (1989). Ecological systems theory through space and time: A future perspective. In R. Vasta (Ed.), *Six theories of child development: Revised formulations and current issues* (pp. 187–250). Greenwich, CT: JAI Press.

Bronfenbrenner, U. (1995). Developmental ecology through space and time: A future perspective. In P. Moen, G. H. Elder, Jr., & K. Luscher (Eds.), *Examining lives in context* (pp. 619–647). Washington, DC: American Psychological Association.

Bulgren, J. A., & Knackendoffel, A. (1986). Ecological assessment: An overview. *The Pointer, 30*(2), 23–30.

Cairns, R. B., & Cairns, B. (1995). Social ecology over time and space. In P. Moen, G. H. Elder, Jr., & K. Luscher (Eds.), *Examining lives in context*. Washington, DC: American Psychological Association.

Cantrell, M. L., & Cantrell, R. P. (1985). Assessment of the natural environment. *Educational and Treatment of Children, 8*, 275–295.

Carlson, C. I., Scott, M., & Eklund, S. J. (1980). Ecological theory and method for behavioral assessment. *School Psychology Review, 9*, 75–82.

Ceci, S. J., & Hembroke, H. A. (1995). A bioecological model of intellectual development. In P. Moen, G. H. Elder, Jr., & K. Luscher (Eds.), *Examining lives in context* (pp. 303–345). Washington, DC: American Psychological Association.

Christenson, S. L. (1993). Ecological assessment: Linking assessment to intervention. *Communique, 21*(5), 26–27.

Cole, M. (1991). A cultural theory of development: What does it imply about the application of scientific research. *Learning and Instruction, 1,* 187–200.

Conoley, J. C. (1987). Schools and families: Theoretical and practical bridges. *Professional School Psychology, 2,* 191–203.

Conoley, J. C. (1988). Positive classroom ecology. *Behavior in Our Schools, 2*(2), 2–7.

Conoley, J. C., & Haynes, G. (1992). An ecological approach to intervention. In R. C. D'Amato & B. A. Rothlisberg (Eds.), *Psychological perspectives on intervention: A case study approach to prescriptions for change.* New York: Longman.

Dawis, R. V. (1992). The individual differences tradition in counseling psychology. *Journal of Counseling Psychology, 39*(2), 7–19.

Dawis, R. V., & Lofquist, L. H. (1984). *A psychological theory of work adjustment.* Minneapolis, MN: University of Minnesota Press.

Diamond, K. E., Spiegel–McGill, P., & Hanrahan, P. (1988). Planning for school transition: An ecological–developmental approach. *Journal of the Division of Early Childhood, 12,* 245–252.

Ekehammer, B. (1974). Interactionism in personality from a historical perspective. *Psychological Bulletin, 81,* 1026–1048.

Elder, G. H., Jr. (1995).The life course paradigm: Social change and individual development. In P. Moen, G. H. Elder, Jr., & K. Luscher (Eds.), *Examining lives in context* (pp. 101–139). Washington, DC: American Psychological Association.

Evans, S. S., & Evans, W. H. (1987). Behavior change and the ecological model. *The Pointer, 31*(3), 9–12.

Evans, W. H., & Evans, S. S. (1990). Ecological assessment guidelines. *Diagnostique, 16,* 49–51.

Evans, W. H., Gable, R. A., & Evans, S. S. (1993). Making something out of everything: The promise of ecological assessment. *Diagnostique, 18,* 175–185.

Felsenthal, H. (1982, March). *Factors influencing school effectiveness: An ecological analysis of an "effective" school.* Paper presented at the annual meeting of the American Educational Research Association, New York.

Fine, M. J. (1985). Intervention from systems ecological perspective. *Professional Psychology: Research and Practice, 16,* 262–270.

Fine, M. J. (1990). Facilitating home-school relationships: A family-oriented approach to collaborative consultation. *Journal of Educational and Psychological Consultation, 1,* 169–187.

Fine, M. J. (1995). Family–school intervention. In R. H. Mikesell, D. D. Lusterman, & S. H. McDaniel (Eds.), *Integrating family therapy: Handbook of family psychology and systems theory* (pp. 481–495). Washington, DC: American Psychological Association.

Fuhrer, U. (1990). Bridging the ecological–psychological gap: Behavior settings as interfaces. *Environment and Behavior, 22,* 518–537.

Gump, P. V. (1975). Environmental psychology and the behavior setting concept. In B. Honkman (Ed.), *Responding to social change, EDRA 6* (pp. 152–163). Stroudsburg, PA: Downden, Hutchinson, & Ross.

Hendrickson, J. M., Gable, R. A., & Shores, R. E. (1987). The ecological perspective setting events and behavior. *The Pointer, 31*(3), 40–44.

Henggeler, S. W. (1994). A consensus: Conclusions of the APA task force report on innovative models of mental health services for children, adolescents, and their families. *Journal of Clinical Child Psychology, 23*(Suppl), 3–6.

Henggeler, S. W., & Borduin, C. M. (1990). *Family therapy and beyond: A multisystematic approach to treating the behavior problems of children and adolescents.* Pacific Grove, CA: Brooks/Cole.

Henggeler, S. W., Schoenwald, S. K., & Pickrel, S. G. (1995). Multisystemic therapy: Bridging the gap between university- and community-based treatment. *Journal of Consulting and Clinical Psychology, 63,* 709–717.

Hewett, F. M. (1987). The ecological view of disturbed children shadow versus substance. *The Pointer, 31*(3), 61–63.

Hilton, A. (1987). Using ecological strategies when working with children. *The Pointer, 31*(3), 52–55.

Hobbs, N. (1966). Helping disturbed children: Psychological and ecological strategies. *American Psychologist, 21,* 1105–1115.

Hobbs, N. (Ed.). (1975). *Issues in the classification of children.* San Francisco: Jossey Bass.

Holland, J. L. (1973). *Making vocational choices: A theory of careers.* Englewood Cliffs, NJ: Prentice-Hall.

Holland, J. L. (1985). *Making vocational choices: A theory of vocational personalities and work environments* (2nd ed.). Englewood Cliffs, NJ: Prentice-Hall.

Holland, J. L. (1996). Exploring careers with a typology: What we have learned and some new directions. *American Psychologist, 51,* 397–406.

Johnson, G., Johnson, J. , & DeMatta, R. (1991). Predictive exploration of educational–failure paradigms. *Canadian Journal of Special Education, 7,* 164–180.

Johnson, M. J., Swartz, J. L., & Martin, W. E., Jr. (1995). Application of psychological theories for career development with native Americans. In F. T. L. Leong (Ed.), *Career development and vocational behavior among ethnic minorities* (pp. 103–133). Hillsdale, NJ: Lawrence Erlbaum Associates.

Kantor, J. R. (1924). *Principles of psychology* (Vol. 1). Bloomington, IN: Principia Press.

Kaser, R. (1993). A change in focus ... without losing sight of the child. *School Psychology International, 14,* 5–19.

Kelly, J. G. (1967). Naturalistic observation and theory confirmation: An example. *Human Development, 10,* 212–222.

Kelly, J. G. (1970). Antidotes for arrogance: Training for a community psychology. *American Psychologist, 25,* 524–531.

Kelly, J. G. (1971). Qualities for a community psychologist. *American Psychologist, 26,* 897–903.

Kelly, J. G. (1979). 'Tain't what you do, it's the way that you do it. *American Journal of Community Psychology, 7,* 239–413.

Kelly, J. G. (1986). Context and process: An ecological view of the interdependence of practice and research. *American Journal of Community Psychology, 14,* 581–589.

Kendler, T. S. (1986). Worldviews and the concept of development: A reply to Lerner and Kauffman. *Developmental Review, 6,* 80–95.

Koffka, K. (1935). *Principles of gestalt psychology.* London: Routledge & Kegan.

LeCompte, W. A. (1972). When the donkey speaks: The perspective of ecological psychology. *Hacettepe Bulletin of Social Sciences and Humanities, 4,* 153–161.

Lewin, K. (1935). *Dynamic theory of personality: Selected papers.* New York: McGraw-Hill.

Lewin, K. (1951). *Field theory in social science.* New York: Harper & Row.

Linehan, S. A., Brady, M. P., & Hwang, C. (1991). Ecological versus developmental assessment: Influences on instructional expectations. *Journal of the Association for Persons with Severe Handicaps, 16,* 146–153.

Lofquist, L. H., & Dawis, R. V. (1969). *Adjustment to work: A psychological view of man's problems in a work-oriented society.* New York: Appleton-Century-Crofts.

Lofquist, L. H., & Dawis, R. V. (1972). Application of the theory of work adjustment to rehabilitation counseling. *Minnesota Studies in Vocational Rehabilitation Bulletin, 58.*

Lofquist, L. H., & Dawis, R. V. (1991). *Essentials of person-environment correspondence counseling.* Minneapolis: University of Minnesota Press.

Lowenthal, B. (1991). Ecological assessment: Adding a new dimension for preschool children. *Intervention in School and Clinic, 26,* 148–152.

Lowenthal, B., Landerholm, E., & Augustyn, K. (1994). Three aspects of early childhood special education assessment: Family interviews, learning styles, and parent–child interactions. *Early Child Development and Care, 99,* 113–122.

Mischel, W. (1968). *Personality and assessment.* New York: Wiley.

Moos, R. H. (1976). *The human context: Environmental determinants of human behavior.* New York: John Wiley.

Moos, R. H. (1980). Major features of a social ecological perspective. *APA Division of Community Psychology Newsletter, 13,* 1.

Moos, R. H. (1984). Context and coping: Toward a unifying conceptual framework. *American Journal of Community Psychology, 12,* 1–36.

Moos, R. H. (1987). Person–environment congruence, in work, school, and health care settings. *Journal of Vocational Behavior, 31,* 222–230.

Moos, R. H., & Moos, B. (1987). *Family Environment Scale manual* (2nd ed.). Palo Alto, CA: Consulting Psychologists Press.

Moos, R. H., & Trickett, E. J. (1987). *Classroom Environment Scale manual* (2nd ed.). Palo Alto, CA: Consulting Psychologists Press.

Murray, H. A. (1938). *Explorations in personality.* New York: Oxford University Press.

Muscott, H. S. (1987). Conceptualizing behavior management strategies for troubled and troubling students a process for organizing the direction of intervention efforts in schools. *The Pointer, 31*(4), 15–22.

Paget, K. D., & Nagle, R. J. (1986). A conceptual model of preschool assessment. *School Psychology Review, 15,* 154–165.

Parsons, F. D. (1909). *Choosing a vocation.* Boston: Houghton-Mifflin.

Polirstok, S. R. (1987). Ecological effects of a home-based, school-based, and community-based training of parents of children with learning and behavior problems. *International Journal of Rehabilitation Research, 10,* 293–301.

Putnam, M. L. (1987). Effective interventions for mildly handicapped adolescents in the home and the community. *The Pointer, 30*(3), 19–24.

Reynolds, C. R., Gutkin, T. B., Elliott, S. N., & Witt, J. C. (1984). *School psychology: Essentials of theory and practice.* New York: Wiley.

Rhodes, W. C. (1970). A community participation analysis of emotional disturbance. *Exceptional Children, 37,* 309–314.

Schmid, R. (1987). Historical perspectives of the ecological model. *The Pointer, 31*(3), 5–8..

Schneider, B., & Bartlett, C. J. (1970). Individual differences and organizational climate: II. Measurement of organizational climate by the multitrait–multirater matrix. *Personnel Psychology, 23,* 493–512.

Schoenwald, S. K., Henggeler, S. W., Pickrel, S. G., & Cunningham, P. B. (1996). Treating seriously troubled youths and families in their contexts: Multisystemic therapy. In M. C. Roberts (Ed.), *Model programs in child and family mental health.* Mahwah, NJ: Lawrence Erlbaum Associates.

Siegel, D. J. (1981). Children's behavior problems and referral for school psychological services. *Psychology in the Schools, 18,* 364–368.

Smead, V. S. (1982). Individuals as agents of change. *Ontario Psychologist, 14*(4), 14–20.

Stern, G. G. (1970). *People in context: Measuring person-environment congruence in education and industry.* New York: Wiley.

Szymanski, E. M., Dunn, C., & Parker, R. M. (1989). Rehabilitation counseling with persons with learning disabilities: An ecological framework. *Rehabilitation Counseling Bulletin, 33*(1), 38–53.

Toro, P. A., Trickett, E. J., Wall, D. D., & Salem, D. A. (1991). Homelessness in the United States: An ecological perspective. *American Psychologist, 46,* 1208–1218.

Trickett, E. J., Kelly, J. G., & Todd, D. M. (1972). The social environment of the high school: Guidelines for individual change and organizational development. In S. Golann & C. Eisdorfer (Eds.), *Handbook of community mental health.* New York: Appleton-Century-Crofts.

Trickett, E. J., Kelly, J. G., & Vincent, T. A. (1985). The spirit of ecological inquiry in community research. In E. C. Susskind & D. C. Klein (Eds.), *Community research: Methods, paradigms, and applications.* New York: Praeger.

Trickett, E. J., Leone, P. E., Fink, C. M., & Braaten, S. L. (1993). The perceived environment of special education classrooms for adolescents: A revision of the classroom environment scale. *Exceptional Children, 59,* 411–420.

Trickett, E. J., & Moos, R. H. (1973). Social environment of junior high and high school classrooms. *Journal of Educational Psychology, 65*(1), 93–102.

Trickett, E. J., & Moos, R. H. (1974). Personal correlates of contrasting environments: Students satisfactions in high school classrooms. *American Journal of Community Psychology, 2*(1), 1–12.

Trickett, E. J., & Todd, D. M. (1972). The high school culture: An ecological perspective. *Theory into Practice, 11*(1), 28–37.

Walsh, W. B., & Betz, N. E. (1995). *Tests and assessment.* Englewood Cliffs, NJ: Prentice Hall.

Wandersman, A., Murday, D., & Wadsworth, J. C. (1979). The environment–behavior–person relationship: Implications for research. *Environmental Design Research Association, 10,* 162–174.

Watts, R. J. (1992). Elements of a psychology of human diversity. *Journal of Community Psychology, 20,* 116–131.

Welch, M. (1994). Ecological assessment: A collaborative approach to planning instructional interventions. *Intervention in School and Clinic, 29*(3), 160–164.

Wicker, A. W. (1973). Undermanning theory and research: Implications for the study of psychological and behavioral effects of excess human populations. *Representative Research in Social Psychology, 4*, 185–206.

Wicker, A. W. (1983). *An introduction to ecological psychology.* New York: Cambridge University Press.

Wicker, A. W. (1992). Making sense of environments. In W. B. Walsh, K. H. Craik, & R. H. Price (Eds.), *Person–environment psychology: Models and perspectives* (pp. 157–192). Hillsdale, NJ: Lawrence Erlbaum Associates.

Young, C. C., Gable, R. A., & Hendrickson, J. M. (1989). An ecological perspective to training teachers of the behaviorally disordered: Where are we now? *Behavior Disorders, 15*(1), 16–20.

II

ASSESSMENT
AND INTERVENTION
WITH STUDENTS

2

Characteristics of the Learning Environment: Students, Teachers, and Their Interactions

Lena R. Gaddis
Leilani Hatfield
Northern Arizona University

Behavior and learning problems among children in schools have long been a concern among educators and mental health professionals. Many origins of these problems have been proposed (Sarasson & Doris, 1979). Perhaps the most prominent explanation, from a historical perspective, is that derived from the medical model which assumes that such problems originate from within the individual and are independent of the environment in which the child exhibits these behaviors (Rubin & Balow, 1971). However, due to the general dissatisfaction with this traditional model, alternative explanations for the origins of children's difficulties have surfaced. Among these is the ecological perspective. Specifically, the ecological perspective describes children's behavior problems as resulting from a complex interaction between the child and the environment (Algozzine, 1976). This perspective has received much attention not only from educational researchers, but also from policymakers. For example, in her keynote address at the 1985 Wingspread Conference, Madeleine Will, assistant secretary for Special Education and Rehabilitative Services, spoke of current practices of educational classification and placement as being "driven by a conceptual fallacy: that poor performance in learning can be understood solely in terms of deficiencies in the student rather than deficiencies in the learning environment" (Will, 1986, p. 9). Also, the National Academy of Science's Panel of Selection and Placement of Students in Programs for the Mentally Retarded has suggested that two independent phases of assessment take place when evaluating *any child* exhibiting academic problems, with the first phase being devoted to a complete evaluation of the learning environment and the second phase being the more traditional child assessment (Heller, Holtzman, & Messick, 1982, cited in Sattler, 1988).

Interpreted in an ecological context, "Behavior is not problematic, deviant, or abnormal in and of itself; a behavior is considered a problem as a function of the time it occurs, the place it occurs, the person who exhibits the behavior, and the person who sees it" (Algozzine, Ysseldyke, & Christenson, 1983, p. 90). This chapter focuses on the ecological assessment of difficulties that arise in a classroom. To this end, the time, place, and behavior of the individuals involved are considered. Specifically, relevant literature is addressed, as are practical assessment techniques that may be utilized. A case study and implications for intervention strategies are also presented.

FACTORS TO CONSIDER IN AN ECOLOGICAL ASSESSMENT MODEL

Walker (1991) asserted that assessing only the psychoeducational characteristics of a child will likely result in failure to gather other essential information. This, in turn, may lead to errors in placement and intervention with that child. Thus, ecological assessment involves gaining access to information from diverse system levels (e.g., behavior/characteristics of the individual, social relationships indicated by dyadic interactions, social group structures that organize the relations among dyadic interactions). Given that numerous factors affect students' behavior, each should be considered in the assessment of a problem exhibited by a child.

Physiological Factors

Such factors as vision, hearing, pharmaceutical interventions, and medical conditions must be considered. This type of data may typically be acquired via a review of the student's records, as well as from interviews with parents and classroom teachers. Of course, federal guidelines, as well as state rules and regulations, require that sensory functioning (e.g., vision and hearing) be included in the evaluation process of any child.

Physical Aspects of Environment

Many aspects of the physical environment may impact student learning and behavior and thus also deserve consideration. For example, seating arrangements influence the flow of classroom conversations, with an across-a-table arrangement superior to an around-a-table one (Steinzor, 1950); on-task behavior is increased when students are seated in rows placing them back to back (Axelrod, Hall, & Tams, 1972). Teacher attention toward certain students may be increased with a relocation to the front or center aisles of classroom (Adams & Biddle, 1970). Other possible physical characteristics to be aware of are classroom lighting and noise. Informal observations in the targeted classroom will provide the needed information to this aspect of the problem.

Child Temperament and Goodness of Fit

Temperament, a set of individual difference constructs, gained prominence via the New York Longitudinal Study (NYLS; e.g., Thomas & Chess, 1977; Thomas, Chess, Birch, Hertzig, & Korn, 1963). Through extensive research efforts, individual variations in activity level, biological rhythmicity, speed of adaptability to environmental change, strength of initial approach tendency in new social situations, emotional intensity, mood, distractibility, and persistence/attention span were revealed for infants and young children. Investigative evidence continues to accumulate to suggest that temperament variables are highly predictive of outcomes such as developmental psychopathology of children (Graham, Rutter, & George, 1973; Terestman, 1980), and child–family interactions (Lerner & Galambos, 1985). Such traits have also been found to have a number of educational correlates, including response to classroom structures (Barclay, 1983; Farley, 1981), classroom behavior (Billman & McDevitt, 1980; Martin, Paget, & Nagle, 1983), student–teacher interaction (Paget, Nagle, & Martin, 1984), teachers' attitudes toward their students (Martin, Paglet, & Nagle, 1983), educational decisions made by teachers (Pullis & Cadwell, 1982), and academic achievement (Burk, 1980; Martin, Drew, Gaddis, & Moseley, 1988; Martin & Holbrook, 1985; Martin, Nagle, & Paget, 1983; Pullis & Cadwell, 1982).

Another major outcome of the NYLS was a proposal by the principle investigators of the *goodness of fit* model (GOF; e.g., Chess & Thomas, 1986; Thomas, Chess, & Birch, 1968). The GOF is widely accepted by temperament theorists and "implies that the adequacy of an organism's functioning is dependent upon the degree to which properties of its environment are in accord with the organism's own characteristics and style of behaving" (Thomas et al., 1968, p. 137). The similarity of this construct and the basic tenets of ecological theory is quite evident.

The GOF conception was based on the discovery that although variability among the individual difference domains of temperament in the first year of life predicted referral rates later in childhood, it did not fully explain the dynamics that led to referrals to child guidance clinics. Specifically, whereas 70% of the subjects identified as possessing difficult temperament charac- teristics later experienced behavioral difficulties (Thomas et al., 1968), there were cases of children with difficult temperaments who did not develop behavior problems (Chess & Thomas, 1984). Therefore, because other factors contribute to the development of behavior disorders, caution against creating a theory that pinpoints temperament or other child characteristics as the primary determinant of later psychopathology would be prudent.

In this framework, a *good fit* takes place when there is compatibility between the characteristics of the individual and the demands of the environment. In contrast, a *poor fit* occurs when there is incompatibility between the individual and the environment which increases the risk for the development of behavior disorders (Chess & Thomas, 1986). Thus, when demands are consistently made upon a child who does not possess the capacity (either temperamentally or experientially) to meet them, the result is excessive stress on the child which is likely to be perceived as maladjustment by the caretaker.

Scarr (1994) noted that GOF is important for all children. Specifically, children are vulnerable to the naturally ocurring changes of the environment to which they are subjected. A poor fit between child characteristics and demands of the environment can result in a disturbance of child adjustment. Teachers who tend to have the general expectations that all children entering their classrooms possess the capacity to quickly adjust to the environment may be placing certain children under stress which may, in turn, lead to maladaptive behavior patterns. Such findings led Lerner and Lerner (1994) to note that the demands of the social environment (e.g., expectations and attitudes of significant others that interact with the child), as well as the characteristics of the child should be considered in the assessment process. In fact, Thomas and Chess (1977) emphasized that a poor fit may be created by a number of factors, including (a) disparity between environmental demands and child temperament, (b) differences between values and behav- iors developed in the home and expectancies at school, (c) inconsistencies in parental practices resulting in stress on the child, and (d) dissonance between child expectations for acceptance and affection and caretaker exhibition of these characteristics.

Influence of Significant Others in the Environment

Among the factors that impact a child with behavioral difficulties in a classroom are individuals (e.g., peers, teachers, aides, the principal) who interact with that child. Thus, consideration of the influences of these individuals is crucial to obtaining a true ecological portrait of the situation or, more specifically, how the target student fits within the social structure of the classroom. Teachers often control the social influences (e.g., granting opportunities to respond, providing feedback, structuring antecedents and consequences) that govern the interactions between students experiencing difficulties and their peers. It has been well established that teachers do not interact the same with all students (Brophy & Good, 1974; Jackson, 1968). For example, students with learning disabilities received twice as much criticism from teachers (Bryan, 1978), and had fewer response opportunities in regular classrooms than they did in special education classrooms (Bryan, Wheeler, Felcan, & Henek, 1976). A complete assessment of all aspects of the child and the environment is necessary to make sound decisions. This includes the characteristics of the child's behavior as well as characteristics of teachers and other significant persons in the environment.

Algozzine (1979) suggested that others' reactions to specific behaviors exhibited are a contributing factor to identification of emotional disturbance in school children. In other words, certain behaviors may be bothersome to some, and not (or less so) to others (Rhodes, 1967, 1970). This so-called "eye of the beholder" perspective is supported by the literature. Specifically, past research demonstrated that emotional states of a rater of child behavior effects the recorded perceptions.

For example, Forehand and his colleagues consistently found that mothers with higher levels of depression rate their children as being more deviant (Brody & Forehand, 1986; Forehand, Wells, McMahon, Griest, & Rogers, 1982; Griest, Wells, & Forehand, 1979; Rickard, Forehand, Wells, Griest, & MacMahon, 1981) and that measures of maternal distress were more strongly related to measures of child of adjustment than were external evaluation of the child's behavior (Forehand et al., 1982; Griest et al., 1979). This line of research indicates that the emotional state of the mother does effect the perception of the child, suggesting that states such as depression may lower the mother's tolerance level for certain behaviors (Martin, 1988b).

In the classroom setting, the individual most likely to see problem behavior is the classroom teacher. More importantly, the teacher is the most likely source of referral for disciplinary action or special education services or both. In fact, teacher referral is considered among the most important steps in the diagnosis of children with mild handicaps (Reschly, 1988), which, by some estimates, accounts for up to 90% of all children placed in special education (Algozzine & Korinek, 1985). Given the extent to which teachers influence the ultimate classification and placement of their students, and in consideration of the utility of the ecological perspective, consideration of teacher-related variables is warranted.

Research has consistently demonstrated relationships between teachers' views of children's temperament and their views of pupil *teachability* (Keogh, 1994; Kornblau, 1982; Kornblau & Keogh, 1980). It is emphasized that teachers are "key players" in child–school interaction. Keogh (1982, 1986) suggested that an understanding of children's adjustment in the school setting is dependent upon recognizing differences in teacher beliefs, attributions regarding schooling, and perceptions of individual students. Decisions made by teachers regarding their students may be based on their perceptions and beliefs about what pupils should be like. Keogh (1994) refers to this as teachability; that is, "a synthesizing construct to get teachers' views of individual children and their ideas and beliefs about desirable attributes" (p. 248).

Keogh (1982) conducted a study in which teacher participants completed ratings of their "ideal" student. Additionally, teachability ratings of actual students of the participants were obtained. This allowed the researchers to derive a discrepancy score for each child (Ideal – Actual = discrepancy score). Children with discrepancy scores reflecting a poor fit were rated by teachers to be lower on the temperament scales of Task Orientation and Personal/Social Flexibility, and higher in Reactivity. Also, it was found that the frequency of interactions was similar for children who were rated as low and high in teachability; however, the type of interaction differed. With low-teachable children, interactions with the teacher were limited to management and instruction, while high-teachable students experienced more positive social interactions with the teacher. This may represent an affective component of the classroom environment in which some children experience a comfortable and accepting environment, while others may feel rejected or less valued (Keogh, 1994).

Walker (1991) investigated the relationship between teacher distress (e.g., components of burnout) and tolerances for child behaviors. This researcher found significant relationships between burnout and rates of disciplinary referrals and tolerance for socially deviant and physically disturbing behaviors. As proposed by Maslach and Jackson (1981) burnout in this study was defined by three distinct aspects: (a) emotional exhaustion, (b) negative attitudes towards clients or students, and (c) loss of feelings of accomplishment on the job. Maslach (1982) noted that burnout may lead to poor quality of service. In being faithful to ecological theory, it must be noted that the system in which both the child and the teacher exist may contribute significantly to the development of burnout and stress. This spawns ideas of intervention at the systems level. However, this is beyond the scope of this chapter, and the reader is referred to original sources regarding effects of organizational conditions on teachers' emotional well-being (Farber, 1984; Schwab & Iwanicki, 1982a; Schwab, Jackson, & Schuler, 1986).

Whiteman, Young, and Fisher (1985) investigated the relationship of teachers' perceptions of others with the experience of burnout. The results indicated a high positive relationship between burnout and elementary school teachers' perceptions of others. Specifically, a higher degree of burnout corresponded to more negative perceptions of others. Thus, in the case of teachers, negative perceptions of their students may result from poor adjustment on the part of the teacher.

For example, Schwab and Iwanicki (1982b) found that younger teachers suffered from more intense feelings of emotional exhaustion; males displayed higher levels of depersonalization (feelings of detachment, blaming the student for the problems they are experiencing) than did female teachers, as did intermediate level teachers (Grades 7 through 12) when compared to grade school teachers (Kindergarten through Grade 6); and high school teachers experienced a lesser degree of personal accomplishment than did grade school teachers. Stressors that lead to teacher burnout were investigated by Shaw, Keiper, and Flaherty (1985). According to these researchers, the events determined most stressful included notification of unsatisfactory performance, being involuntarily transferred, and being threatened with personal injury.

Algozzine (1979) indicated that perceived deviance "may be as much a function of reactions to behavior as it is the behavior in and of itself " (pp. 1–2). The author referred to this as an ecological perspective of deviance, in which behavior is identified as *disturbing* as opposed to *disturbed*, thus suggesting that the focus should be on both the child and the individuals who interact with the child. Rubin and Balow (1971) concluded that teachers possess a very narrow definition of what is considered appropriate behavior, and that any child falling outside that narrow definition is viewed as needing special attention. An implication with regards to assessment is that if teachers' tolerance levels for child behaviors results in negative reactions, and a potential source of bias is present in the referral and assessment process, then steps must be taken to account for this bias.

Algozzine (1976) found that regular education teachers identified certain behaviors (e.g., social facility, social defiance, physical symptoms, social delinquence) as more disturbing than did special education teachers or teachers-in-training. Likewise, Kerr and Zigmond (1986) found that regular educators were intolerant of inappropriate sexual behavior, stealing, aggression, and refusing to obey rules. Teachers were concerned with behaviors that would lead to adaptation in the the classroom, but not as concerned with behaviors such as poor peer relations.

In summary, the literature supports the notion that numerous environmental variables need to be taken into account when engaging in assessment and problem-solving of behavior and learning problems. These include physiological factors, physical aspects of environmental surrounding, degree and quality of the fit between child and environment, and characteristics of others in the environment (e.g., teachers' perception of the student, tolerances for child misbehavior, and personal adjustment).

ECOLOGICALLY SENSITIVE MEASURES AND TECHNIQUES

Discussed next are a number of measures thought to be sensitive to the ecology in which students find themselves. Each of the described instruments provides a slightly different view of the home–student–school interaction. Utilizing some of these assessment tools to augment the evaluation process will, it is hoped, help the professional clarify the characteristics of the interacting dyads (parent–child, teacher–student, parent–teacher), thus, providing a better understanding of the interaction of the student characteristics with those of the school environment. Some of the measures are commercially available; others have yet to be published commercially and thus must be obtained directly from the test developers. It is not suggested that any one of these instruments be used in isolation, but rather used in combination with one another or other appropriate measures and techniques as required. The reader should also be aware that this is by no means an exhaustive listing of such instrumentation; rather, those included should be regarded as a sampling of what is available.

Eyberg Child Behavior Inventory (ECBI)

The ECBI (Robinson, Eyberg, & Ross, 1980) is a rating scale that is sensitive to the interaction of the parent–child dyad. It looks at the child's externalizing behaviors from the parent's perspective. In this regard, the ECBI is a relatively unique instrument consisting of 36 items focusing on social and emotional behaviors that indicate conduct disorder including aggression, impulsivity, and hyperactivity. Each item is rated on two dimensions: (a) a 7-point Likert Scale ranging from 1 (*never*) to 7 (*always*), reflecting the severity of the problem behavior; and (b) a dichotomous scale (yes or no) used to identify the extent to which a specific behavior is problematic to the parent. The scale yields two scores: the number of problem items indicated (Problem Scale) and a derived Intensity Score (Intensity Scale). The latter component allows evaluation of parental tolerance of child behavior.

The ECBI is used with children from 2 to 16 years of age and is quick and easy to score. In a review of the instrument, Martin (1988b) noted that the ECBI demonstrates validity, differentiating effectively between children with and without conduct disorders, and is also sensitive to treatment effects. Both the Problem and Intensity Scales are considered reliable, with an internal consistency (coefficient alpha) of .98 being noted for each. Test–retest reliability ranged from .86 (for Intensity) to .88 (Problem Behaviors). Strengths of the ECBI are that all items are focused on testing one construct and that the phrasing of questions is behavioral. Estimates of frequency of occurrence, extent to which the behavior is viewed as problematic, and degree to which that behavior is viewed as troublesome provide information relevant to parent tolerance and parent–child interaction. A limitation of the ECBI is its focus on externalizing behaviors and the absence of items related to issues such as anxiety, depression, and learning disabilities. Although the norm sample is not particularly adequate, when the focus of concern is conduct disorder this instrument may be considered.

Sutter–Eyberg Student Behavior Inventory (SESBI)

The SESBI (Sutter & Eyberg, 1984) is a 36-item teacher report measure and is a useful companion to the ECBI. The SESBI has an age range of 2 to 17 years, with acceptable norm samples for the 2 to 7 year ranges; however, 8 to 17 year norms should be used with caution. This checklist examines the teacher's perspective of the child–school interaction by having the teacher identify those student behaviors that are particularly problematic in the classroom. Additionally the SESBI is able to distinguish between behaviors that are conduct disorder related and those that are primarily attentional.

The SESBI yields two scores (Problem and Intensity). Because no manual is available, potential users should obtain pertinent journal articles regarding scale development and psychometric characteristics across studies (e.g., Burns & Owens, 1990; Funderburk & Eyberg, 1989). To summarize, internal consistency (Cronbach's alpha) ranged from .90 to .98 for Intensity and from .93 to .96 for the Problem scale; test–retest estimates ranges from .90 to .94 and .89 to .98 for the Intensity and Problem scales, respectively; interrater reliability ranges from .85 to .95 (Intensity) and .84 to .87 (Problem). Criterion-related validity is evidenced by significant correlations with numerous other rating scale instruments. Sensitivity to treatment effects have been documented (Watson, 1992).

Temperament Assessment Battery for Children (TABC)

The TABC (Martin, 1988a) is a product of modifications of the Temperament Questionnaires originally developed by Thomas, Chess, and Korn (Thomas & Chess, 1977). Consistent with the ecological perspective, the Martin TABC provides three rating scales, allowing for the comparison of the viewpoints of parents, teachers, and clinicians in reference to the temperament characteristics of one particular child (age range 3 to 7 years). The Parent and Teacher Forms each consist of 48 items on which observable behaviors of the young child are rated on a 7-point scale of frequency ranging from 1 (*hardly ever*) to 7 (*almost always*). The Clinician Form, consisting of 24 items, is completed by an examiner immediately following an evaluation session. The scales of the TABC were designed to measure activity level, adaptability to changing social circumstances, approach/withdrawal tendencies to novel social stimuli, emotional intensity, distractibility, and persistence. The author reports internal consistency reliability, indexed through alpha coefficients, around .85 for the scales across several samples. Six month test–retest reliability ranged between .70 and .81, whereas intervals of 1 to 2 years revealed test–retest coefficients ranging from .37 to .70. Martin (1988a) summarized a good deal of validity data in the manual for the TABC that provides substantial support for the criterion and construct validity of the TABC.

The Instructional Environment Scale (TIES)

Ysseldyke and Christenson (1987) developed the TIES to "systematically describe the extent to which a student's academic and behavioral problems are a function of factors in the instructional environment and to identify starting points in designing appropriate instructional interventions for individual students" (p. 1). McKee and Witt (1989) noted that the TIES is "not so much a test or an instrument as it is a process to follow in systematically examining a classroom environment" (p. 373). The TIES uses multiple sources of information thereby providing a more ecologically valid view of the learning environment. It is for use in an elementary school setting and is composed of the following 12 components:

1. Instructional Presentation.
2. Classroom Environment.
3. Teacher Expectation.
4. Cognitive Emphasis.
5. Motivational Strategies.
6. Relevant Practice.
7. Academic Engaged Time.
8. Informed Feedback.
9. Adaptive Instruction.
10. Progress Evaluation.
11. Instructional Planning.
12. Student Understanding.

Howell (1989) reported that the TIES is an attempt to operationalize the long held assumption that the instructional environment plays a significant role in the development of classroom academic and social behaviors. Procedurally, the TIES requires the user to engage in a number of observations and interviews (teacher and student). Interviews with the teacher are highly structured and allow the user to gather information regarding planning, expectations, monitoring, and evaluation procedures. Interviews with the student, also structured, are designed to assess the pupils' understanding of assignments and to check for their rates of success. Guidelines for the classroom observations center around the 12 components of the TIES system and entail recording narrative responses to 10 of the 12 components. Interclass correlation coefficients for interobserver reliability ranged from .83 to .96. Content validity of the TIES is generally well established via a detailed review of the relevant literature for each of the 12 components noted. Once data is collected from the multiple sources, the user then combines the information in order to make judgments regarding the quality of the instructional environment.

Student Observation System (SOS)

The SOS is one portion of The Behavior Assessment System for Children (BASC; Reynolds & Kamphaus, 1992). The SOS component lends itself particularly well to ecological assessment of a child within a classroom. This provides a multidimensional system for recording classroom behavior and may be appropriately utilized in either regular or special education classes. The SOS is composed of three parts that facilitate different aspects of intervention planning including: Time Sampling of Behavior, Behavior Key and Checklist, and Teacher's Interaction with Student. These parts provide three different types of quantitative and qualitative information important to clinicians in diagnosis and intervention. The Time Sampling of Behavior portion is made up of thirty 3-second behavioral observations that are completed in a period of 15 minutes and yield reliable information about a child's deviant or adaptive classroom behavior. Thus, it "provides a tally of the frequency of a child's behaviors in broad descriptive terms" (Reynolds & Kamphaus, 1992, p. 39). The Behavior Key and Checklist portion allows the observer to identify the most frequently occurring behaviors as well as those that are the most disruptive within the classroom. Additionally, a space is provided on the SOS record form to record teacher–student interactions, including the teacher's behavior change techniques (e.g., type reinforcement), and the teacher's location relative to the target student. Space is also provided in which to record specific disruptive classroom incidents (antecedents, disruptive behavior, consequences).

The SOS takes an ecological perspective documenting a wide range of behavioral interactions taking place in a classroom and can be used repeatedly over time, thus facilitating the evaluation of intervention strategies. Moreover, it may be used to compare the behavior of the target child with that of the classroom peer group. Although it is not norm referenced, the observer can make comparison within the classroom norm by observing two or three children within the target child's peer group.

Disturbing Behavior Checklist I (DBC I) and II (DBC II)

To get at the individual teacher's reaction to and perspective on a particular student, Algozzine (1979) developed these two scales to aid the process of determining the relative *disturbingness* of behaviors characteristic of emotionally (DBC I) and learning disabled (DBC II) students. The DBC I is a modification of the Behavior Problem Checklist (Quay & Peterson, 1979) and consists of 55 behaviors rated on a Likert scale, ranging from 1 (*not disturbing*) to 5 (*very disturbing*). The scale yields the following four factor-analytically derived scores: (a) Socially Immature Behaviors, (b) Socially Defiant Behaviors, (c) Physically or Motorically Disturbing Behaviors, and (d) Socialized Delinquent Behaviors. Kuder-Richardson reliability coefficients for the four factors ranged from .62 to .93. The DBC II items, on the other hand, were developed from texts covering the characteristics of children with learning disabilities. The scale is comprised of 51 items, organized into the following three indicator factors: General Perceptual Problems, Unmanageable Behavior, and Social Immaturity. Internal consistency (KR20) is quite strong, ranging from .87 to .96.

Teacher Social Behavior Standards and Expectations (SBS)

The SBS purports to measure the type and intensity of demands and expectations unique to the learning environment of a particular classroom. Walker and Rankin (1980) developed this scale to evaluate the behavioral demands/expectations of teachers (Walker, 1986). It contains 107 items focusing on two domains, with the first referring to desirable behaviors and the second to maladaptive and inappropriate behaviors. Items on Section I, which contains the desirable or adaptive behaviors, are rated as to whether they are "critical," "desirable," or "unimportant" in adjustment to the classroom. On the other hand, the maladaptive behaviors, contained within Section II, are rated as "unacceptable," "tolerated," or "acceptable." A third section requests that the rater re-rate certain items endorsed in the previous sections. Specifically, for behaviors rated as "critical" or "unacceptable," teachers are asked to decide whether (a) the behavior must be within normal limits before the child can enter the classroom or (b) appropriate behavior related technical assistance would be sufficient for the child's maintenance in a regular education classroom.

The scale was normed on 2,000 teachers in Canada, which may limit the generalizability. However, development of local norms would easily resolve this problem. Reliability of the instrument was studied by Walker and Rankin (1983). They reported a test–retest estimate of approximately .80, and internal consistency estimates exceeding .90. Additionally, the SBS they found to correlate significantly with criterion variables, such as direct observation of teachers' management and instructional behavior.

Maslach Burnout Inventory Form Ed (MBI)

The use of instruments such as the MBI can provide insight into teacher characteristics which may effect the functioning of the teacher–student dyad. The MBI focuses on the teacher's indicators of burnout, thus providing the evaluator with valuable information which might be used in interpreting teacher reports and in anticipating teacher tolerance for classroom interventions and variations in student behavior. The MBI Form Ed (Maslach & Jackson, 1986) was developed for use with teachers and is entitled the "Educators Survey." It is composed of 22 items and taps three aspects of the burnout syndrome identified by the principle author as Emotional Exhaustion (EE), Depersonalization (D), and Lack of Personal Accomplishment (PA). Greater feelings of accomplishment are denoted by higher scores on the PA scale, which measures feelings of competence and successful achievement in one's work with students. EE measures feelings of being overextended, and D assesses unfeeling and impersonal responses toward students (Walker, 1991).

The three-factor structure of the instrument has been verified. Internal consistency reliability estimates are adequate for EE (Cronbach alpha range .88 to .90), D (.74 to .76), and PA (.72 to .76) across two studies (Gold, 1984; Iwaniki & Schwab, 1981). Test–retest reliability is adequate for EE (.82) and PA (.80), but was not sufficient for D (.60; Maslach & Jackson, 1981). Evidence for validity cited by Maslach and Jackson (1981a) include findings that indicate burnout scores are higher in stressful job settings and predict job turnover and absenteeism.

CASE STUDY

The following case study illustrates some of the components and instruments which can be involved in an ecological approach to assessment. It also examines how the individual's characteristics interact with other aspects of the environment (physical, social, personal) to produce subsystem dyads. Specific aspects assessed are physiological characteristics of the target individual, the physical environment, child temperament qualities, the influence of significant others in the environment, and the quality of goodness of fit between the individual and all the subsystems of which he is a part.

Tony, a 7-year, 10-month-old male, was referred to the child study team (CST) by his classroom teacher, Ms. P., due to what she termed *emotional* problems. He is presently in second grade. The CST at Tony's school is made up of at least one "master" teacher who is identified by the school's principal, the classroom teacher of the child being discussed, a special educator, a school psychologist, the assistant principal at the school, and other professionals deemed necessary for the child being discussed. This particular elementary school is committed to facilitating family involvement, and thus, as a rule, elicits parental involvement with the CST. Over the course of a 3-week period, multiple sources of information, much of which is ecologically sensitive, were collected.

Review of Records

This record review provides information on some of the physiological factors that may be influencing Tony's interaction with subsystems in his educational environment. Tony's cumulative file included academic information and histories provided by Tony's mother. Tony is the youngest of four children and lives with his siblings (8, 11, and 15 years) and his natural parents. Information in the file revealed that the mother had experienced a difficult pregnancy with Tony, complicated by maternal depression and failure to gain sufficient weight during gestation. Tony was born 4 weeks premature, was small for gestational age, and was jaundiced. He was kept in the nursery for 5 days before being allowed to go home. Medical history is significant for allergies, numerous bouts of tonsillitis, pneumonia, and an accident resulting in stitches to his chin. Tony is currently receiving immunotherapy for the numerous food and environmental allergies from which he suffers.

Delays in language and motor development were noted. The language delays were identified when Tony was 4 years old, and resulted in services from a speech/language therapist. He reportedly made some gains in therapy, and language skills were found to be only slightly delayed at the time Tony entered first grade. Due to the illnesses and resulting absences, Tony was retained in kindergarten. Since that time, satisfactory academic progress has been made; however, his performance over the past few weeks had begun to suffer. Additionally, although he is a year older than most of his classmates, he is physically smaller.

Teacher and Parent Interviews

Significant others in the Tony's ecosystem were interviewed to provide information relative to Tony's functioning in two of the subsystems of his environment: the teacher–student dyad and the parent–child dyad. The interviews also provided some sense of the demand level of both of these subsystems and how well he was coping with those demands. His teacher reported that emotional problems were evident early in the school year. In fact, she reported that she was somewhat "taken aback" by Tony's first day in her classroom when he had trouble separating from his mother who had brought him to school. Ms. P. had planned outdoor physical activities for the first hour of school. When Tony arrived late that day, his mother and he had to find the class on the playground where the group was engaged in a competitive sports activity. She reported that he was reluctant to join in the activity, even when coaxed by herself. Ms. P. expressed that Tony's mother "coddled" him that day, and that this had emerged as a pattern during the school year. She reported that "after that I knew that I would have my work cut out for me" and that "children had to learn to be independent or they would never make it in this world." Ms. P. indicated that she had tried to help Tony on several occasions, but that her efforts had resulted in his becoming emotionally upset and, at times, visibly tearful. Tony reportedly "looks sad," has easily hurt feelings, shows withdrawal from social and competitive situations, and is overly fearful. She also reported that when Tony is called on in class, he "trembles" and refuses "to open his mouth." She indicated that when this happens she moves on to another student to have the question answered. Ms. P. said that she wishes to help Tony, but is at a loss as to how to do so.

Tony's mother, Ms. E., also participated in an interview. She reported that she knew that, of late, Tony had not been doing as well in school as he had in the past. She also had noticed that he does not seem to like school anymore, and that it is more difficult for him to "get going" in the mornings. She stated that she knows Ms. P. is genuinely concerned about Tony, which she appreciates. Ms. E. indicated that she had been very pleased with the teacher Tony had last year because she was so supportive of Tony that he actually began to come out of his shell a bit. She further stated that she "felt bad" that she could not get off work more often to come in to school like Ms. P. thinks she should, but that she "has to work" and transportation is a problem. She noted that she tried to help Tony with his school work, but that she did not "go very far in school myself." However, his older sister "gets straight As" in school and is good at helping the younger children. Both she and Mr. E. work, with Mr. E. working 12 hours a day 6 days a week "just to make ends meet." When Tony comes home, he is under the care of his older siblings until one of his parents gets home from work. He was "sick a lot" when he was younger and is, at this time, more susceptible to illness than his siblings. Because of this, he has tended to get considerable attention from both his parents and his older siblings. She noted that he engages in normal play activities in the neighborhood, such as riding bikes and playing board games, but prefers to play with one or two friends rather than a larger group. He is not a "thrill seeker" like his older brother (20 months his senior). It is further reported that he is perfectly happy doing activities by himself, and that this is also true of other family members. Although he is "easier to cry" than his siblings, she believes that he is not especially sad or overly emotional.

Tony's former teacher, Ms. T., was contacted and indicated that Tony was a "sweet and sensitive" child. She indicated that he was initially "fearful" of the classroom, but that he had warmed up over time. Although he continued to show difficulties with changes in situations and settings, he had gotten to the point that he initiated interactions with her and familiar peers.

Observational Data

The observational aspect of the assessment provides not only information on the physical environment of the classroom, but also on the target child's behavior and interaction with teacher's and peers within that environment. The observer thereby gleans understanding of the subsystems involved and the behavioral characteristics of the target child when he is interacting within them.

The classroom was observed on three occasions. The first was informal and focused on the physical characteristics and general dynamics of the classroom. On this occasion, there were 24 students present in the classroom, approximately equally split between boys and girls. Physically, the room was arranged into five rows of about six desks. Tony was seated in the third desk in the far right row. Lighting was sufficient, and the temperature was comfortable. The classroom could be characterized as busy, but certainly not rowdy. This particular morning there was an aide present in the classroom (this is generally the case for the class between 8 and 11:15 a.m.). The teacher enthusiastically engaged a large group of children in a hands-on mathematics activity, while the aide led the smaller group in a reading activity. Ms. P. provided praise and encouragement to those students actively participating. Likewise, the aide appeared to be positive in her interactions with the group as a whole.

Two additional observations (15 minutes each) utilizing the SOS (described previously), allowed for direct observation of Tony, of peer comparisons, and of interactions with peers and the teacher. Data were aggregated across the two observation periods. A randomly selected male student (Peer 1) and a "strong" student (Peer 2) selected by the teacher served as peer comparisons. The time sampling portion of the SOS revealed that Tony exhibited similar responses to instruction as did both peers. Considerably less peer interaction was noted for Tony than for either peer, although it should be noted that Peer 1 was also relatively lower in exhibition of this type of behavior when compared to Peer 2. Tony displayed a higher frequency of inattentive and somatization behaviors than either Peer 1 or 2. The teacher was positioned at the blackboard and engaged several students in the lesson; Tony was not among them. Tony generally sat quietly, looking about the room during periods of 30 to 45 seconds. Peer 2, on the other hand, was very active, enthusiastically waving his hand with answers to questions being posed by the teacher; he was called on an average once per 5 minute interval of the observation.

Rating Scales

The rating scales used in this section provide information related to the target child's behavior within different dyads or subsystems of his environment. Additionally, they provide an idea of the differences in demands and expectations within these dyads and subsystems.

Tony's behavior/temperament was evaluated in multiple settings (home and school). Tony's mother, father, and teacher completed the Temperament Assessment Battery for Children (TABC). Both parents rated Tony in a similar fashion with regard to all the temperament dimensions. However, there were inconsistencies in ratings between his parents and his teacher. Specifically, the teacher rated Tony as being less active, less adaptable to changes in the environment, and more likely to withdraw from new social situations than did his parents. All raters noted difficulties in Tony's inclination to persist at difficult tasks, and the teacher rated Tony as more distractible than his same-age peers. It should be noted that such discrepancies could reflect that either behaviors exhibited in the settings vary due to the differing demands of the environments, or that the raters in the respective settings have differing expectations or tolerances for certain behaviors.

Tolerance Levels

Information on the tolerance of the teacher in the teacher–student dyad will provide a better understanding of the behavioral expectations held for the target child's particular classroom.

The last instrument utilized was the DBC I. The reader is reminded that it is a general rating of what child behaviors a teacher finds disturbing and not a measure of the behavior of the target child. The most notable information obtained from the DBC is that Ms. P. found the class of behaviors referred to as "Socially Immature" as being particularly disturbing. Specific behaviors appearing on this scale included lack of self-confidence, feelings of inferiority, social withdrawal, general fearfulness, inability to relax, chronic sadness, and passivity.

Hypotheses Generation

Many hypotheses for the origins of Tony's behavioral difficulties may be generated from the multiple sources of data noted above. Two of these are discussed here. Either could result in the perceived difficulties reported to the CST.

First, there may be a mismatch between the demands of the classroom and Tony's temperamental characteristics. Ms. P.'s expectations may be that a child possess certain qualities or characteristics. Tony does not possess these qualities, perhaps due to his temperamental characteristics which are reflective of a "slow to warm up" or cautious child. Formulation of symptoms are often a result of such a mismatch. In Tony's case, he seems unhappy and is developing a dislike of school which places him at risk for a school phobic reaction in the future. This hypothesis is supported by ratings of Tony's temperament, his history of former successful experiences in school, and behavioral observations of Ms. P.'s interactions with Tony and his peers. It appears that Tony is a young man with temperamental qualities reflective of a child who is "slow to warm" to new or different situations or both. However, there is also evidence to suggest that he is able to adjust to situations given time and a supportive or nurturing environment.

In this hypothesis there exists an incompatibility between the components of the subsystem, made up of the student and the educational environment. In other words, according to this hypothesis, a mismatch between child characteristics and the demand level of this current learning environment are the cause of this child's difficulty with school.

A second hypothesis is that Ms. P. possesses a particularly strong intolerance for socially immature behaviors, which are the type that Tony is reported to have. Others (parents, a former teacher) have reported similar behaviors, yet have not perceived Tony as a problematic child. A caretaker's sensitivity or aversion to a particular type of behavior may lead him or her to report those behaviors more negatively and, thus, as in need of attention.

In this second hypothesis the incompatibility is again focused in the student–teacher dyad, but more specifically with the teacher whose particular intolerance (socially immature behavior) level alone may be sufficient to cause her to perceive this child as problematic, when others would not.

There are other plausible hypotheses of which space does not permit discussion. It is important to illustrate that data such as those collected for this case study are crucial to accurate evaluation of presenting problems. This will, in turn, guide us in selection of appropriate intervention strategies. As was the case with assessment, interventions often focus on changing the child in some way. When we alter our assessment strategies, alternative interventions strategies need to follow. Discussed next are some general recommendations for alternative interventions which would apply to the case presented here, as well as to others. In the case of Tony, other factors contributing to intervention conceptualization would be his extensive medical history, the seating arrangements in the classroom, and the antecedents and consequences of the problem behaviors noted by Ms. P.

CONCLUSIONS

Because the focus of this chapter was assessment from an ecological perspective, it is quite evident that the nature of interventions will be greatly influenced by ecological assessment techniques. The ecological perspective demands that a clinician's intervention repertoire be expanded to take into account the many possible environmental influences. This is not to imply that traditional intervention strategies are passe, rather interventions should be broadly construed to include staff sensitivity training, environmental change and specific accommodation, as well as the development of sound behavioral management plans for a specific student. Many practitioners are becoming aware that, in certain circumstances, such multifaceted alternative interventions must be considered. In the ecological framework, the child is viewed as part of a social system that may require alterations in not only the child, but also within the environment and within individuals that make up that environment. Implications for intervention, and perhaps more importantly prevention, may be directed toward increasing teacher's sensitivity to individual differences in temperament and other child characteristics, as well as helping them become more aware of their own reactions to these differences. Another approach might emphasize altering a caretaker's reaction to disturbing behaviors. Still another strategy worth exploring involves matching a child (who exhibits problematic behaviors) with a teacher according to the teacher's assessed levels of tolerance or based on teacher and child adjustment characteristics.

Interventions at the systems level should also be considered. In fact, many issues discussed in this chapter may best be dealt with at that level. This is especially true when one considers the sensitive issue of determining the impact of characteristics associated with a teacher. Some of the techniques presented above involve the assessment of teachers' own attitudes and adjustment; this is not something that the teachers are accustomed to and may raise questions regarding the relevance of this information to the evaluation of a "child's" difficulties. Unfortunately, when this reaction happens, there is a risk of the teacher perceiving the evaluators are seeking to place blame. The practitioner should avoid this perception or else they jeopardize the consultative relationship with the teacher. Although there will be times in which a specific caretaker must be the focus of the interventions, it would be more effective to deal with issues regarding sensitivity to individual domains, tolerance levels, and personal adjustment (stress, burnout) at a systems level prior to such factors resulting in extensive difficulties among faculty and staff. This might be achieved via inservice training or consultation with relevant school administrators regarding the organizational factors that influence adjustment, such as job satisfaction.

REFERENCES

Adams, R. S., & Biddle, B. J. (1970). *Realities of teaching.* New York: Holt, Rinehart & Winston.

Algozzine, B. (1976). The disturbing child: What you see is what you get? *The Alberta Journal of Educational Research, 22,* 330–333.

Algozzine, B. (1979). *The disturbing child: A validation report* (Research Report No. 8.). Minneapolis: University of Minnesota, Institute for Research on Learning Disabilities.

Algozzine, B., & Korinek, L. (1985). Where is special education for students with high prevalence handicaps going? *Exceptional Children, 51,* 388–394.

Algozzine, B., Ysseldyke, J., & Christenson, S. (1983). The influence of teachers' tolerance for specific kinds of behaviors on their ratings of a third grade student. *The Alberta Journal of Educational Research, 9*(2), 89–97.

Axelrod, S., Hall, R. V., & Tams, A. (1972, May). *A comparison of common seating arrangements in the classroom.* Paper presented at the Kansas Symposium on Behavior Analysis in Education, Lawrence, KS.

Barclay, J. R. (1983). Meta-analysis of temperament–treatment interactions with alternative learning and counseling treatments. *Developmental Review, 3,* 410–443.

Billman, J., & McDevitt, S. C. (1980). Convergence of parent and observer ratings of temperament with observation of peer interaction in nursery school. *Child Development, 51,* 395–400.

Brody, G. H., & Forehand, R. (1986). Maternal perceptions of child maladjustment as a function of the combined influence of child behavior and maternal depression. *Journal of Consulting and Clinical Psychology, 54,* 237–240.

Brophy, J. E., & Good, T. L. (1974). *Teacher–student relationships: Causes and consequences.* New York: Holt, Rinehart & Winston.

Bryan, T. H. (1978). Social relationships and verbal interactions of learning disabled children. *Journal of Learning Disabilities, 7,* 26–34.

Bryan, T. H., Wheeler, R., Felcan, J., & Henek, T. (1976). "Come on Dummy" An observational study of children's communication. *Journal of Learning Disabilities, 9,* 661–669.

Burk, E. (1980). *Relationship of temperamental traits to achievement and adjustment in gifted children.* Unpublished doctoral dissertation, Fordham University, New York.

Burns, G. L., & Owens, S. M. (1990). Disruptive behavior in the classroom: Initial standardization of a new teacher rating scale. *Journal of Abnormal Child Psychology, 18,* 515–525.

Chess, S., & Thomas, A. (1984). *The origins and evolution of behavior disorders: Infancy to early adult life.* New York: Brunner/Mazel.

Chess, S., & Thomas, A. (1986). *Temperament in clinical practice.* New York: Guilford.

Farber, B. A. (1984). Stress and burnout in suburban teachers. *Journal of Educational Research, 77,* 225–331.

Farley, F. H. (1981). Basic process individual differences: A biologically based theory of individualization for cognitive, affective, and creative outcome. In F. H. Farley & N. J. Gordon (Eds.), *Psychology and education: The state of the union.* Berkely, CA: McCutchan.

Forehand, R., Wells, K. C., McMahon, R. J., Griest, D., & Rogers, T. (1982). Maternal perception of maladjustment in clinic-referred children: An extension of earlier research. *Journal of Behavioral Assessment, 4,* 145–151.

Funderburk, B. W., & Eyberg, S. M. (1989). Psychometric characteristics of the Sutter–Eyberg Student Behavior Inventory: A school behavior rating scale for use with preschool children. *Behavioral Assessment, 11,* 297–313.

Gold, Y. (1984). Burnout: A major problem for the teaching profession. *Education, 104,* 271–273.

Graham, P., Rutter, M., & George, S. (1973). Temperament characteristics as predictors of behavior disorders in children. *American Journal of Orthopsychiatry, 43,* 328–339.

Griest, D. L., Wells, K. C., & Forehand, R. (1979). An examination of predictors of maternal perceptions of maladjustment in clinic-referred children. *Journal of Abnormal Psychology, 88,* 277–281.

Howell, K. W. (1989). Review of The Instructional Environment Scale. In J. C. Conoley & J. J. Kramer (Eds.), *Tenth mental measurements yearbook.* Lincoln, NE: The Buros Institute.

Iwanicki, E. F., & Schwab, R. L. (1981). A cross-validation study of the Maslach Burnout Inventory. *Educational and Psychological Measurement, 41,* 1167–1174.

Jackson, P. W. (1968). *Life in classrooms.* New York: Holt, Rinehart & Winston.

Keogh, B. K. (1982). Children's temperament and teachers' decisions. In R. Porter & G. M. Collins (Eds.), *Temperamental differences in infants and young children* (pp. 269–279). London: Pitman.

Keogh, B. K. (1986). Temperament and schooling: Meaning of goodness of fit? In J. V. Lerner & R. M. Lerner (Eds.), *New directions for child development: Temperament and social interaction in infants and children* (pp. 89–108). San Francisco: Jossey–Bass

Keogh, B. K. (1994). Temperament and teacher's views of teachability. In W. B. Carey & S. C. McDivitt (Eds.), *Prevention and early intervention: Individual differences as risk factors for the mental health of children* (pp. 246–254). New York: Brunner/Mazel.

Kerr, M. M., & Zigmond, N. (1986). What do high school teachers want? A study of expectations and standards. *Education and Treatment of Children, 9,* 239–249.

Kornblau, B. W. (1982). The Teachable Pupil Survey: A technique for assessing teachers' perceptions of pupil attributes. *Psychology in the Schools, 19,* 170–174.

Kornblau, B. W., & Keogh, B. K. (1980). Teachers' perceptions and educational decisions. In J. J. Gallagher (Ed.), *New directions for exceptional children: No. 1. The ecology of exceptional children* (pp. 87–101). San Francisco: Jossey-Bass.

Lerner, J. V., & Galambos, N. (1985). Mother role satisfaction, mother–child interaction, and child temperament: A process model. *Developmental Psychology, 21,* 1157–1164.

Lerner, J. V., & Lerner, R. M. (1994). Explorations of the goodness-of-fit model in early adolescence. In W. B. Carey & S. C. McDivitt (Eds.), *Prevention and early intervention: Individual differences as risk factors for the mental health of children* (pp. 161–169). New York: Brunner/Mazel.

Martin, R. P. (1988a). *The temperament assessment battery for children.* Brandon, VT: Clinical Psychology.

Martin, R. P. (1988b). *Assessment of personality and behavior problems: Infancy through adolescence.* New York: Guilford.

Martin, R. P., Drew, K. D., Gaddis, L. R., & Moseley, M. (1988). Prediction of elementary school achievement from preschool temperament: Three studies. *School Psychology Review, 17,* 125–137.

Martin, R. P., & Holbrook, J. (1985). Relationship of temperament characteristics to the academic achievement of first grade children. *Journal of Psychoeducational Assessment, 3,* 131–140.

Martin, R. P., Nagle, R., & Paget, K. (1983). Relationship between temperament and classroom behavior, teachers, attitudes, and academic achievement. *Journal of Psychoeducational Assessment, 1,* 377–386.

Martin, R. P., Paget, K., & Nagle, R. (1983). Relationships between temperament and classroom behavior, teacher attitudes, and academic achievement. *Journal of Psychoeducational Assessment, 1,* 377–386.

Maslach, C. (1982). *Burnout: The cost of caring.* Englewood Cliffs, NJ: Prentice-Hall.

Maslach, C., & Jackson, S. E. (1981). *MBI: Maslach Burnout Inventory Manual.* Palo Alto, CA: Consulting Psychologists Press.

Maslach, C., & Jackson, S. E. (1986). *MBI: Maslach Burnout Inventory Manual.* Palo Alto, CA: Consulting Psychologists Press.

McKee, W. T., & Witt, J. C. (1989). Review of The Instructional Environment Scale. In J. C. Conoley & J. J. Kramer (Eds.), *Tenth mental measurements yearbook.* Lincoln, NE: The Buros Institute.

Paget, K. D., Nagle, R. J., & Martin, R. P. (1984). Interrelationships betweem temperament characteristics and first-grade teacher–student interactions. *Journal of Abnormal Child Psychology, 12,* 547–560.

Pullis, M., & Caldwell, J. (1982). The influence of children's temperament characteristics on teacher's decision strategies. *American Educational Research Journal, 19,* 165–181.

Quay, H. C., & Peterson, D. R. (1979). *Manual for the Behavior Problem Checklist.* Miami, FL: H. C. Quay.

Reschly, D. J. (1988). Special education reform: School psychology revolution. *School Psychology Review, 17,* 459–475.

Reynolds, C. R., & Kamphaus, R. W. (1992). *BASC Behavior Assessment System for Children: Manual.* Circle Pines, MN: American Guidance Services.

Rhodes, W. C. (1967). The disturbing child: A problem of ecological management. *Exceptional Children, 33,* 449–455.

Rhodes, W. C. (1970). A community participation analysis of emotional disturbance. *Exceptional Children, 36,* 309–314.

Rickard, K. M., Forehand, R., Wells, K. C., Griest, D. L., & McMahon, R. J. (1981). A comparison of mothers of clinic-referred deviant, clinic-referred nondeviant, and nonclinic children. *Behaviour Research and Therapy, 19,* 201–205.

Robinson, E. A., Eyberg, S. M., & Ross, A. W. (1980). The standardization of an inventory of child conduct problem behavior. *Journal of Clinical Child Psychology, 9,* 22–29.

Rubin, R., & Balow, B. (1971). Learning and behavior disorders: A longitudinal study. *Exceptional children, 15,* 293–299.

Sarasson, S. B., & Doris, J. (1979). *Educational handicap, public policy, and social history.* New York: Free Press.

Sattler, J. M. (1988). *Assessment of Children* (3rd ed.). San Diego: Author.

Scarr, S. (1994). Genetics and individual differences: How Chess and Thomas shaped developmental thought. In W. B. Carey & S. C. McDevitt (Eds.), *Prevention and early intervention: Individual differences as risk factors for the mental health of children* (pp. 170–178). New York: Brunner/Mazel.

Schwab, R. L., & Iwanicki, E. F. (1982a). Perceived role conflict, role ambiguity and teacher burnout. *Educational Administration Quarterly, 18,* 60–74.

Schwab, R. L., & Iwanicki, E. F. (1982b). Who are our burned out teachers? *Educational Research Quarterly, 7,* 5–16.

Schwab, R. L., Jackson, S. E., & Schuler, R. S. (1986). Educator burnout: Sources and consequences. *Educational Research Quarterly, 10,* 14–30.

Shaw, D. G., Keiper, R. W., & Flaherty, C. E. (1985). Stress causing events for teachers. *Education, 106,* 72–77.

Steinzor, B. (1950). The spatial factor in face-to-face discussion groups. *Journal of Abnormal Social Psychology, 45,* 552–555.

Sutter, I., & Eyberg, S. M. (1984). *Sutter–Eyberg Behavior Inventory.* Gainesville, FL: S. M. Eyberg.

Terestman, N. (1980). Mood quality and intensity in nursery school children as predictors of behavior disorder. *American Journal of Orthopsychiatry, 50,* 125–128.

Thomas, A., & Chess, S. (1977). *Temperament and development.* New York: Brunner/Mazel.

Thomas, A., Chess, S., & Birch, H. (1968). *Temperament and behavioral disorders in childhood.* New York: New York University Press.

Thomas, A., Chess, S., Birch, H., Hertzig, M., & Korn, S. (1963). *Behavioral individuality in early childhood.* New York: New York University Press.

Walker, B. A. (1991). *A study of the relationship between teacher burnout and tolerance of disturbing classroom behaviors.* Unpublished doctoral dissertation, University of Southern Mississippi, Hattiesburg.

Walker, H. M. (1986). The Assessment for Integration into Mainstream Settings (AIMS) assessment system: Rationale, instruments, procedures and outcomes. *Journal of Clinical Child Psychology, 15,* 55–63.

Walker, H. M., & Rankin, R. (1980). *The SBS inventory of teacher social behavior standards and expectations.* Eugene, OR: University of Oregon Press.

Walker, H. M., & Rankin, R. (1983). Assessing the behavioral expectations and demands of the less restrictive setting. *School Psychology Review, 12,* 274–284.

Watson, T. S. (1992). Review of Sutter-Eyberg Student Behavior Inventory. In J. C. Conoley & J. J. Kramer (Eds.), *Eleventh mental measurements yearbook.* Lincoln, NE: The Buros Institute.

Whiteman, J. L., Young, J. C., & Fisher, M. L. (1985). Burnout and student behavior. *Education, 105,* 299–305.

Will, M. (1986). *Educating students with learning problems: A shared responsibility.* Washington, DC: U. S. Department of Education.

Ysseldyke, J. E., & Christenson, S. L. (1987). *The Instructional Environment Scale Manual.* Austin, TX: PRO-ED.

3

Ecological Interventions With Students

Jane Close Conoley
Texas A&M University
Pamela Carrington Rotto
University of Nebraska–Lincoln

Previous chapters in this volume outlined the important theoretical and conceptual elements of ecological psychology. This chapter contains only a small portion of this background to provide a foundation for the exploration of various interventions useful in assisting students to meet the demands of the school context. Although theoretically there is an infinite number of interventions that might be useful to assist students, selection of the best intervention is determined by who presents the problem, the nature of the problem, and by the forces present in each student's unique life space (Apter & Conoley, 1984).

Proponents of the ecological orientation take the position that behavior is determined by the *interaction* of individual and environmental characteristics. Although all major approaches to understanding human behavior used to design treatment approaches for school-aged children cite internal and external forces as operating together to produce behavior, they differ significantly in emphasis (Apter, 1977, 1982; Barker, 1978; Gump, 1980; Hewett, 1987; Hobbs, 1975, 1982; Lewin, 1951; Rhodes, 1967, 1970).

For example, both psychodynamic and biophysical models are concerned, for the most part, with the definition and understanding of internal forces. Although classical psychodynamic approaches have lost some popularity as bases for interventions, biophysical strategies are used frequently with students. Psychodynamic theorists focus primarily on *needs* and *drives* and on the investigation of patterns of behavior that occur at various stages of development. Biophysical theorists, on the other hand, emphasize physiological or temperamental conditions that may lead to certain typical behavior patterns (Thomas & Chess, 1977; Thomas, Chess, & Birch, 1968).

55

Biophysical approaches include psychotropic medication administered to students to modify their behavior. Both these approaches may be termed *medical model* to illustrate their emphasis on internal, individual characteristics as most important in understanding a student's behavior.

Behavioral and sociological models are concerned mainly with external forces. The behavior theorist tries to understand stimulus–response patterns and the reinforcing and punishing conditions in the environment that produce particular sequences of behaviors. This functional analysis of behavior is a commonly used approach to planning interventions for students. Sociologists, on the other hand, are more concerned with the broader environment including institutions, communities, culture, and society in their efforts to understand conditions that produce individual and group behavior. Although this perspective is cited frequently, for example when we note a child's poverty and neighborhood as risk factors for behavioral deviance, few school-based interventions have emerged from this model.

In contrast to these other approaches, ecological theory maintains an equal emphasis of concern for internal and external forces when attempting to understand human behavior and making plans to facilitate change. Ecologists assume there is a unique pattern of explanatory forces for each student (Allen-Meares & Lane, 1987) and agree that behavior is a product of the interaction between internal forces and environmental circumstances. Thus, ecologists examine ecosystems rather than individuals. Ecosystems are composed of all the interacting systems of living things and their nonliving surroundings. Ecosystems have histories and internal development that make each unique and constantly changing. When a student is successful in a particular situation, ecologists see the ecosystem as congruent or balanced. On the other hand, when such congruence does not exist, the student is likely to be considered deviant (i.e., out of harmony with social norms) or incompetent (i.e., unable to perform to a certain criterion in the unchanged setting). When this is the case, ecologists say the system is not balanced and that particular elements are in conflict with one another. Such conflicts are termed *points of discordance*; that is, specific places where there is a failure to match between the child and the ecosystem (Conoley & Haynes, 1992).

Figure 3.1 is an illustration of the many interacting elements that characterize most students' lives. The relationships graphed in Fig. 3.1 could be harmonious or filled with discord. The student might receive assistance from one system to succeed in another or may find that activities in one interfere with competence in the other. Relationships drawn between a student and his or her important systems create an ecomap (Newbrough, Walker, & Abril, 1978) that can guide critical aspects of intervention

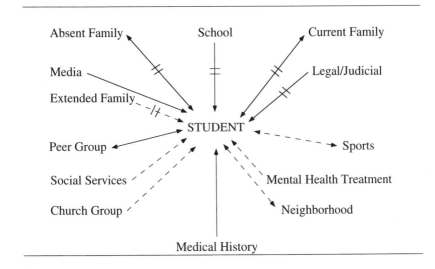

FIG. 3.1.   Ecomap of student system.

planning. This technique bears some resemblance to the genogram approach advocated by McGoldrick and Gerson (1985) but focuses beyond the biological family into other life spaces of the child.

INTERVENTION ASSUMPTIONS

The breadth of ecological theory may lead some to believe that all interventions are ecological, thus confusing ecology with eclecticism. Although almost every known psychological and educational intervention may be a potential tool to assist students, ecological interventions are designed and selected according to some basic assumptions.

It may be helpful to remember that only three things can be changed for any student: the student, the student's environment, and important adults' perception of the student. Changing the student is the usual, but difficult, strategy chosen by most educators. Altering the student's environment is the prime target for behavioral practitioners. Finally, changing the expectations and perceptions of the students held by important adults is an adult-focused perspective in serving children.

With these limited targets and target combinations in mind, several assumptions guide intervention development (Apter & Conoley, 1984; Hobbs, 1966, 1982).

Each child is an inseparable part of a small social system: Every student lives in a context that is both unique and critical to our understanding of the youngster and our intervention efforts.

Disturbance is viewed not as a disease located within the body of the child but, rather, as discordance in the system. Contrary to psychodynamic or biophysical models in which the disease defines the student, from the ecological position the troubled youngster represents a troubled system. For example, environments may elicit disturbing behaviors and then identify and label such behaviors as symptoms of emotional disturbance or behavior disorder. Which behaviors get labeled depends on the time, place, and culture in which they are emitted and on the tolerance of those who observe them (Rhodes, 1967; Swap, Prieto, & Harth, 1982).

Discordance may be defined as a disparity between an individual's abilities and the demands or expectations of the environment—a failure of match between child and system. Some settings are extremely demanding and unresponsive to the individual abilities of a child. In such environments, a child may appear incompetent, while in other more nurturing environments the same child will not be identified as deviant. An example may be the so-called "street smart kids"—children who may fail in school but are quite competent in surviving in dangerous community settings.

These targets and assumptions can be used to design interventions related to the settings inhabited by students, services offered, relationships experienced by students, curricula offered, and instructional strategies that characterize students' classrooms (Muscott, 1987). Each of these areas yield rich possibilities for conceptualizing and implementing interventions (Swap, 1974, 1978).

GOALS AND PURPOSES FOR INTERVENTION

The goal of an ecologically based intervention is not a particular state of mental health or a particular set of behavior patterns, but an increased concordance between the behavior of a student and the settings in which he or she resides. These goals are reached not through implementation of a new set of techniques or treatments but through use of a framework of existing techniques applied in an ecological manner. More specifically, the treatment plan is guided by the child's interactions with all the important elements of his or her life space. The ecological perspective provides a useful umbrella to organize a variety of intervention efforts into a purposeful attempt to increase the possibility of system change, the competence of individuals, and the congruence of individuals with their settings (see Hilton, 1987).

BUILDING INTERVENTIONS

Because the child's ecosystem or life space (current and past) is the assessment target (see Gaddis & Hatfield, chapter 2, this volume), data relevant for intervention planning are potentially quite extensive. Only after the ecosystem is understood can decisions of how and where to intervene be made. Obviously, the smallest change with the greatest likelihood of success is the preferred strategy. The intervention can be aimed at multiple environments or systems, the individual student, the relationship among systems, those who referred the student, or a combination of targets (Comer & Haynes, 1991).

Ecological Levels

Rosenberg and Reppucci (1985) identified four ecological target levels with examples of known dysfunctional events that influence child welfare. These are individual, familial, community, and societal levels. Although throughout this chapter these four levels are organized and presented in somewhat different formats in order to tailor the information to students, all ecological planning falls along these dimensions.

For example, a student who appears depressed and withdrawn when entering a new school may be assisted by a buddy system of peers, cooperative learning activities, or a chance to be a peer or cross-age tutor. All of these might accelerate the youngster's access to the new peer group and build the necessary social support to prevent intensification of socioemotional problems (Bennett & Bates, 1995).

Psychological, academic, medical/physical, historical, and social information create the foundation for ecologically oriented interventions. The important purpose is to reach an understanding of the reciprocal interactions between students and their significant relationships. This requires that interventions be planned and implemented in as many of the students' life settings as possible to maximize the chances to create change (e.g., classroom, peer group, family, community activities). Most student intervention plans are strengthened with support from inside and outside of school.

Because intervention planning is grounded in information pertaining to all the elements of the ecosystem, the astute practitioner must understand the typical and successful development of children, families, classrooms, peer groups, and so on. Such knowledge alerts the professional to particular stressors that may overwhelm a student's ability to cope with environmental demands and provides a relevant context for interpreting these events.

For example, separations and transitions (e.g., divorce) are frequently encountered sources of stress which may be compounded in effect by the timing and frequency of the youngster's experiences with such occurrences. Although a practitioner cannot change actual transitional events, connecting a student with a stable force (e.g., special teacher, extended family member, Big Brother/Sister) and offering group or individual treatment that allows for new meanings to be associated with the transition (i.e., change in attributions) are viable intervention methods to provide needed support for the child.

Supporting and Inhibiting Forces

Most ecosystems contain both supporting and inhibiting forces in terms of a student's match to various settings. These forces, which refer to resources available or obstacles faced in accomplishing certain system demands, exist at individual to system levels. At an individual level, for example, a student may have normal intelligence that is supportive of success in school but demonstrate deficiencies in specific areas of achievement such as written language or social problem solving. These relative deficits may inhibit success for the student at school.

Thus, in addition to balancing the intervention focus among the various levels in a student's life space, it is critical to attend to and utilize existing student strengths. Individual variables or behaviors that predict student success in the classroom include the ability to follow teacher directions and assignment instructions, adhere to and follow classroom and group rules, complete class work without additional teacher intervention, remain flexible and adjust to change, and respond to conventional classroom management techniques (Walker & Rankin, 1983).

Other examples of supportive forces in the school environment include specific strong student aptitudes, history of school success, academically capable peer group, desire to succeed and strong life goals, and interest in extracurricular activities. Conversely, examples of forces that could inhibit school success include low motivation to succeed, interpersonal problems with friends and teachers, a fear of failure and evaluation, problems with authority figures, unsupportive or unavailable family members, chronic illness, and more than 20 hours per week at work.

Each of the student's ecosystems can be examined for supportive and inhibiting forces. Interventions are then based on strengthening or using the supportive forces and reducing or circumventing the inhibiting forces.

Consider, for example, an analysis of a student's family. Supportive forces for increased academic performance include concerned parents, affectionate bonds among family members, and parents who were success-ful in school and in other life challenges (e.g., are drug free and not incarcerated). In contrast, family forces such as family conflict, poor educational background of mother, and a history of antisocial activity potentially inhibit school success. Without buffering agents, the youngster from this or similar situations finds it difficult to meet the demands of academic environments (Patterson, DeBaryshe, & Ramsey, 1989).

Additionally, a student's medical history and classroom situation can be examined for clues as to which factors will support concordance and which may create dissonance for the student. For example, attractive healthy children are more likely to be successful in school. Children who have attentional or impulse control problems have much more difficult chal-lenges to face in educational settings.

Classrooms characterized by high expectations, smooth transitions, task and progress feedback, strong personal relationships between students and teachers, and many motivational strategies are likely to enhance children's adjustment and performance. In contrast to these supportive forces, chaotic classrooms with large numbers of special needs children and little emphasis on cognitive strategies are likely to make it difficult, even for fairly compe-tent students, to achieve at optimum levels (Ysseldyke & Christenson, 1986).

TYPICAL PROGRAMS OF CHANGE

Ecological change efforts involve attempts to make small adjustments in the patterns of behavior, environmental demands and supports, expecta-tions, or attitudes of significant people in several of a child's settings. To effect such change, these interventions generally involve coordinated team meetings among parents, teachers, the student, and other persons significant to the child. Team functions typically include sharing information, identi-fying strengths and problems, engaging in group problem solving, using consensus decision making, and giving and receiving feedback. Careful plans must be constructed, individual responsibilities specified, and evalu-ation criteria decided. Ecological intervenors must be sensitive to each person's unique goals or criteria for success. It is of utmost importance that all members of an intervention team realize they must be ready to adjust their behavior, expectations, or attitudes if success is to be achieved. This realization contrasts the more traditional notion that intervention teams meet to plan for how the child must change to meet specified criteria (Evans & Evans, 1987).

Consider Tables 3.1 and 3.2. These have been constructed to illustrate two slightly different ways of conceptualizing an ecological treatment plan. Although not exhaustive, the information suggests how to elaborate on these basic targets when constructing ecological interventions for students. Notice the types of interventions available to psychologists across all the targets. Although the tables contain only a very few options, using such frameworks may help a practitioner consider all the intervention possibilities once issues of concern have been identified.

It is difficult to discuss ecological interventions without a problem context because the ecological intervention package is tailored individually to each student. In addition, what further distinguishes ecological planning from traditional treatment packages or manuals is that a student's skills are often emphasized as strongly as their deficits with the belief that increased competence in a particular area will increase the student's match to the school system.

What follows are examples of ecological interventions in home, school, and community settings that represent obvious choices for interventions. The unique particulars for each would be fine-tuned based on individual characteristics and specific assessment data (including an analysis of both supporting and inhibiting forces in terms of the child's match with various settings).

Home

A broad range of home interventions may be directed at individual, subsystem, and system levels which in turn may be influenced by changing skills, expectations, and environments. Within this context, parent management skills are frequently targeted to enhance family functioning. For example,

TABLE 3.1
Examples of Ecological Interventions for Students

Targets/Agents of Change	Strategy Categories			
	Academic	Socio/Emotional	Behavioral	Resource
Child	Mnenomics	Therapy	Social skills	Peer tutor
Parent	Paired reading	Marital communication	Compliments	Extended family
Teacher	Academic time	Life space interview	Response cost	Inservice training
Setting	Cooperative learning	Crisis teams	Discipline policy	Police liaisons

Table 3.2
Ecological Interventions: Designing an Overall Treatment Plan

Targets or Agents of Change	Dimensions of Change		
	Setting/Environment	Skills/Strategies	Relationships
Child	Alter space in class	Self-monitoring	Social skills
Parent	Homework program	Stress management	Marital communication
Teacher	Alter teacher–student ratio	Inservice	Consultation
Peers	Peer tutoring	Negotiation	Safety teams
Community	Adopt a school program	Mentoring program	Crisis teams

parents and their children often benefit from parent acquisition and use of management skills such as time in and time out, nondirective and child-centered play, delivery of effective instructions, use of reinforcements and punishments, and methods for supporting school achievement (Polirstok, 1987). Other new skills may include using preferred activities to motivate child behavior change or linking a desired outcome (e.g., improved grades, prosocial interactions, completion of daily chores) to access to activities identified by the child as important. Changes in structure or daily routine also may be implemented, such as establishing regular study times during which TV, radio, and phones are off limits while all family members spend an hour reading, completing assignments, assisting one another with homework, or discussing some family plan for an outing or other event.

Beyond acquisition of specific management skills, parents also typically need support to facilitate consistent use of newly learned skills or previously acquired competencies across various situations. This critical support may come from the practitioner or be the product of a subsystem change. For example, parenting skills may be improved if parents learn to support one another, give each other respite, and learn to discuss their parenting options together as a team. Such changes may require some refinement in the marital relationship if parenting problems have been an outgrowth of basic quarrels between the husband and wife.

Single parents also may need to learn to seek help for their parenting efforts from alternative support sources such as relatives, friends, religious groups, or other parenting experiences. It often is challenging for one parent to socialize children and manage daily household routines even when basic parenting skills are present because of the overwhelming demands from other systems, such as work or extended family.

Additionally, parents may need information about normal developmental sequences and age-appropriate expectations. They may benefit from knowing which behaviors are common at particular ages and those that are atypical. Given increased parental understanding of the communicative intent of many difficult childhood behaviors, parent effectiveness may be enhanced. For example, it may assist parents to learn that some whining and misbehaviors are learned attempts to attract attention. Knowing this, parents can substitute more appropriate personal responses (e.g., structure enjoyable shared times between parents and children and ignore whining).

Parents and their children also may benefit from information pertaining to what they should expect from the school system. In addition to enhancing parent understanding of child performance in relation to peers, this information may increase parent expectations and use of school-based resources, or provide a more realistic picture of what teachers can accomplish (Fine, 1985).

Parents of special needs children may appreciate assistance in rallying all systems available in support of their student, particularly when there is a need for involvement with multiple services. Many parents describe feelings of frustration and exhaustion resulting from interactions with medical, school, and social service agencies as they attempt to access individualized resources for their child.

An ecological practitioner may play the role of case manager in situations such as this, empowering and coordinating the efforts of the parents and professionals alike. Thus, case managers may assume the dual focus of direct family intervention (i. e., parent–professional partnership) and service network intervention (i. e., interagency and interprofessional collaboration). In such cases, the needs of the child and the involvement of the family are primary considerations when identifying an appropriate continuum of family-centered and culturally competent services. This continuum may range from prevention to treatment. Likewise, case management should be viewed as an active, dynamic, and ongoing process within the intervention context.

School

Consistent with the development of home-based interventions, the ecological practitioner also must consider individual, subsystem, and system targets when designing school-based interventions. Examples of possible targets include student skills, teacher competencies, classroom processes, faculty teaming efforts, and procedures used to coordinate home and school plans

(Cantrell & Cantrell, 1985). All of these levels are, however, embedded within a particular context of beliefs and assumptions.

Hidden Curriculum.   Practitioners must be cognizant of what has been called the *hidden curriculum* (Hamilton, 1983). This is the curriculum of values and behavior taught implicitly by the social systems of the school. This social side of schooling has implications for student behavior and academic learning and may not be apparent to all students, particularly those with exceptional educational needs, without explicit instruction and opportunities for practice and feedback.

Exceptional educational needs may arise from disabilities the child has, such as, physical or cognitive challenges. A child with limited cognitive skills may lack the problem solving necessary to negotiate games in the playground without resorting to fighting. Such a child may require specific training in managing competitive game situations. Many teachers and administrators could see the fighting as a behavioral deficit without realizing it is a legitimate teaching target. Children with handicapping conditions may have a difficult time recognizing or responding to implicit expectations and require direct intervention.

Additionally, the hidden curriculum may be characterized by the ethnic, cultural, and economic positions of the teachers and administrators. These positions may not be similar to those of the children. If there is a discrepancy (e.g., most teachers are Euro-American and most children are African American), the children and adults may be at a disadvantage in knowing how to succeed in or transmit this hidden curriculum. If most teachers come from middle-class economic backgrounds, their understandings of the effects of poverty on childrens' home situations may be limited.

Developing ecological interventions for students must be done with an awareness of social class, the cultural realities, and the histories of various groups in the United States. This is a tall order, but competent ecological planning is likely to lead to culturally competent interventions for a number of reasons.

First, strengths are emphasized in good intervention planning. This focus avoids pathologizing difference and turns attention to building on existing resources. Second, the use of information from multiple life spaces maximizes the chance that all the constituent voices can be heard and valued in the intervention planning. Finally, the assumption that everyone is expected to change to help a child succeed can reduce any tendency to blame a particular part of the child's ecosystem for the perceived difficulty (Conoley & Bryant, 1995).

Students. Individual interventions for students may include training in a content area, metacognitive skills, or appropriate behavior. Although the need for such interventions is simple to determine, implementation is comparatively difficult without developing a good relationship with key individuals such as the student and teacher. Group interventions in the form of school psychologist or counselor's groups may be used to address special needs such as impulsive problem solvers, children of divorce, and anger management. Within this context, children may gain knowledge and strategies for use when faced with novel problems. For example, poor problem solvers or those who have difficulty attending to auditory stimuli may be assisted by learning simple procedures such as looking at those who are speaking, asking people to repeat statements, and reminding themselves to slow down and pay attention (Barone, Aguirre-Deandreis, & Trickett, 1991).

Similar training could be done as a prerequisite to participation in activities in a peer or cross-age tutoring intervention. In fact, students might be more open to information if they perceived its importance in targeting someone other than themselves. Likewise, junior high students are highly motivated to be with peers. A group of boys and girls of varying skill levels brought together to improve their problem solving and increase their reflectiveness in stressful situations could receive social as well as academic benefit (Bell, Young, Blair, & Nelson, 1990; Greenwood, Delquadri, & Hall, 1989; Greenwood, Terry, Utley, Montagna, & Walker, 1993).

Teachers. Certain teacher behaviors and instructional management strategies can positively impact student behavior. Application of these behaviors in the classroom has been identified as an *interactive* teaching style and features characteristics such as a strong academic focus, interactive activities, active academic responding, teacher-selected activities, student–teacher interactions, delivery of instruction, and effective classroom management strategies (Gettinger, 1995).

Because teachers may not have the necessary skills or knowledge of effective instructional approaches to meet the needs of a diverse set of learners, they may benefit from feedback about use of specific instructional strategies or consultation about the characteristics of a particular child. Again, relationship issues are paramount.

Teachers may need to become more attentive to a student in ways tailored to increase task completion. For example, some students use low-level inappropriate behavior to avoid beginning assignments they evaluate as being too difficult. Strategies to assist them in beginning work might include physical proximity at the start of the individual seat work, progress feedback frequently during the period, reinforcement of any contributions from students, adaptation of some assignments in terms of particular strengths and weakness of a student, development of personal relationships with students that are based on a recognition of strengths, private conferences or confrontations regarding work or behavior rather than public discussions, and consistent enforcement of rules and contingencies (e.g., gaining free time for completed work or losing free time when work is not completed). On this last point, teachers must not threaten, but follow through on every contingency they mention.

Classroom.   Trickett and Quinlan (1979) identified three domains of interest in classrooms: personal development dimensions, system maintenance dimensions, and relationship dimensions. These provide some guidance in conceptualizing ecological interventions in the classroom. A student may be having difficulty because of lack of study and learning tools or because the tasks being assigned to the student are inappropriate. Perhaps many written assignments or essay exams are the norm in a particular class and this child has a weakness in writing. If so, the task dimensions would be particularly frustrating. It might be more feasible to change the way a student can meet expectations than to work on a particular disability.

Such a change would require cooperation from teachers. This might come from a single teacher or be the product of a team decision to adjust curriculum for a single or small group of students. Facilitating teaming decisions and follow through is a critical component to intervening with students. Ecological interventions often depend on the cooperation of many adults to improve situations for students. Without skills in cooperation and collaboration, even very elegant interventions will fail.

The common problem of helping a student achieve more successfully involves personal change, adjustments in how the classroom system may function, and demands on or changes in the relationship skills of adults and youngsters. Trickett and Moos (1974) reported on the environmental correlates of student satisfaction. They found that students were most satisfied in classrooms that emphasized personal relationships and had clear rules. Notice how a practitioner wanting to assist a student might use these findings. The implementation of change efforts, however, would depend on personal and system commitments from teachers and students.

School Setting.   The school, itself, must be a context that elicits success. The climate and norms of a school are predictive of students' success. Schools that pay attention to the stresses of transitions, with effective leadership, clear and high expectations, and rules that facilitate rather than oppress students tend to have high achievement and low levels of student deviance (Brophy, 1986; Felner, Ginter, & Primavera, 1982; Good & Weinstein, 1986; Purkey & Smith, 1983; Rutter, 1983). System and administrative consultation are strategies of choice to facilitate such environments.

Schools that facilitate high involvement from students have the highest achieving and best behaved students. Most students benefit from participation in extracurricular activities. Connections with other youngsters and teachers often get students "hooked" into school. Coaches or other sponsors of activities can be out-of-classroom advocates for a youngster who is troubled during the regular program. Receiving special attention from high status adults or peers in a school may provide incentives to improve academics and keep behavioral problems to a minimum (Barker, 1968; Barker & Gump, 1964; Boyer, 1983; Glass, Cahen, Smith, & Filby, 1982; Goodlad, 1984).

Community

Communities may have resources useful for supporting student success in school, but may require intervention to increase their nurturing of young people's competence in other settings. Community level intervention is conceptualized in the same manner as each of the previously discussed levels. Examples of strategies for promoting community-based care include soliciting assistance from influential individuals, improving the internal functioning of service agencies to increase their positive influence with young people, and integrating or augmenting services across agencies with similar or complimentary missions to increase their impact.

For children and youth with complex needs who require high levels of intervention and multiple services, community-based teams consisting of family, school, and community members may be organized to create comprehensive plans of care to meet life domain needs using strength-based approaches. These intervention teams can identify and access services to provide positive mental health resources and family friendly services for targeted youth. Mobile response teams can be created to provide assistance during crisis times, helping families learn new coping techniques. Additionally, mentoring programs consisting of volunteer or paid individuals who provide intensive specified interventions for youth or family members with ongoing monitoring by the community team may be established. An analogous program for schools is the adopt-a-school approach used in many communities to bring businesses and schools together to pool resources around particular targets for improvement (Goldstein, Harootunian, & Conoley, 1994).

Many students have little productive or beneficial community involvement. A useful target would be to increase youth involvement in organizations such as a church, YMCA or YWCA, Boys or Girls Clubs, city sporting leagues, physical fitness clubs, and so on. In these settings, students might be able to take leadership roles, meet academically oriented peers, and increase their personal sense of efficacy while adding to a positive community environment.

In some communities there is a paucity of activities for young people. This lack becomes especially critical during adolescent years when youngsters want very much to be out with friends. A school's willingness to sponsor activities (either independently or cooperatively) or to locate community sponsors for activities such as dances, sports leagues, computer clubs, art projects, and so forth on a year-round basis is an example of a marvelous strategy for changing the life spaces of large numbers of students. Existing resources also might be used in different ways. The involvement of police officers in educational efforts around gangs and drug use is a good example of helping young people change their behaviors and expectations toward police.

Another important target for intervention is the transition of students from schools to employment settings in the community. Depending on the student's level of need, significant efforts may be needed to arrange work, training, monitoring, and retraining options for handicapped students (Barone, Trickett, Schmid, & Leone, 1993; Putnam, 1987).

EXPECTED OUTCOMES

As mentioned earlier, ecological interventions, although aimed at specific target(s) for change, are not defined by a particular type of outcome. The outcomes may be behavioral change, system change, or change in participants' expectations or beliefs. When working with students the likely outcomes include: (a) improved academic performance or behavioral match to environmental demands; (b) enhanced relationships between the student and important other groups such as teachers, peers, and families; (c) increased adult skills in dealing productively with student behaviors; (d) improved system functioning and flexibility so that resources are made available to meet student needs; (e) increased accountability among all elements of systems for developing, implementing, maintaining, and evaluating change efforts; and (f) increased collaboration and coordination among all the system components so that services to students reduce rather than exacerbate fragmentation (Conoley & Conoley, 1991).

Sources of data to measure whether such outcomes are achieved could include reports from students and adults about change in their own and others' behaviors, direct observations of classroom behavior of students and teachers, evaluation of team meetings convened to problem solve about particular students, standardized or curriculum based measures of achievement, behavioral checklists, instructional climate surveys, and school climate surveys (see Scott, 1977; Trickett, Leone, Fink, & Braaten, 1993; and Ysseldyke & Christenson, 1986 for interesting examples of ecological measurement).

What if improvement is not noted on all or any of the measures just noted? A first step, if outcomes are not developing as expected, is to analyze treatment integrity. If implementation problems are found, further supportive consultation is in order. If everyone is doing as planned, then a new round of problem identification and solution generation must be implemented.

Although the potential number of targets when planning ecologically is very large, many aspects of a student's life space are not altered in any treatment plan. It is possible the most important components are overlooked in early efforts. The beauty of ecological intervention is that, ideally, change is implemented on many levels, making the package of treatment more important than any particular treatment element (Bryant & Zayas, 1986).

CONCLUSIONS

Time-consuming assessments typically completed on individual children must be paired with equally detailed analyses and resultant understandings of the settings the children inhabit and the people with whom they interact. In many cases of student difficulty, most of the student's significant adult relationships are impaired as well, in part, due to deficits in adult behavior, attitudes, or expectations. Furthermore, some underachievement is due to a poor match between student strengths and task demands. Most ecological analyses suggest a more systemic orientation in which adults and tasks should be modified as well as children.

A shift in our assessment and treatment targets to include children's life spaces will be difficult. Primary reliance on a biophysical model is an obstacle to creating comprehensive treatment plans. Overreliance on narrow behavioral understandings can interfere with an appreciation of the effects of past emotional experiences and current cognitive strategy deficits.

An ecological framework assists in organizing large amounts of data in useful and valid ways. Humans are remarkably complex and seem to resist easy theoretical explanations. Expert human ecologists are precise observers of what people do and sensitive interpreters of how people feel and process events. An openness to what may work for a particular child in a particular setting is far more important to the ecologist than implementing a prescribed treatment package.

It is also true that ecological interventions can be more complex and demanding than putting a child in a resource room or increasing the rewards and punishments a child receives. A psychologist's skill in motivating adults to take part in such interventions is the key element in predicting success. It is not hard to think of interventions, but it is hard to get others to cooperate (Conoley, Conoley, Ivey, & Scheel, 1991; Conoley, Padula-Hall, Payton, & Daniels, 1994).

Psychologists must be as expert in understanding the life spaces of each adult as they are in understanding the child's situation. This necessary element in treatment implementation makes clear why assisting children with their life difficulties usually takes much longer than anyone has predicted or planned. Establishing the resources necessary to support troubled children entails continuous adult attention.

REFERENCES

Allen-Meares, P., & Lane, B. A. (1987). Grounding social work practice in theory: Ecosystems. *Social Casework, 68*, 515–521.

Apter, S. J. (1977). Applications of ecological theory: Toward a community special education model for troubled children. *Exceptional Children, 43*, 366–373.

Apter, S. J. (1982). *Troubled children/Troubled systems*. New York: Pergamon.

Apter, S. J., & Conoley, J. C. (1984). *Childhood behavior disorders and emotional disturbance*. Englewood Cliffs, NJ: Prentice-Hall.

Barker, R. G. (1968). *Ecological psychology: Concepts and methods for studying the environment of human behavior.* Stanford, CA: Stanford University Press.

Barker, R. G. (1978). *Habitats, environments, and human behavior.* San Francisco: Jossey-Bass.

Barker, R. G., & Gump, P. (1964). *Big school, small school: High school size and student behavior.* Stanford, CA: Stanford University Press.

Barone, C., Aguirre-Deandreis, A. I., & Trickett, E. J. (1991). Means–ends problem-solving skills, life stress, and social support as mediators of adjustment in the normative transition to high school. *American Journal of Community Psychology 1991, 19*, 207–225.

Barone, C., Trickett, E. J., Schmid, K. D., & Leone, P. E. (1993). Transition tasks and resources: An ecological approach to life after high school. *Prevention in Human Services, 10*, 179–204.

Bell, K., Young, K. R., Blair, M., & Nelson, R. (1990). Facilitating mainstreaming of students with behavioral disorders using classwide peer tutoring. *School Psychology Review, 19*, 564–573.

Bennett, D. S., & Bates, J. E. (1995). Prospective models of depressive symptoms in early adolescence: Attributional style, stress, and support. *Journal of Early Adolescence, 15*, 299–315.

Boyer, E. L. (1983). *High school: A report on secondary education in America.* New York: Harper & Row.

Brophy, J. E. (1986). Teacher influences on student achievement. *American Psychologist, 41*, 1069–1077.

Bryant, C., & Zayas, L. H. (1986). Initial moves with school–family conflict: Entering, engaging and contracting. *Child and Adolescent Social Work Journal, 3*, 87–100.

Cantrell, M. L., & Cantrell, R. P. (1985). Assessment of the natural environment. *Education and Treatment of Children, 8*, 275–295.

Comer, J. P., & Haynes, N. M. (1991). Parent involvement in schools: An ecological approach. *Elementary School Journal, 91*, 271–277.

Conoley, C. W., Conoley, J. C., Ivey, D. C., & Scheel, M. J. (1991). Enhancing consultation by matching the consultee's perspectives. *Journal of Counseling and Development, 69*, 546–549.

Conoley, C. W., Padula-Hall, M. A., Payton, D. S., & Daniels, J. A. (1994). Predictors of client implementation of counselor recommendations: Match with problem, difficulty level, and building on client strengths. *Journal of Counseling Psychology, 41*, 3–7.

Conoley, J. C., & Bryant, L. E. (1995). Multicultural family assessment. In J. C. Conoley & E. B. Werth (Eds.), *Family assessment* (pp. 103–129). Lincoln, NE: Buros Institute of Mental Measurements.

Conoley, J. C., & Conoley, C. W. (1991). Collaboration for child adjustment: Issues for school- and clinic-based psychologists. *Journal of Consulting and Clinical Psychology, 59*, 821–829.

Conoley, J. C., & Haynes, G. (1992). Ecological perspectives. In R. D'Amato & B. Rothlisberg (Eds.), *Psychological perspectives on interventions* (pp. 177–189). White Plains, NY: Longman.

Evans, S. S., & Evans, W. H. (1987). Behavior change and the ecological model. *Pointer, 31*(3), 9–12.

Felner, R. D., Ginter, M., & Primavera, J. (1982). Primary prevention during school transitions: Social support and environmental structure. *American Journal of Community Psychology, 10*, 277–290.

Fine, M. J. (1985). Intervention from a systems–ecological perspective. *Professional Psychology: Research and Practice, 16*, 262–270.

Gettinger, M. (1995). Best practices for increasing academic learning time. In A. Thomas & J. Grimes (Eds.), *Best practices in school psychology* (Vol. 3, pp. 943–954). Washington, DC: National Association of School Psychologists.

Glass, G. V., Cahen, L. S., Smith, M. L., & Filby, N. N. (1982). *School class size: Research and policy.* Beverly Hills, CA: Sage.

Goldstein, A. P., Harootunian, B., & Conoley, J. C. (1994). *Student aggression: Prevention, management, and replacement training.* New York: Guilford.

Good, T. L., & Weinstein, R. S. (1986). Schools make a difference: Evidence, criticisms, and new directions. *American Psychologist, 41*, 1090–1097.

Goodlad, J. I. (1984). *A place called school: Prospects for the future.* New York: McGraw-Hill.

Greenwood, C. R., Delquadri, J. C., & Hall, R. V. (1989). Longitudinal effects of classwide peer tutoring. *Journal of Educational Psychology, 81*(3), 371–383.

Greenwood, C. R., Terry, B., Utley, C. A., Montagna, D., & Walker, D. (1993). Achievement, placement, and services: Middle school benefits of classwide peer tutoring used at the elementary level. *School Psychology Review, 22*, 497–516.

Gump, P. V. (1980). The school as a social situation. *Annual Review of Psychology, 31*, 553–582.

Hamilton, S. F. (1983). Synthesis of research on the social side of schooling. *Educational Leadership, 40*(5), 65–72.

Hewett, F. M. (1987). The ecological view of disturbed children: Shadow versus substance. *Pointer, 31*(3), 61–63.

Hilton, A. (1987). Using ecological strategies when working with young children. *Pointer, 31*(3), 52–55.

Hobbs, N. (1966). Helping disturbed children: Psychological and ecological strategies. *American Psychologist, 21*, 1105–1115.

Hobbs, N. (1975). *The futures of children.* San Francisco: Jossey-Bass.

Hobbs, N. (1982). *The troubled and troubling child.* San Francisco: Jossey-Bass.

Lewin, K. (1951). *Field theory and social science.* New York: Harper.

McGoldrick, M., & Gerson, R. (1985). *Genograms in family assessment.* New York: Norton.

Muscott, H. S. (1987). Conceptualizing behavior management strategies for troubled and troubling students: A process for organizing the direction of intervention efforts in schools. *Pointer, 31*(4), 15–22.

Newbrough, J. R., Walker, L., & Abril, S. (1978, April). *Workshop on ecological assessment.* Paper presented at the meeting of the National Association of School Psychologists, New York.

Patterson, G. R., DeBaryshe, B. D., & Ramsey, E. (1989). A developmental perspective on antisocial behavior. *American Psychologist, 44*, 329–335.

Polirstok, S. R. (1987). Ecological effects of home-based, school-based, and community-based training of parents of children with learning and behavior problems. *International Journal of Rehabilitation Research, 10*, 293–301.

Purkey, S. C., & Smith, M. S. (1983). Effective schools: A review. *Elementary School Journal, 83*, 427–452.

Putnam, M. L. (1987). Effective interventions for mildly handicapped adolescents in the home and the community. *Pointer, 31*(3), 19–24.

Rhodes, W. C. (1967). The disturbing child: A problem of ecological management. *Exceptional Children, 33*, 449–455.

Rhodes, W. C. (1970). A community participation analysis of emotional disturbance. *Exceptional Children, 37*, 309–314.

Rosenberg, M. S., & Reppucci, N. D. (1985). Primary prevention of child abuse. *Journal of Consulting and Clinical Psychology, 53*, 576–585.

Rutter, M. (1983). School effects on pupil progress: Research findings and policy implications. *Child Development, 54*, 1–29.

Scott, M. (1977). Some parameters of teacher effectiveness as assessed by an ecological approach. *Journal of Educational Psychology, 69*, 217–226.

Swap, S. M. (1974). Disturbing classroom behaviors: A developmental and ecological view. *Exceptional Children, 41*, 163–172.

Swap, S. M. (1978). The ecological model of emotional disturbance in children: A status report and proposed synthesis. *Behavioral Disorders, 3*, 186–196.

Swap, S. M., Prieto, A. G., & Harth, R. (1982). Ecological perspectives of the emotionally disturbed child. In R. L. McDowell, G. W. Adamson, & F. H. Wood (Eds.), *Teaching emotionally disturbed children*. Boston: Little, Brown.

Thomas, A., & Chess, S. (1977). *Temperament and development*. New York: Brunner/Mazel.

Thomas, A., Chess, S., & Birch H. (1968). *Temperament and behavior disorders in children*. New York: New York University Press.

Trickett, E. J., Leone, P. E., Fink, C. M., & Braaten, S. L. (1993). The perceived environment of special education classrooms for adolescents: A revision of the Classroom Environment Scale. *Exceptional Children, 59*, 411–420.

Trickett, E. J., & Moos, R. H. (1974). Personal correlates of contrasting environments: Student satisfactions in high school classrooms. *American Journal of Community Psychology, 2*, 1–12.

Trickett, E. J., & Quinlan, D. M. (1979). Three domains of classroom environment: Factor analysis of the Classroom Environment Scale. *American Journal of Community Psychology, 7*, 279–291.

Walker, H. M., & Rankin, R. (1983). Assessing the behavioral expectations and demands of less restrictive settings. *School Psychology Review, 12*, 274–284.

Ysseldyke, J. E., & Christenson, S. (1986). *The Instructional Environment Survey*. Austin, TX: Pro-Ed.

III

ASSESSMENT AND INTERVENTION WITH TEACHERS IN CLASSROOMS

4

Principles and Application of Ecological Assessment for Teachers

Mary J. McLellan
Irene Sanchez
Northern Arizona University

The purpose of this chapter is to provide information to classroom teachers, and those who work with classroom teachers, about the principles of ecological assessment and its application to the classroom environment. This chapter stresses the importance of understanding students within their own context. This chapter stresses the understanding of each student as a member of a cultural group with similarities to and differences from other individuals within the group. This view of the child should provide a clearer idea of the manner in which each child learns. Bronfenbrenner (1979) said that the child's ability to learn, even in the earliest stages, depends on the existence and nature of the ties between the school and the home, as well as on the manner in which the child is taught. These ties can exist only by understanding the various components of each child's context and the connections between contexts. In addition, a case study provides specific ideas about tools and techniques to gain an ecological awareness of a child's classroom situation.

THEORETICAL UNDERPINNINGS OF ECOLOGICAL PSYCHOLOGY APPLIED TO CLASSROOMS

Bronfenbrenner (1979) postulated that the classroom, as seen from an ecological perspective, is a *microsystem*—a pattern of interpersonal relations, activities, and roles experienced by each student. Each student in the classroom lives within various microsystems. The number of microsystems increases as the child develops and becomes involved in more and varied activities.

As students in the classroom interact, different settings are created called *mesosystems*. Mesosystems are the set of interrelations between multiple settings. The first order network of the mesosystem is created when each person in the classroom participates, at the very minimum, in two settings, such as home and school. There is also a second order network resulting from the influence on an individual in the classroom by the family and other contexts of all students in the classroom. Usually, one student has a connection with another student's family, without face-to-face interaction. Additionally, a direct connection from one setting to the other also occurs when there is communication between settings, such as when the parent and teacher meet. Finally, an interconnection occurs when there is information about one setting transferred to the other setting. This type of interconnection occurs when children talk at school about their homes or other settings in which they are involved, or when individuals take the time to learn about the other settings in which a member of their microsystem lives. Such an interconnection would occur when the teacher gains knowledge about a child's home or parents gain information about school. Because they unify the child's experiences within different contexts into a unified whole, these links between settings are of utmost importance. Specifically, the connection of the teacher and a member of the child's home setting increases the potential for learning. This enhancement of potential was determined to be due to greater compatibility between role demands and goals in different settings (Bronfenbrenner, 1979).

As a result of focusing attention on the interpersonal systems in which the child participates, rather than exclusively on the child, the teacher can seek to include the family in the communication network. Such communication is best if it is made up of bidirectional channels of communication. Bidirectional communication creates a partnership between teachers and parents.

Each person also lives within an *exosystem* made up of one or more settings that affect the individual although the individual is not a participant. The exosystem encompasses federal government mandates, such as school lunches, school board's decisions that affect each child, and the community's attitude about school effectiveness. In addition, the exosystem involves indirect connections parallelling to the direct connections of the mesosystem.

Furthermore, each person within the classroom lives within a *macrosystem*. The macrosystem refers to the consistency noted in the form and content of the microsystems, mesosystems, and exosystems, as well as the consistency of the belief systems within a given culture or subculture. This consistency is based on similar values held by members of the macrosystem. It is at the level of the macrosystem that the minority culture child appears to experience difficulty because of the inconsistencies between the mainstream and minority culture. Szapocznik and Kurtines (1993) pointed out that families (therefore family members) must be understood within a culturally pluralistic context.

Social Learning Theory Applied to the Classroom

Heider (1958), an early attribution theorist, believed that a grasp of an individual's subjective experiences is essential to understanding the individual's perception of the world. An individual's thoughts about the causes of an event or the motives of other persons participating in the event explain what the individual does in a situation. Weiner (1985) stated that attributions of an individual's performance influence that individual's expectations of future performance, persistence, affective reactions, and choice of tasks.

Bandura's (1982) self-efficacy theory is linked to attribution theory. This theory's main premise is that people's actions are mediated by expectations of personal self-efficacy. These expectations influence individuals to choose activities they can perform, how much effort they will expend, and the level of persistence when there are aversive experiences. Schunk (1983) viewed attributional content as an antecedent for self-efficacy expectations.

As part of social learning theory, Bandura (1977) presented the environment as important, since behavior is seen as resulting from the interaction of persons and situations, rather than from either alone. According to Bandura, people are viewed as producing environmental conditions that affect their behavior, and they are in turn affected by the environmental conditions they create. In the classroom, the environment consists of the individuals and the context of the social systems in which they live, both inside and outside the classroom. The behavior that results from the interaction within the classroom generates experiences that also determine what a person becomes and what a person can do; these in turn affect subsequent behavior. Moreover, as a product of these experiences, perceptions of self-efficacy are formed. People, consequently, act in a protective manner when in the presence of aversive stimuli. Thus, for example, children who have negative experiences when speaking up in class may not speak in a classroom setting.

Social-Cognitive Development in the Classroom

The development of social knowledge has been determined to be primarily contextual. Research by both Bronfenbrenner (1967) and Luria (1976) regarding the cognitive activity of children revealed that there are major shifts in mental activity, including the creation of new motivations for or against action, during periods of great sociohistorical change. The basic structure of cognitive processes within the individual changes as a result of personal experiences, together with the experiences of the culture as a whole.

In an approach offered by Higgins and Parsons (1983), the developing social cognitions of children are viewed as going through developmentally distinct contexts with different social arrangements, social expectations, and rules for appropriate social behavior. Therefore, changes in the cognitive structure and process that occur with development are largely the result of contextual demands that occur for different age subcultures. That is, children at different stages of development think differently about social events because adaptation to the social demands of the environment require alterations in thought processes.

Acculturation in the Classroom

There is consistency noted within macrosystems, yet, on an individual basis, there are variations in the experience of culture. This is especially true for individuals who are in transition from one culture to another. The level of acculturation to the prevailing culture is a critical factor in understanding individuals' experience of their culture. The understanding of the principal acculturation research is a crucial aspect of understanding individuals within a classroom and, therefore, teaching effectively. There are several key elements of acculturation theory.

Over the last 20 years there has been much discussion and research about the process of acculturation. The theory of acculturation is the attempt to understand the adjustment process of minority groups to the majority, or dominant culture (Sadowsky & Plake, 1991). Recent immigrants and individuals from varied ethnocultural backgrounds have been the primary focus of study.

Three major approaches have been identified in the theory of acculturation. First, acculturation has been viewed as a unidirectional or linear process of assimilation that involves rejecting traditional values, customs, beliefs, and behaviors of the minority culture, and replacing them with the values, customs, beliefs, and behaviors of the new, dominant culture (Garcia

& Vega, 1979). Second, acculturation has been viewed as bidirectional, or bicultural (Szapocznik, Kurtines, & Fernandez, 1980). This view suggests that acculturation takes place along two independent dimensions: the first is a linear process of accommodation to the new culture, and the second consists of a complex process of rejecting all or portions of the culture of origin and deciding to retain certain characteristics of the culture of origin (Szapocznik et al., 1986). Finally, the third major approach to acculturation has been conceived as a complex, multidimensional process that results from a combination of cultural, economic, educational, cognitive, behavioral, and attitudinal factors (Cuellar, Harris, & Jasso, 1980). It is important to note that language continues to be perceived as the major dimension of acculturation. Factor analytic studies of language levels among minority cultures have, to date, provided the best prediction of levels of acculturation (Olmedo, 1979; Sadowsky & Plake, 1991).

In the classroom, it is important to consider the level of acculturation of all minority culture children, without neglecting the fact that there are some children who may appear to belong to the mainstream culture, yet exist in the minority. There is, for example, the mainstream child in a minority neighborhood. Any child can be considered different by peers: it is this feeling of difference from the majority that can result in low self-esteem that may contribute to socialization and learning problems (Phinney, 1991; Tajfel, 1981). Edwards (1969) pointed out that a person's self-concept or sense of personal worth will be impacted by the status of the individual's cultural or racial group within the total pecking order of U.S. society. When the group is low on the pecking order, the development of personality, certain behavioral patterns (including language), and attitudinal syndromes vary markedly from that of less restricted members of society.

Ogbu (1987) further stated that caste-like minorities exist in the United States. These minorities were incorporated into this country through slavery and the conquest of colonization, and consist of groups such as African Americans, Native Americans, Puerto Ricans, and Mexican Americans. According to Ogbu, the experience of being second class citizens leads to new and different cultural patterns or adaptations that can result in *cultural inversion*. He defined cultural inversion as a minority group's tendency to reject dominant group behaviors, events, meanings, and symbols, as a means of repudiating their perceived second class status. Cultural inversion can lead to avoidance of the dominant group's frame of references, such as avoidance of working for good grades.

Matute-Bianchi's research (1986, 1989) in a California high school validated Ogbu's findings. The results showed that, among Mexican American students, academic success was linked to the expectation of a higher status occupation by immigrants or children of immigrants. Unsuccessful Mexican American students who had not made that connection were generally nonimmigrants.

Teachers function in a critical capacity, as facilitators of a child's understanding and acceptance of other children in the classroom who exhibit differing levels of acculturation. Therefore, enhancing an understanding of acculturation factors and transitions that each child is experiencing is a critical aspect of teaching.

Determination of Prior Knowledge

Ausubel (1968), in his classic text on cognitive psychology, stated that the single most important factor influencing learning is what the learner already knows. When the existing knowledge base is deep, learning of new information is easier due to the existing schemata to which the new material can be linked. The optimal organization consists of hierarchically arranged concepts. These concepts and their arrangement in relation to one another are the main components of the scaffolding that Vygotsky (1962) determined to be necessary for effective learning to take place. Scaffolding refers to the support the teacher gives to the learner during the process of learning. This involves a dynamic process in which the scaffolding is eliminated, piece by piece, as the learner grasps a concept. At this point, the new learning is assimilated, extending the knowledge base (DiVesta, 1989). The scaffolding is re-established at a higher level for new learning to take place.

Some of the schemata found within the knowledge base consists of scripts. These scripts are crucial for comprehension to take place, because they enhance the ability of the learner to classify new information (Scripts-Bower, Black, & Turner, 1979). There are also scripts (cognitive representations or attributions) that explain an individual's experience of the self (Palmer & Goetz, 1988). Children from minority cultures, depending on the level of acculturation, sometimes come to school with scripts resulting from very different experiences than those of children from the mainstream culture. It is important to determine which children are not prepared to meet the demands of the classroom (Pena, Quinn, & Iglesias, 1992). These children are at risk to fail unless their prior knowledge base can be expanded to include information from the mainstream culture that will enhance the ability to learn what is being taught. Furthermore, research about the different thinking skills of experts and novices has revealed information that helps us understand the nature of the differences that exist when there is a large knowledge base versus a small knowledge base. There is not only a difference in what is known, but also in how information is organized, and the depth of support children are able to provide as an explanation for what they know (Chase & Simon, 1973; Chi, Feltovich, & Glaser, 1981).

Social Variables in the Classroom

John Dewey (1960) viewed all human experience as ultimately social, as it involves contact and communication. It is the teacher who must select the kind of current experience that will result in fruitful and creative experiences in the future. The best experiences for learning are those that provide enjoyment in the present and lead to a positive effect on future experiences. The learning that takes place in the future is referred to as *collateral learning*. Through the influence of earlier learning upon later learning, a continuity of learning is achieved. Dewey perceived learning as an interaction between an individual's needs and environmental influences. Environmental influences are equivalent to the total social context of the situation in which the individual is engaged. Within the classroom, the teacher functions as a guide, evaluating and directing the experiences of the students. In order to do this appropriately, the teacher must possess the knowledge of the subject matter to be taught, ways to include experiences from outside the school in the school environment, and, more importantly, knowledge of the individuals being taught. It is essential, therefore, that the teacher assess each student early in the school year, with the purpose of determining how to make learning objectives meaningful to the learner.

In his research on integrated classrooms, Giles (1959) posited that it is necessary for teachers to achieve a positive social climate within the classroom. Giles further indicated that students who work together tend to like school more than those who are not allowed to work together. In addition to positive feelings toward school, Giles found that cooperative learning creates a feeling of goodwill and a desire that classmates do well. Students benefit from knowledge of one another as individuals. Social climate setting activities are good for the teacher and the students, resulting in better understanding of themselves and each other. This is particularly true when some students may be forthcoming with information about themselves and others may not reveal information unless asked (Bernal, Saenz, & Knight, 1991).

In addition to experience, Weiner (1985) considered personality factors as influential upon attribution. Temperament is an especially significant personality factor. The individual differences in responsiveness and self-regulation that are present at birth have been found to be relatively stable over time and across situations (Thomas & Chess, 1977). These temperament characteristics are influenced, however, by the interaction of heredity, maturation, and experience. In their classic New York Longitudinal Study, Thomas and Chess examined patterns of nine aspects of temperament. The results indicated that there are three patterns of infant temperament found to have different effects on the child's social interactions. The three patterns were as follows: average or easy children tend to respond in a positive manner to new experiences; slow-to-warm-up children adapt slowly to new situations, and react moderately to these situations; and difficult children reacted with intensity to new or stressful situations. The latter children, in fact, elicited criticism and negative reactions in their caregivers.

Influences from the environment play a significant role in the support or modification of temperament throughout the developmental period. The impact of the environment can cause some children's temperament to change significantly over time. As a result, the degree to which temperament style contributes to the development of personality is influenced by the environment; especially the reaction that the child elicits from parents and other caregivers. The goodness of fit between the child's temperament style in the areas of parental attitudes, expectations, and responses is much better when there is congruence (Thomas & Chess, 1977). Characteristics of temperament have been shown to increase (or decrease) in a positive (or negative) direction as a consequence of maternal personality, marital factors, and quality of mother–infant interaction styles (Belsky, Fish, & Isabella, 1991). Differences in parental perception and reaction to their child's personality can either emphasize or de-emphasize a child's temperamental qualities. A child may act in ways consistent with his or her own temperament when confronted with the expectations and reactions of each parent (Plomin, 1989).

Taken together, these social variables lead to an increased understanding of the complexities of individuals and how individual differences are created. The critical role teachers play in the ecological understanding of each child, and how various social variables interact with this understanding, were also highlighted. However, simply recognizing the impact of this interaction is not enough. To optimize the individual's learning experience, the teacher needs to actively seek information on these variables for each of their students. As such, the next section addresses how professionals obtain this necessary information.

COMPONENTS OF ECOLOGICAL ASSESSMENT

The components of an ecological assessment are discussed in the following section. The focus is on how a teacher may approach the ecological assessment of an individual within a classroom. The components are multifaceted and attempt to account for the variables that encompass the child's ecological system. The various components emphasized in this section are the child's total context, acculturation, family and school environment, temperament variables, academic achievement, and learning capacity. The goal is to facilitate an understanding of each student that engenders a rich sense of awareness of ecological issues.

Child Context

As a child enters a classroom for the first time, there is a variable amount of information available to the teacher. Ecological assessment is, under these circumstances, gathering all attainable information in order to create an ecological understanding of this child. A change in perspective from the internal forces that determine a child's functioning to the external forces that may also contribute to the total picture of the child is required for a successful ecological assessment. The assessment of the child's context includes review of school records and knowledge of the child's developmental history.

The optimal ecological assessment can occur when there has been enough stability in the student's academic career so educational records are available. Educational records provide information about the child's performance on standardized achievement tests, grades achieved, attendance in school, and past teachers comments. However, some children enroll in a school with little or no information. Registration forms provide information about where a child is currently living, declared ethnicity, phone contact, where the child transferred from, how many siblings are in the family, and who is residing in the home. Verification of obtained information through a verbal interview is recommended.

It is in the best interest of the child that a developmental history be outlined. Some school systems require parents to complete brief developmental histories upon school registration. As with educational records, verification of the information gained through developmental histories with a verbal interview is desirable as it is often a rich source of information. It is amazing what parents forget when they are registering their children for school!

Acculturation

The determination of the acculturation level of a child provides valuable information. The impact of placing a child in an environment that is discordant with the home environment was discussed earlier and teachers should be aware of their role in this process. To what extent children are living within their culture of origin and how comfortable they are with their current cultural context is information a teacher can obtain. Swartz and Martin (1995) are currently developing the Cultural and Contextual Guide (CCG) process, a method for assessing a child's cultural and contextual psychosocial adaptation. The CCG measures the extent of congruence between children and their past, current, and future environments in relation to contextualized ethnocultural factors. Information generated by the CCG can enable a teacher to more fully understand the specific cultural and contextual factors that each student brings to the classroom, as well as how the student's cultural and contextual background interacts with the cultural and contextual demands of the classroom environment.

Home and School Environment

Knowledge of the child's home environment is an essential part of ecological assessment. The physical structure of students' homes and immediate community sheds light on the environment within which students live. The risk comes when assumptions are made about the child's knowledge base and expected performance in school based on information about the physical living situation. Home visits by the teacher for each student in the class are a daunting task which is extremely time consuming but worthwhile. Home visits provide invaluable exposure to how children live, versus where they live.

Creating an information sheet that becomes part of a student's classroom file provides a good source of information. A good example of home and community assessment is found in Garbarino and Sherman's Neighborhood and Community Assessment (1980). This is a structured interview that probes into the areas of neighborhood, church, child care arrangements, employment, schooling, volunteer work, recreation, finances, health, family organizations, child rearing practices, parenting information, and future goals for the family. It is designed to provide comprehensive information about *how* the child lives without values attached to the information.

The compatibility of a student's needs and teaching styles or strategies has received attention in the educational and psychological fields. The idea that a set style of teaching strategies would work for all students is certainly not within anyone's list of expectations, and the task of accommodating to each student's instructional needs can be somewhat overwhelming. The Teacher Instructional Environment Scale (TIES; Ysseldyke & Christenson, 1987) represents a means of gathering information about how the teacher, student, and classroom environments interact. The TIES is considered a process of gaining information to assist teachers in adapting their classroom environment to better suit a particular child's style of learning.

Temperament Issues

Knowledge of temperament may be obtained through the Temperament Assessment Battery for Children (Martin, 1988) and the McDevitt Behavioral Style Questionnaire (Carey & McDevitt, 1978). These are pencil-and-paper questionnaires completed by the teacher, parents, or examiner depending on the measure. Typically, interpretation of these measures is completed by a school psychologist who explains how the results may relate to a child's functioning in school. Evaluation of the congruence between the different responses given from the teacher, parent, and examiner can yield interesting information about the child's context. The perceptions of how a child behaves may be different at home and school; in fact, the child may behave differently at home and at school. Part of these perceptions are based on the expectations of children, and a school psychologist can assist in the interpretations of these measures in relation to apparent expectations.

Academic Achievement

Academic achievement is one of the most consistently used outcome measures for a teacher's success. Standardized measures of achievement are the most accepted way to measure how a child's achievement compares to age and grade peers. Unfortunately, one of the problems with nationally standardized tests is their lack of sensitivity to how a child is functioning within the school district. The Woodcock–Johnson Tests of Educational Achievement–Revised (WJ–R; Woodcock & Johnson, 1989) and the Kaufman Test of Educational Achievement (KTEA; Kaufman & Kaufman, 1985) are two well constructed, commercially available achievement measures.

Other types of assessment of academic function may include curriculum-based assessment (CBA). CBA is a term applied to any testing strategy that uses the child's curriculum as the foundation for material assessed (Shinn, 1995). Short measures of a child's progress are gathered at strategic points that lend information about the progress a child has made within that specific curriculum. This information is tailored to the curriculum of the school and yields specific information about how particular children progress. School psychologists are becoming increasingly familiar with the procedures of CBA and can be valuable sources of information regarding a specific set of measures that would be appropriate for a particular curriculum.

Portfolio assessments are designed to provide a structured sample of a child's work directly reflecting the products the student has accumulated over a given period of time. According to Popham (1995), certain factors are critical to the success of a classroomwide portfolio assessment program. First, students should have an investment in the process and understand what they are required to do. Second, feedback is critical. Therefore, prior to initiating the process, evaluation criteria should be determined as well as guidelines for what work will be evaluated. A schedule of portfolio conferences should be built into class planning, including parent involvement. Portfolio assessments are increasingly being instituted on a district- or statewide basis. These protocols for information collected may prove to be a valuable asset when attempting to interpret a particular child's response to his or her educational ecosystem.

Learning Capacity

A child's learning capacity, and its effect on performance, is probably one of the most controversial topics in the field of education. Learning capacity can be assessed through intellectual assessment and dynamic assessment. The Wechsler Scales, WISC-III and WPPSI-R, (Wechsler, 1989, 1991) are the most widely used measures of intellectual ability in school systems. The Wechsler scales are measures with superior psychometric properties that provide a great deal of information about how children perform on various tasks that correlate to school achievement. However, intellectual assessments are typically not completed unless there is some reason to suspect a child has a significant learning problem. When completed, scores should always be interpreted with consideration of the child's total context. Specifically, the intellect of any given child is a relatively small component in the total context of that child.

Dynamic assessment has been discussed in the literature for several years and is an area of continued investigation (Campione & Brown, 1987). Dynamic assessment is a measure of a child's ability to learn. The information about the child's capacity is gathered by providing the child with strategies to incorporate new information or processes. A pre–posttest paradigm provides the examiner with information regarding how a child incorporates strategies to solve problems. Dynamic assessment is particularly promising when the amount of information a student has been exposed to may be limited.

The components of an ecological profile of a student should be geared toward a thorough understanding. The information provided in the preceding section attempted to provide some guidance related to the important factors that need to be considered by teachers. The child's developmental and educational history, acculturation, home and school environment, temperament, academic achievement, and learning capacity are all critical aspects of the ecological profile. The following section provides a case study to illustrate what information is necessary for an ecological understanding of a student.

CASE STUDY

Educational and Family History

Julia is beginning her fourth year in school and is in the second grade. She lives in an eastern city with a population of more than 500,000 people and attends school in a multiethnic, diversified, urban school with approximately 600 students.

Julia had a difficult start in her first 2 years in school due to frequent illnesses (i.e., repeated ear infections that caused high fevers and possible intermittent hearing loss). She passed kindergarten, but was placed in a transitional first grade to provide extra time to establish readiness skills. Her academic performance improved during the pre-first year, and she did well in first grade with the exception of reading skills, which were of some concern to her teacher. She received Chapter One Reading services during her first-grade year and is now beginning the second grade. As her reading placement is in the lower quartile of the class, she will remain in Chapter One Reading classes in addition to her regular curriculum.

Julia's attendance has improved during the current school year. She is a willing participant in school, but does not demonstrate enthusiasm or excitement about school attendance. She does not participate in any of the after school activities. Although she has been identified as having a good singing voice, she has refused any attempts to get her involved with school or church choirs. She goes directly home after school each day.

Julia is a child of Hispanic origin, and lives in a three bedroom apartment with her mother and three siblings. Julia has one older brother and two younger sisters. Julia's mother and father were divorced when Julia was 6 years old. Her father visits Julia and her siblings occasionally, mostly around holidays. He has remarried and has a small child from his new marriage, but does try to attend special occasions for the children, such as school plays and church programs. However, he has never attended a teacher conference about his children.

Julia is a child who has a few friends. These friends are children who live in her apartment complex and with whom she walks to and from school. Although they spend some time together outside of school, Julia is required to go home after school to help her older brother care for her two younger sisters. The friends primarily interact on the way to and from school and at church. In school, Julia is quiet and respectful to adults and congenial with her peers. She has one friend in her classroom and is always seen next to her when there is opportunity for peer interaction. Her friend is a gregarious child of African-American origin who has many friends and often ignores Julia. Julia seems to take this in stride and plays by herself when her friend is not available.

Julia's mother speaks Spanish with Julia's grandparents and at family gatherings. Julia's father speaks Spanish, but only with Julia's mother and not with his own family. Julia's first language is English, although Spanish is often spoken within the home. When conversing with her siblings or her friends, she uses English. Family relationships on her mother's side are quite traditional, with a great deal of importance placed on keeping the family bonds strong and on understanding the family history and traditions.

Classroom Variables

Ms. Jenkins, Julia's teacher, has been teaching for 3 years and is beginning to feel confident in her ability to teach the third-grade curriculum. Ms. Jenkins is of Euro-American descent and was raised in a small town in the Northeastern portion of the United States. She obtained her degree in elementary education from a large state-funded university. Ms. Jenkins had never lived in a large city prior to acquiring a teaching job at Julia's school. She shares an apartment with another teacher who teaches at one of the middle schools for the same district. They live and spend most of their time in a section of the city that is populated primarily by Euro-Americans.

Case Study Evaluation

This section addresses the evaluation of Julia from an ecological perspective. Assessment of the variables that affect Julia as an individual are considered to attempt to improve Julia's chances of receiving the optimal benefits from school.

As Julia has attended the same school throughout her educational career, Ms. Jenkins has specific information related to Julia's academic achievement. Ms. Jenkins knows that Julia had poor attendance in kindergarten and pre-first, but there has been a great deal of improvement. Julia has had satisfactory ratings on the social and behavioral dimensions reviewed on the report cards. However, Julia is considered at risk because she attended pre-first and received remedial Chapter One services in the area of reading for the past year. Her progress in reading has been described as "slow and steady." The standardized testing completed in the first grade indicated that Julia's reading comprehension and decoding skills were in the 5th percentile. Mathematics computations were in the 19th percentile, indicating low average performance. All other scores reported were consistently in the low average range. Further psychoeducational assessment of Julia's functioning in school could provide specific information regarding the extent of the problem and remediation strategies. A child study team meeting at the school level would be the first step in determining if an assessment is necessary.

Julia is reported to be a quiet child who tends to have few friends, but does not appear to be an isolate. Ms. Jenkins has been able to gather the following observations during the time Julia has been in her room. During structured classroom instruction, Julia appears to be quietly attentive and rarely asks questions. Her work is most often completed according to directions but not always correct. She responds to feedback well and will correct her work. Homework is not always completed, but if given the opportunity, she will work on it before class time.

Julia is a quiet child who rarely shows her emotions. She accepts compliments with a pleasant but shy smile and does not appear to enjoy being singled out. She seems to be a child who would be very pleased with a quiet smile or touch on the shoulder versus having her name called out with a compliment.

Assessment Factors and Implications for the Classroom

Behavioral interactions with environmental factors such as instructional time and activities, teacher behaviors, and active student participation are the components of learning (Delquadri, Greenwood, Whorton, Carta, & Hall, 1986). Ms. Jenkins knows that she is the critical link to Julia's skill acquisition. Therefore, evaluation of her own ability to interact with students as individuals and to enhance their ability to learn from her and one another must be reflected upon regularly. She understands that she must know Julia as an individual and that she must facilitate the acceptance and knowledge of Julia as an individual from each of her classmates. For example, do classmates know that Julia has two younger sisters whom she cares for every afternoon? Do her classmates know her favorite activities outside of school or her favorite foods? Julia is a child who will not offer information about herself unless she is encouraged and has models from other students in a somewhat structured format. The goal for Ms. Jenkins should be to assist Julia in becoming an active recipient in the educational process. Julia needs to become enthusiastic about coming to school and sharing part of herself in the process.

Class members should be encouraged to participate in each other's lives. Julia is a child who may benefit from familiarity and comfort with her teacher and fellow classmates. This comfort could be increased with Ms. Jenkins making the effort to express concern and involvement with Julia's life outside of the classroom. For example, Ms. Jenkins could visit Julia's home and talk with her mother about the important dimensions of their family. Conducting a structured interview (Garbarino & Sherman, 1980), discussed earlier, could provide a good starting point for Ms. Jenkins to gather information.

Julia is struggling with the process of learning to read. Attention needs to be given to the scope of the problem and the determination of how to best facilitate Julia's progress. Whether or not she becomes a competent reader, her educational process must continue. Julia has personal strengths that should be reinforced, and every measure possible should be taken to remediate her reading problems. Ms. Jenkins and her classmates all play a critical role in how Julia will proceed through her education.

CONCLUSIONS

The job of a classroom teacher is a truly amazing collection of factors. The information presented in this chapter was intended to shed some light on considerations that should be taken into account when developing strategies for creating an optimal learning environment for children. Ecological psychology provides a framework in which to incorporate the factors that every teacher already knows. That is, teachers need to understand each one of their students as an individual. To this end, techniques and tools were presented that can facilitate the teacher's understanding of each child.

REFERENCES

Ausubel, D. (1968). *Educational psychology: A cognitive view.* New York: Holt, Rinehart & Winston.

Bandura, A. (1977). *Social learning theory.* Englewood Cliffs, NJ: Prentice-Hall.

Bandura, A. (1982). Self-efficacy mechanism in human agency. *American Psychologist, 37,* 122–147.

Belsky, J., Fish, M., & Isabella, R. A. (1991). Continuity and discontinuity in infant negative and positive emotionality: Family antecedents and attachment consequences. *Developmental Psychology, 27,* 421–431.

Bernal, M. E., Saenz, D. S., & Knight, G. P. (1991). Ethnic identity and adaptation of Mexican American youth in school settings. *Hispanic Journal of Behavioral Sciences, 13,* 135–154.

Bronfenbrenner, U. (1967). Response to pressure from peers vs. adults among Soviet and American school children. *International Journal of Psychology, 2,* 199–208.

Bronfenbrenner, U. (1979). *The ecology of human development: Experiments by nature and design.* Cambridge, MA: Harvard University Press.

Campione, J. C., & Brown, A. L. (1987). Linking dynamic assessment with school achievement. In C. S. Lidz (Ed.), *Assessment: An interactional approach to evaluating learning potential* (pp. 82–115). New York: Guilford.

Carey, W. B., & McDevitt, S. C. (1978). Revision of the Infant Temperament Questionnaire. *Pediatrics, 61,* 735–739.

Chase, W. G., & Simon, H. A. (1973). Perception in chess. *Cognitive Psychology, 4,* 55–81.

Chi, M. T., Feltovich, P., & Glaser, R. (1981). Categorization and representation of physics problems in experts and novices. *Cognitive Science, 5,* 121–152.

Cuellar, J., Harris, L. C., & Jasso, R. (1980). An acculturation scale of Mexican-American normal and clinical populations. *Hispanic Journal of Behavioral Sciences, 2,* 199–217.

Delquadri, J., Greenwood, C. R., Whorton, D., Carta, J. J., & Hall, R. V. (1986). Classwide peer tutoring. *Exceptional Children, 52,* 535–542.

Dewey, J. (1960). *The school and society.* Chicago: University of Chicago Press.

DiVesta, F. J. (1989). Applications of cognitive psychology to education. In M. C. Wittrock & R. Farley (Eds.), *The future of educational psychology.* Hillsdale, NJ: Lawrence Erlbaum Associates.

Edwards, T. J. (1969). Pedagogical and psycho-social adjustment problems in cultural deprivation. In J. Hellmuth (Ed.), *Disadvantaged child* (pp. 161–171). New York: Brunner/Mazel.

Garbarino, J., & Sherman, D. (1980). High-risk neighborhood and high-risk families: The human ecology of child maltreatment. *Child Development, 51,* 188–198.

Garcia, M., & Vega, L. T. (1979). Development of a Cuban ethnic identity question. *Hispanic Journal of Behavioral Sciences, 1,* 247–261.

Giles, H. (1959). *The integrated classroom.* New York: Basic Books.

Heider, F. (1958). *The psychology of interpersonal relations.* Hillsdale, NJ: Lawrence Erlbaum Associates.

Higgins, E. T., & Parsons, J. E. (1983). Social cognition and the social life of the child: Stages as subcultures. In E. T. Higgins, D. N. Ruble, & W. W. Hartup (Eds.), *Social cognition and social development: A sociocultural perspective.* Cambridge, UK: Cambridge University Press.

Kaufman, A. S., & Kaufman, N. L. (1985). *Kaufman Test of Educational Achievement.* Circle Pines, MN: American Guidance Services.

Luria, A. R. (1976). *Cognitive development: Its culture and social foundations.* Cambridge, MA: Harvard University Press.

Martin, R. (1988). *Temperament Assessment Battery for Children.* Brandon, VT: Clinical Psychology.

Matute–Bianchi, M. E. (1986). Ethnic identity and patterns of school success and failure among Mexican descent and Japanese American students in a California high school: An ethnographic analysis. *American Journal of Education, 95,* 233–255.

Matute–Bianchi, M. E. (1989). *Situational ethnicity and patterns of school performance among immigrant and non-immigrant Mexican-descent students* (Bilingual Research Group Report, #89–05). Santa Cruz, CA: University of California.

Ogbu, J. U. (1987). Variability in minority school performance: A problem in search of an explanation. *Anthropology and Education Quarterly, 18,* 312–334.

Olmedo, E. L. (1979). Acculturation: A psychometric perspective. *American Psychologist, 34,* 1061–1070.

Palmer, D. J., & Goetz, E. T. (1988). Selection and use of study strategies: The role of the studier's beliefs about self and strategies. In C. E. Weinstein, E. T. Goetz, & P. A. Alexander (Eds.), *Learning and study strategies: Issues in assessment, instruction, and evaluation.* New York: Academic Press.

Pena, E., Quinn, R., & Iglesias, A. (1992). The application of dynamic methods to language assessment: A nonbiased procedure. *The Journal of Special Education, 26,* 269–280.

Phinney, J. S. (1991). Ethnic identity and self-esteem: A review and integration. *Hispanic Journal of Behavioral Sciences, 13,* 193–208.

Plomin, R. (1989). Environment and Genes: Determinants of behavior. *American Psychologist, 44,* 105–111.

Popham, W. J. (1995). *Classroom assessment: What teachers need to know.* Boston: Allyn and Bacon.

Sadowsky, G. R., & Plake, B. (1991). Psychometric properties of the American-International Relations Scale. *Education and Psychological Measurements, 51,* 207–216.

Schunk, D. H. (1983) Ability versus effort attributional feedback: Differential effects on self-efficacy and achievement. *Journal of Educational Psychology, 75,* 848–856.

Scripts–Bower, G. H., Black, J. B., & Turner, T. J. (1979). Scripts in memory for text. *Cognitive Psychology, 3,* 177–220.

Shinn, M. R. (1995). Best practices in curriculum-based measurement and its use in a problem-solving model. In A. Thomas & J. Grimes (Eds.), *Best practices in school psychology-III* (pp. 547–567). Washington, DC: National Association of School Psychologists.

Swartz, J. L., & Martin, W. E., Jr. (1995). *The impact of culture and context on psychosocial adaptation: Measuring person-environment correspondence.* Unpublished manuscript.

Szapocznik, J., & Kurtines, W. M. (1993). Family psychology and cultural diversity: Opportunities for theory, research, and application. *American Psychology, 48,* 400–407.

Szapocznik, J., Kurtines, W., & Fernandez, T. (1980). Bicultural involvement and adjustment in Hispanic American youth. In A. M. Padilla (Ed.), *Acculturation: Theory, models and some new findings.* Boulder, CO: Westview.

Szapocznik, J., Rio, A., Perez-Vidal, A., Kurtines, W., Hervis, O., & Santiseben, D. (1986). Bicultural effectiveness training (BET): An experimental test of an intervention modality for families experiencing intergenerational/intercultural conflict. *Hispanic Journal of Behavioral Sciences, 8,* 303–330.

Tajfel, H. (1981). *Human groups and social categories.* Cambridge, MA: Cambridge University Press.

Thomas, A., & Chess, S. (1977). *Temperament and development.* New York: Brunner/Mazel.

Vygotsky, L. S. (1962). *Thought and language.* Cambridge, MA: MIT Press.

Wechsler, D. (1981). *Wechsler Adult Intelligence Scale-Revised.* San Antonio, TX: The Psychological Corporation.

Wechsler, D. (1989). *Wechsler Preschool and Primary Scale of Intelligence-Revised.* San Antonio, TX: The Psychological Corporation.

Wechsler, D. (1991). *Wechsler Intelligence Scale for Children-Third Edition.* San Antonio, TX: The Psychological Corporation.

Weiner, B. (1985). An attributional theory of achievement motivation and emotion. *Psychological Review, 92,* 548–573.

Woodcock, R. W., & Johnson, M. W. (1989). *Woodcock–Johnson Test of Educational Achievement-Revised.* Allen, TX: DLM Teaching Resources.

Ysseldyke, J. E., & Christenson, S. L. (1987). *The Instructional Environment Scale.* Austin, TX: Pro-Ed.

5

Ecosystemic Intervention
With Teachers: A Collaborative
Approach

Julia S. Shaftel
Marvin J. Fine
University of Kansas

When a student experiences behavioral or learning difficulties in a school setting, it is not uncommon for the child to be viewed as the locus of the problem. From this viewpoint, interventions are intended to change the child. There has been a growing recognition that the problem is likely to be the outgrowth of several factors or conditions. The child is still an important part of the picture, but other factors based in the classroom and even outside the classroom may be important contributors to the child's behavior and, in turn, may need to be the focus of intervention.

This chapter emphasizes an ecosystemic perspective that views the child in context and with an appreciation of the interaction between child-based and setting-based variables. Although teachers may benefit from reading this chapter, the anticipated audience is composed mainly of school and community psychologists, mental health and learning specialists, and other school personnel who may be available to help teachers.

This chapter also considers the concept of *collaboration* as it applies to two important service delivery systems: consultation and teacher support teams. Professionals from outside the schools who are called on to offer services to teachers will benefit from familiarity with these two approaches and will be able to engage more readily in joint problem-solving efforts with school personnel.

Teachers are usually skilled at dealing with children who are experiencing learning or behavior problems and are able to cope successfully on a daily basis with a broad spectrum of student issues. However, there will still be instances where the usual interventions do not work, and the teacher is left frustrated or unsure of how to proceed. What typically occurs then is that a mental health, pupil personnel, or learning specialist is called in through the school's referral process to assist the teacher. That person, identified in this chapter as the *consultant*, can invoke an ecosystemic perspective to assist in understanding the situation and in formulating interventions. There may be some type of teacher support team in the school with whom the teacher can meet to develop interventions for the situation. The consultant can participate as a member of this team and might also become the follow-up person to support the teacher in carrying out the team's suggestions. The consultative process, enacted in the consultant's one-to-one contact with the teacher or in relation to the consultant's participation on a team, serves as the delivery system for an ecosystemic intervention.

AN ECOSYSTEMIC PERSPECTIVE

There are several assumptions that derive from both ecological and systems theories that are germane to the theme of classroom help for children who are experiencing difficulties. Bronfenbrenner's (1979, 1986) conceptualization of four nested, interactive systems (micro, meso, exo, and macro), within which persons exist and that can affect an individual's development and behavior, is a useful frame of reference. Behavior is reciprocal within and across these systems so that the person is affected by the system, but also affects the system. Understanding these four systems in relation to a child and the home and school settings opens opportunities for varied avenues of intervention. Awareness of these systems and their interplay helps in conceptualizing the issues and possible interventions by avoiding the self-limiting viewpoint of a single problem source. Following an overview of these four nested systems, we present some assumptions specific to intervention from an ecosystemic perspective.

The *microsystem* refers to immediate settings of which the person is a member, such as home and school. Children come to school with different experiences and attitudes about teachers, learning, effort, and their own future goals. For some children the school experience is consonant with home values and experiences; for other children the school is an alien environment. In instances where there is a continuity of experiences and values between home and school, we can anticipate a more positive academic and social adjustment by children.

The *mesosystem* is the realm of interaction between microsystems such as the home and school. Consultants will often generate activity in the mesosystem as they explore the implications of the home–school relationship with respect to the behavior of the child and how the child's behavior is understood in each context. Effective intervention may require greater collaboration between the parents and school personnel.

The *exosystem* represents a level of potentially significant but indirect influence that includes the local community and the educational system. As an example, in a school district in which teachers have been exhorted to "get back to basics," the explicit emphasis on raising test scores may undermine some teachers' attempts to work more flexibly with children with learning difficulties.

The *macrosystem* refers to larger and more pervasive areas of society such as national educational policy, political structures, and the economy. For example, federal legislation has mandated that all identified disabled and at-risk young children receive free and appropriate educational services. Federal funds are allocated to support these services, and these funds move from the federal to state levels and then to the specific school districts. While additional funding sources contribute to the school's resources, there is never enough to meet the needs of all children with special needs. School districts have to be careful how they expend special services funds and how they determine which children require special education. There are likely to be some natural tensions between a district's definition of eligibility for services and the educational personnel's perceptions of a child's needs.

Assumptions Underlying an Ecosystemic Perspective

Several assumptions are particularly germane to consultants as they develop an understanding of a situation and work with teachers to develop interventions. These assumptions broadly address behaviors, values, and the interaction of the two.

Behavior Has a Value Specific to the Setting. The value of behavior is defined within the setting in which it occurs. There are many anthropological examples of how behavior considered bizarre or deviant in one setting is acceptable and even valued in other settings (Benedict, 1961). This assumption posits a cultural relativism in the definition of the normalcy or deviancy of behavior and underscores the importance of understanding the setting and context within which the behavior occurs. A child may be seen as more acceptable in one classroom and less acceptable in another classroom because of the values, beliefs, and expectations regarding students in those two settings.

"Deviancy" Refers to Behavior That is Discordant With the Values of Its Setting. It is the behavior, not the person, that is deviant. Apter (1982) stated, "Discordance may be defined as a disparity between an individual's abilities and the demands or expectations of the environment" (p. 69). The problem is not considered to reside within the individual, but to exist within the interaction of the individual with the environment. From this perspective, the child is *disturbing* rather than *disturbed* (Swap, 1984).

It is Important to Consider the "Goodness of Fit" of the Person to the Setting. The extent of match or mismatch of person to setting has serious implications for the child and other involved persons. Related to Apter's (1982) statement on discordance, Chess and Thomas (1987) concluded from their extensive research on children's temperament and parenting that "Goodness of fit exists when the demands and expectations of the parents and other people important to the child's life are compatible with the child's temperament, abilities, and other characteristics. With such a fit healthy development for the child can be expected" (p. 56). As a consequence of a poor fit, "the child is likely to experience excessive stress, and healthy development is jeopardized" (p. 57).

There are many examples of children who may be mismatched in some way with their school or classroom settings. Not only will their behavior be judged differently in different settings, but they will, in fact, behave differently. A child who perceives the teacher as accepting and who is assisted with difficulties in a helpful way is likely to respond differently than a child who perceives the environment as hostile and punitive.

People Within the Setting Make the Value Judgment. Key individuals within a setting demonstrate the values of that setting regarding a child's behavior. Swap (1984), in her article on ecological approaches to working with families of disturbing children, stated "that in order for a behavior to be considered disturbing, a concerned adult must identify it as such" (p. 108). It is people, rather than an amorphous concept of system or setting, who observe or experience the child's behavior and then apply a value judgment regarding the acceptability of the behavior. This point underscores the degree of subjectivity associated with the concepts of normalcy and deviancy. It also points to the teacher as the most likely person to establish a value perspective on the child. For example, does the teacher present the child in a sympathetic light as needing help or as a "bad" child needing correction?

There Is a Bidirectionality to Interactions Within a Setting. The teacher influences the structure and activities within a setting that impact the child, but the child's reactions, in turn, impact the setting and others in the setting. For example, a teacher's belief that children learn best in a structured learning environment influences the way in which the teacher structures the environment. The children who are perceived by the teacher as responding positively to the structure are probably reacted to more positively by the teacher. A child's adaptive response (i.e., performing well) also reinforces the teacher's beliefs about the value of the structure. The teacher's approving reactions simultaneously reinforce that student's behavior. Also, as mentioned earlier, a student with difficulties is likely to respond differently to a setting perceived as helpful and sympathetic than to a setting perceived as punitive. The teacher, in turn, responds differently depending on that teacher's perceptions of the child's response.

Ecological Systems, Rather Than People, May Need to be Changed. In terms of the objectives of an ecological intervention, Swap (1984) emphasized that interventions should be directed at altering the ecological system to create more effective solutions sympathetic to the needs of all of the involved persons. This position would be consistent with those of Chess and Thomas (1987), Rhodes and Paul (1978), and Apter (1982). Conoley and Haynes (1992) stated "the goal of an ecologically based intervention is not a particular state of mental health or particular behavior patterns, but rather an increased concordance between the behavior of a child and the settings within which he or she resides" (p. 180).

They further stated that, from an ecological perspective, interventions can be organized "to increase the possibility of system change, the competence of individuals, and the congruence of individuals with their settings" (p. 180).

Changing a system usually requires influencing the key person in the system. In the classroom context, this person is the teacher. The concepts of first- and second-order change are relevant when considering the classroom system. *First-order change* is essentially "more of the same." For example, a teacher may need help in refining a behavior modification program that is not achieving its goal. The teacher's perception of the child has not changed, but the sophistication of the intervention may need improvement. First-order changes may be appropriate in certain instances. In contrast, *second-order change* implies that the teacher now perceives the child differently and therefore responds differently. As an example, a consultant helped a teacher to view a noncompliant child as reactive to perceived failure. The teacher had believed the child to be willfully negative and was, in turn, reacting even more punitively toward him. With a new and sympathetic perspective, the teacher created a less threatening situation for the child, one involving a careful selection of academic tasks and more positive feedback. The teacher was also made aware that it would take time to build the child's confidence, which helped her to be more patient with the child's progress. These changes represent second-order change, a real change in the classroom system.

Ecological Interventions are Heuristic and Eclectic. There is general agreement that an ecological intervention does not follow a prescribed format. With the tenets of an ecological perspective in mind, those attempting to carry out an intervention choose whatever methods and procedures seem useful. Conoley and Haynes (1992) stated succinctly that the goals of an ecologically oriented intervention "are reached not through a new set of techniques or treatments but through a framework of using existing techniques in an ecological manner" (p. 180). Existing techniques can refer to modification of curricular methods and materials, breaking larger tasks into smaller units, the use of positive reinforcement, peer tutoring, and developing more effective home–school communication, to name some possibilities.

The actual focus of intervention may vary to achieve specific objectives. Depending on the situation, several interventions might be sequenced, and, as Swap (1984) described, there could be "simultaneous interventions … directed at parents, teachers, and/or other significant members of the child's community. Goals of these efforts might be to add to parents' or teachers' skills or help them to change their priorities or expectations, revise their perceptions, or acquire new resources" (pp. 109-110).

Ecological Interventions May Result in Outcomes That Are Unexpected, Broad, or Pervasive. An ecological modification is likely to precipitate other changes, some expected and others that may be surprising. This awareness encourages the consultant to think through the possible effects of planned changes and to be on the lookout for unanticipated changes following the intervention. For example, an intervention plan for a low-achieving, disruptive child may include several classroom modifications and a behavior change contract. The success of the program might be compromised by the rejection and animosity the child experiences with low-achieving friends who are also disruptive. Some individual counseling may be needed to help the child understand those reactions and to support the child in continuing to progress.

Classroom Factors to Consider in an Ecosystemic Intervention

Any consultant attempting to assist teachers needs to be sensitive to the myriad factors that influence student behavior. These variables, interacting in a reciprocal fashion, define the classroom ecosystem. Although the teacher has the primary responsibility for implementing programs, the consultant's role is to work with the teacher to identify elements that potentially contribute to the problem and to support the teacher in developing, applying, monitoring, and evaluating interventions. The consultative process involves interviews, observations, and, as deemed useful, ratings or assessment devices. These are vehicles for the consultant to become aware of the situational relevance of several factors.

Factors the Teacher Brings to the Classroom. Teacher factors include beliefs about children, expectations of appropriate student achievement and performance, personality, tolerance for differences among children, and perception of the regular educator's role within the school community. In a given situation, the consultant may need to spend time processing the teacher's expectations and values. Those expectations may be self-limiting and, therefore, liable to undermine an intervention plan. The consultant's interpersonal skills and, in particular, the ability to reframe events into a positive light are extremely important.

Factors the Child Brings to the Classroom. Student variables include the child's academic skills and talents, self-esteem and temperament, emotional maturity, physical development, social skills, learning style, attitude toward learning, perceptions of the helpfulness of teachers, and history of educational or behavioral problems (Bulgren & Knackendoffel, 1986; Evans & Evans, 1987). For example, to ignore that a child has a history of school failure and that the child expects failure may doom an intervention plan. The intervention needs to consider the child as an active player, not just the object of the intervention.

Physical Organization of the Classroom. The physical environment needs to be considered, including such variables as seating arrangement, spatial density, noise level, lighting, location of the teacher's desk, traffic patterns, and the availability of study carrels for students who need or prefer them (Bulgren & Knackendoffel, 1986; Evans & Evans, 1987; Evertson, Emmer, Clements, Sanford, & Worsham, 1989; Heron & Heward, 1988). For example, having an attention-seeking, disruptive child seated in a major classroom traffic pattern is predictive of problems. Other variables include the availability of audiovisual devices for classroom instruction (Evertson et al., 1989) and computers for individual work. The use of these technological aids may affect the student's ability to see, hear, and understand a presentation and may influence the teacher's choice of whole group versus small group or individual learning.

Teacher Management Style. Teacher management style refers to group and individual management skills, the use of small groups or peer teams, handling of transitions, timing of activities, feedback and reinforcement of students, and both positive and negative disciplinary techniques (Bulgren & Knackendoffel, 1986; Evertson et al., 1989). Teachers perceived by students to be fair and reasonable are likely to obtain greater student compliance than teachers seen in a less positive light. Effective management is an integral aspect of the total instructional environment.

Curriculum and Instructional Materials. Curriculum factors involve the appropriateness of the curriculum for the student in terms of level and type of presentation, sequencing, feedback, and amount of engaged time (Evans & Evans, 1987). Materials may be modified for the student or the curriculum may be presented in an alternate mode, for example, by auditory or visual means such as through video presentation, rather than by reading. The consultant may need to help the teacher think through various instructional strategies. Sometimes the modification may appear quite simple but produces major outcomes. An example is a teacher who expected a child with learning problems to work unassisted for 15 to 20 minutes at seat assignments. When the teacher agreed to check with the student every five to ten minutes to offer support and feedback, greater on-task and successful behavior by the student occurred.

Use of Auxiliary Personnel. Auxiliary personnel may refer to paraprofessionals or volunteers, team teaching with other regular or special education teachers, or the use of cross-age student tutors. With a greater emphasis on including a wide range of students in the regular classroom, auxiliary personnel are becoming more available to the teacher, but they may not be working together effectively. Parent volunteers can also be a valuable resource in classrooms where there are children needing extra attention and support.

Family–School Factors.   These factors include a range of considerations, such as the continuity between home and school in terms of values regarding learning and social behavior (Fine, 1990, 1995). The consultant should consider the history of the family–school relationship in terms of communication and working out problems. For example, are the school and teacher pro-parent in relation to collaborative efforts? Have either school personnel or the family adopted an adversarial posture? In an ideal situation the parents can be an information and intervention resource for the teacher.

The mesosystemic relationship of school and family are vital to consider within an ecosystemic perspective. It may prove supportive and motivational to students to see their parents actively involved in a partnership role with the teacher. For example, one strategy is a conference involving the teacher, the parent(s), the child, and other involved personnel. The child's participation and awareness of parental involvement can produce significant outcomes in relation to student behavior and success. Robinson and Fine (1994) described the benefits of parent–teacher collaboration and ways for teachers to address some common barriers that occur. Connors and Epstein (1995) have elaborated on how families and schools can learn to collaborate and how parents can be helped to become active participants in the school lives of their children. A typology presented by Epstein (1992, 1995) represents a framework for parent–school involvement at six levels, from the basic duties of the home and school to high-level collaboration resulting in shared responsibility for children's education across the community. Parent involvement, while potentially very valuable, presents many challenges to the schools, not the least of which is how to activate such involvement (Christenson, 1993).

Assessment of Classroom Factors

Ecosystemic interventions grow out of a tentative understanding of many factors that may be related to the problem. Interventions are, in a sense, the testing of hypotheses; the differential effects of the intervention represent valuable feedback to both the teacher and the consultant. There are formal and informal assessment procedures as well as interview techniques that can enhance an understanding of the factors that may be interacting within the setting. The observational and interpersonal skills of the consultant are crucial, whether the consultant is performing student observations or interviewing the teacher and student. Although earlier chapters in this book detail ecological assessment, it may be useful to outline briefly some available means of data collection.

Ecological assessment has several important features, such as using multiple sources of data, focusing on the interactions between the student and the environment, recognizing that behavior may be situation specific, and providing information useful in the design of intervention programs to meet the unique needs of the target student (Bulgren & Knackendoffel, 1986; Christenson, 1993; Conoley & Haynes, 1992; Evans, Gable, & Evans, 1993; Fine, 1995). Ecological assessment is a dynamic process that does not end with the initiation of an intervention plan but can continue during an intervention or can be repeated cyclically to evaluate progress (Bulgren & Knackendoffel, 1986; Fine, 1995). Ecological assessment includes formats such as checklists and rating scales, observational techniques, and interviews, in addition to information obtained from student records, permanent products, and tests (Bulgren & Knackendoffel, 1986; Heron & Heward, 1988).

Checklists may be used by the teacher to identify factors that impact the student's problematic behavior and to show which environmental variables have already been altered or controlled (Evans & Evans, 1990). There are also checklists and rating scales for students that have been designed to measure teacher attitudes and classroom atmosphere such as The Classroom Environment Scale (Trickett, Leone, Fink, & Braaten, 1993).

Classroom observation assessment instruments generally require trained observers for effective use. For example, the Ecobehavioral Assessment Systems Software (EBASS; Greenwood, Carta, Kamps, & Delquadri, 1993) provides coding procedures via laptop computer that simplify the process of data collection, scoring, analysis, and reporting. EBASS observational systems are based on matrices and include variables such as academic demands and student responses. Another ecobehavioral observation design tallies student behaviors in a matrix format providing both quantitative and qualitative information (Hendrickson, 1992). This format assesses two ecological variables, the subject area and the required instructional task, and two behavioral variables, quality of academic response and inappropriate behavior. The completed matrix quickly shows which situations or required student responses cause problems and what type of inappropriate behavior results. Classroom observations can also consist of anecdotal and time-sampling procedures designed to record and measure specific behaviors.

Interviews can provide information from the teacher's perspective and allow the consultant to obtain greater detail about problematic situations or behavior than is available from a rating scale or observation. Semistructured interview formats allow probing of factors unique to a particular situation, yet are designed to capture a range of relevant material. Welch (1994) provides a semistructured interview in a matrix format suggesting who, what, where, when, and why questions about classroom variables such as materials, teaching format, student grouping, homework, evaluation, and feedback. Sattler (1990) provides a comprehensive, semistructured teacher interview to elicit information about peers and family. Obtaining the viewpoint of the students, who are the individuals most affected by the teacher's actions, is crucial within an ecosystemic perspective and more likely to foster change within the classroom (Burden & Fraser, 1993; Trickett et al., 1993). The most direct tool is a student interview, which may be informal yet structured enough to obtain pertinent information. The success of the child interview depends on the consultant's skills with students of different ages.

The Instructional Environment System-II (TIES-II; Ysseldyke & Christenson, 1993) is a comprehensive ecological appraisal based on the idea that "diagnostic personnel should assess the learning environment as well as the learner ... [because] student performance in school is a function of an interaction between the student and the instructional environment" (p. 9). TIES gathers data on 12 aspects of the instructional process: instructional match, teacher expectations, classroom environment, instructional presentation, cognitive emphasis, motivational strategies, relevant practice, informed feedback, academic engaged time, adaptive instruction, progress evaluation, and student understanding. The system includes structured interviews of the teacher, parent, and student along with a classroom observation. A checklist of instructional needs reminds the teacher to consider modifications of the learning environment that have already been made or that may be advisable. Additional information may be collected as part of the evaluative process, including student work completed during the classroom observation period.

Finally, family factors must be considered, along with the relationship between home and school (Anderson, 1983; Evans & Evans, 1987; Fine, 1990, 1992, 1995). A parent interview is an excellent source of information about home environment variables and aspects of the child's behavior, from the parents' perspective, that might influence school performance (Bulgren & Knackendoffel, 1986; Sattler, 1990).

A COLLABORATIVE ORIENTATION
TO INTERVENTION PLANNING

An ecologically valid intervention is sensitive to the ecosystemic context and is acceptable to the teacher, who is not only a key determinant of the classroom ecology but also the likely implementor of the plan. The importance of teacher acceptability of the proposed intervention is paramount. If teachers reject an intervention as too time consuming, too difficult, or opposed to their personal value systems, they may refuse to carry out a strategy that someone else believes will be successful or may implement it halfheartedly, thereby sabotaging its potential effectiveness. The teacher needs to feel enthusiasm and have a sense of ownership for the plan. These observations underscore the relevance of the collaborative process and the need for the teacher to play an active role in developing the intervention.

The heart of collaboration is the willingness of the participants to engage in shared problem solving and decision making. This requires a respect for and appreciation of the potential contributions of everyone involved in the process. Although individuals may vary in their experiences and expertise, the participants need to believe that a viable plan can evolve out of the collaborative activity. The remainder of this chapter focuses on collaborative service delivery models that, by their nature, incorporate ecosystemic considerations. These service delivery options, unlike student-centered interventions such as individual counseling or remedial academic services, focus on the teacher as the person most able to modify the classroom environment with the goal of improving student learning and behavior.

Teacher consultation and school-based teams are the two basic delivery systems for assistance to teachers seeking help with challenging students (Pugach & Johnson, 1989b; Sindelar, Griffin, Smith, & Watanabe, 1992). Participation in collaborative consultation and on problem-solving teams requires a particular frame of mind for the consultant. There are specific skills and ways of functioning characteristic of a collaborative orientation. West and Cannon (1988) identified skills educational professionals deemed necessary for success within a collaborative consultation model. These skills, critical for both consultants and consultees, fell into five broad domains. *Interactive communication skills* include effective communication, listening and responding skills, nonverbal communication, interviewing, and providing feedback. *Equity issues* involve displaying respect for differences, advocating for needed services for all students, and following the principle of least restrictive environment for students with disabilities. *Personal characteristics* of the participants refer to caring and empathic engagement in interactions, respect for different viewpoints, positive self-concept, enthusiasm for the consultation process, and demonstrating willingness to learn. *Collaborative problem-solving skills* include defining shared goals, using a variety of data collection techniques and strategies for generating alternatives, evaluating interventions, and recognizing that adjustment and reworking may be needed. *Evaluation of consultation effec-*

tiveness consists of self-evaluation of strengths and weaknesses and the use of feedback to modify or terminate consultation.

There is growing evidence of teacher preference for collaborative problem solving over other approaches (Buysse, Schulte, Pierce, & Terry, 1994; Kutsick, Gutkin, & Witt, 1991; Wade, Welch, & Jensen, 1994). The shared decision-making nature of collaboration is appealing to teachers. Collaboration affords all participants the opportunity to tap their specific expertise and to develop more thoughtful and comprehensive plans than one person alone could achieve.

Collaborative Consultation

Collaborative consultation consists of a voluntary, nonhierarchical relationship in which the consultant and consultee jointly develop an intervention and share responsibility for its implementation (Friend & Cook, 1992; Graden & Bauer, 1992). The consultant can be an educator from any of a number of professions within the school, such as school psychology, special education, or counseling, or may represent a community agency. The consultee is typically the classroom teacher who is confronted with a problematic situation. Although consultation is usually an interactive process between two people, Graden, Casey, and Christenson (1985) emphasized that parents should always be advised of any classroom difficulties involving their child and the steps being taken to address them and should be included in the planning process, if possible.

A significant aim of the consultant's role is to sustain an atmosphere of parity between the involved persons by refraining from assuming an expert stance which conveys the image of the consultant as someone who knows what should happen and what others should be doing. Pugach and Johnson (1989a) warned that, "For collaborative working relationships to be realized, specialists will have to work hard to shed the 'expert' image to which they have been socialized and which many classroom teachers have come to expect of them. As specialist roles shift to accommodate the current needs of students in the schools, conceptions of expertise should shift with them" (p. 235).

The consultant must also initiate and maintain a confidential relationship with the consultee to develop a sense of trust and comfort in the consultative process (Graden & Bauer, 1992; Schubert, Landers, Curtis, Anderson, & Curtis, 1984). Within an appropriately supportive and trusting climate, the consultant engages the consultee in the steps of intervention planning.

While the number of steps varies from design to design, the tasks of developing, implementing, and evaluating a particular intervention can be subsumed in four major phases (Bergan & Kratochwill, 1990). These four phases comprise the framework of consultation by which the consultant and consultee proceed from agreeing on the problem, examining the ecosystemic context, and devising an intervention to evaluating the effects of the intervention. It should be noted that, as a problem-solving format, consultation is not inherently collaborative. The manner in which the consultant interacts, listens, processes, shares, and achieves agreement is what makes the problem-solving process truly collaborative.

Phase 1: Problem Identification.   This phase refers to defining and clarifying the child's target behavior. This is done by collecting data about the child's performance and generating the objectives of the intervention. Many techniques, such as observations, student and teacher interviews, rating scales, collection of work samples, and curriculum-based assessments, are useful at this stage.

Other problem-solving models (Fine, 1992; Robinson & Fine, 1994) elaborate on this procedure, breaking it down into more steps with greater specificity. Time as well as effective listening and processing skills are necessary to clarify the teacher's perceptions and experiences and to tentatively agree on the problem.

Phase 2: Problem Analysis.   This phase consists of determining the child and instructional variables affecting the intervention plan and the process of designing the plan itself. All of the ecological factors discussed earlier may be included in the analysis of the problem. Plan design consists of outlining general strategies and defining specific tactics to be used during the intervention. The ecological validity of the plan is critical to consider, including the teacher's agreement and willingness to participate. However theoretically correct an intervention might be, it has to make sense to the teacher. The teacher's implementation role in terms of time and energy also has to be acceptable.

Phase 3: Plan Implementation.   This phase includes preparing for and carrying out the intervention. The consultant monitors the operation of the intervention to verify that the plan is being implemented as designed. Both the consultant and consultee collect measurement data during the implementation phase to evaluate the progress of the student.

The concept of collaboration implies a sharing of responsibility for both the plan and its outcomes. The consultant needs to maintain contact in order to support the teacher and trouble-shoot in case of difficulty. If teachers feel that all responsibility has been "dumped" on them, a negative reaction to the role of consultee is likely to occur and the purpose of collaboration will be undermined.

Phase 4: Problem Evaluation. This phase consists of reviewing the efficacy of the intervention strategy based on collected data and making modifications as necessary. It should not be surprising that modifications and fine tuning may be needed. The initial plan is essentially a hypothesis about a solution to be tested in the classroom. The consultant's positive attitude toward making modifications can influence the teacher, who may be thinking that the plan failed because it did not achieve the hoped-for results. Along with hard data, the teacher's attitudes and perceptions need to be considered. Data may show the program is working, but the teacher is becoming frustrated with the extra demands and is ready to terminate. When the goals of the plan are eventually reached, the consultative relationship will likely be ended.

There are instances in which the child's behavior has improved to the teacher's satisfaction, but the consultant still sees room for progress. From a collaborative perspective, the teacher's opinions need to carry considerable weight. Typically, consultation is a voluntary activity in which the teacher has chosen to participate. Because the teacher has responsibility for the whole classroom, not just the one child of initial concern, the teacher may feel comfortable with the changes that have occurred and confident carrying on alone. If the consultant insists on the need for more change or on continued involvement, the teacher may feel trapped and encroached upon in terms of professional prerogatives. The consultant's capacity to negotiate termination on positive terms is important and can lead to future requests for consultation.

Collaborative consultation takes the emphasis off the knowledge of the expert and places it on the skills of the teacher (Schubert et al., 1984). Exploring instructional and management options for students having trouble increases not only teacher skills, but also confidence in the ability to select strategies and put them into action in the future. The teacher is the person who experiences the problem and must feel competent to implement the chosen strategy. Therefore the teacher must be actively involved in developing the intervention plan with the consultant as well as having the final say over the selection of strategies to be tried. Contributing to the generation of possible solutions gives teachers a stake in the outcome of the intervention, which, in turn, increases the likelihood that they will follow through with the plan in the classroom (Fine, 1995; Schubert et al., 1984).

Collaborative Teams

Schools use different names for their teacher support teams. The actual term *collaborative team* may not be used, but the philosophy of collaboration permeates the team structure and manner of functioning. On entering a situation, the consultant may discover that participation on a collaborative team seems more appropriate than individual consultation, or that individual consultation can operate in a parallel and supportive manner with team activities.

Teams meet at regular intervals and represent an ongoing method of teacher support and program planning for students. When a specific child is being discussed, it is often valuable to include the child's parents and the child. In this way teams can connect the child's two major microsystems, the home and the school. Community members can also be involved as team members when deemed appropriate. Collaborative teams emphasize the shared ownership of problems and their solutions with the goal of empowering teachers in addition to modeling communication and collaboration skills for students.

As part of the TIES-II ecosystemic assessment package, Ysseldyke and Christenson (1993) outlined a team problem-solving procedure they call the *Collaborative Intervention Planning Process*. The nine steps of this process are intended to focus the exchange of information and guide intervention design. The steps include describing the teacher concern, sharing information, arriving at consensus, describing the home support for learning, identifying ways to involve parents, brainstorming ideas and options, selecting an intervention, sharing resources, and addressing other questions. The authors provide specific instructions for accomplishing each of the steps in a collaborative manner, utilizing the information obtained during the instructional assessment.

Team size is an issue of great concern, especially for teams that focus on the continuing needs of one child, because collaboration places significant demands on each member, including regular attendance at meetings. Thousand and Villa (1992) defined a core team as the six or seven members from various disciplines who can communicate and operate most efficiently. The core team for a particular student would include the student, parents, paraprofessionals, and teachers who work together regularly. The extended team may come together less frequently and consists of personnel who are not needed for ongoing decision making about the student. Members of the extended team may be invited to participate in core team meetings when needed. For example, a health professional or technology expert may take part in a team meeting once a year to update other members on the student's progress and needs with respect to a particular medical concern. Similarly, a consultant may not participate at each team meeting, but might attend once every few months to interact with core team members.

Collaborative teams, when they are in place, offer the opportunity for an outside consultant or school-based professional to influence the classroom environment for a particular child. These teams are especially valuable for children with significant and chronic needs whose programming requires participation from several professionals. They recognize that the classroom teacher, even with the help of a consultant, does not have all the information needed to plan for an individual child. Ideally, the parents' participation on the team addresses the necessity for continuity between the home and school ecosystems.

SUMMARY

This chapter emphasized the importance of an ecosystemic viewpoint with respect to student problems in the classroom. Bronfenbrenner's (1979, 1986) model of nested systems begins with the microsystem, the smallest system of which the child is a part, such as home or school, and expands to include the mesosystem, the level of interaction between microsystems. Indirect influence at the local level is part of the exosystem, whereas the macrosystem refers to the broader societal level of influence. An ecosystemic perspective emphasizes the interactive and bidirectional relationship of the child with the environment. Change can be described as occurring on two levels, where first-order change is simply "more of the same," and second-order change involves altering one's viewpoint of the problem and subsequently changing the system. Even small changes can have a pervasive effect.

Classroom factors affecting student behavior and learning include teacher and child characteristics, physical organization of the classroom, teacher management style, curriculum and materials, additional personnel in the classroom, and the interaction of the family and school. Assessment of these variables is essential before context-appropriate intervention plans can be devised. Methods for ecological assessment include checklists and rating scales, observations, and, most important, interviews by the consultant with key persons such as the teacher and parents.

The consultant, whether on a one-on-one basis or as a member of a team, can help the teacher and other school personnel recognize and incorporate an ecosystemic viewpoint into intervention planning. The consultant brings an ecosystemic outlook to the forefront during all stages of planning and implementation. Many strategies are opened for consideration when environmental variables are regarded as targets for manipulation. Teacher acceptability of the intervention is critical and is more likely to be accomplished through a collaborative decision-making process.

Collaborative formats in the delivery of support services recognize that the teacher is a key component in ecological modification. This understanding dictates that the teacher play an integral role in developing the intervention to insure its satisfactory implementation. The teacher must feel a sense of ownership in the chosen intervention. It should be acceptable in terms of its format and the time and effort required to put it in place. The consultant needs to provide ongoing support and feedback to the teacher to maintain shared responsibility for the plan. The consultative process can be enhanced through the use of effective interpersonal skills, especially active listening and reframing, and consultant sensitivity to the teacher's perceptions of the situation. The ability of the consultant to step out of the expert role and empower the teacher to develop skills and apply change cannot be overemphasized.

As children with difficulties in learning or behavior are increasingly served within the regular education classroom, teachers will likely request greater support from other professionals and the family to meet the unique needs of these students. An ecosystemic point of view allows those persons concerned with the child to move beyond a narrow definition of the problem and to consider the context within which the child is functioning. Effective and lasting interventions are more likely to emerge from this ecosystemic perspective. Collaborative problem solving, whether through teacher consultation or team participation, is rapidly becoming the service delivery model of choice to develop and implement successful ecosystemic interventions.

REFERENCES

Anderson, C. (1983). An ecological developmental model for a family orientation in school psychology. *Journal of School Psychology, 21*, 179–189.

Apter, S. J. (1982). *Troubled children: Troubled systems.* Elmsford, NY: Pergamon.

Benedict, R. (1961). *Patterns of culture.* Boston: Houghton–Mifflin.

Bergan, J. R., & Kratochwill, T. R. (1990). *Behavioral consultation and therapy.* New York: Plenum.

Bronfenbrenner, U. (1979). *The ecology of human development: Experiments by nature and design.* Cambridge, MA: Harvard University Press.

Bronfenbrenner, U. (1986). Ecology of the family as a context for human development: Research perspectives. *Developmental Psychology, 22,* 723–742.

Bulgren, J. A., & Knackendoffel, A. (1986). Ecological assessment: An overview. *The Pointer, 30*(2), 23–30.

Burden, R. L., & Fraser, B. J. (1993). Use of classroom environment assessments in school psychology: A British perspective. *Psychology in the Schools, 30,* 232–240.

Buysse, V., Schulte, A. C., Pierce, P. P., & Terry, D. (1994). Models and styles of consultation: Preferences of professionals in early intervention. *Journal of Early Intervention, 18,* 302–310.

Chess, S. A., & Thomas, A. (1987). *Know your child: An authoritative guide for today's parents.* New York: Basic Books.

Christenson, S. L. (1993). Ecological assessment: Linking assessment to intervention. *Communiqué, 21*(5), 26–28.

Connors, L. J., & Epstein, J. L. (1995). Parent and school partnerships. In M. H. Bornstein (Ed.), *Handbook of parenting: Vol. 4. Applied and practical parenting* (pp. 437–458). Mahwah, NJ: Lawrence Erlbaum Associates.

Conoley, J. C., & Haynes, G. (1992). An ecological approach to intervention. In R. C. D'Amato & B. A. Rothlisberg (Eds.), *Psychological perspectives on intervention* (pp. 176–189). New York: Longman.

Epstein, J. L. (1992). *School and family partnerships.* Baltimore, MD: Johns Hopkins University Center on Families, Communities, Schools and Children's Learning.

Epstein, J. L. (1995). School-family-community partnerships: Caring for the children we share. *Phi Delta Kappan, 76,* 701–712.

Evans, W. H., & Evans, S. S. (1987). Behavior change and the ecological model. *The Pointer, 31*(3), 9–12.

Evans, W. H., & Evans, S. S. (1990). Ecological assessment guidelines. *Diagnostique, 16,* 49–51.

Evans, W. H., Gable, R. A., & Evans, S. S. (1993). Making something out of everything: The promise of ecological assessment. *Diagnostique, 18,* 175–185.

Evertson, C. M., Emmer, E. T., Clements, B. S., Sanford, J. P., & Worsham, M. E. (1989). *Classroom management for elementary teachers.* Englewood Cliffs, NJ: Prentice-Hall.

Fine, M. J. (1990). Facilitating home–school relationships: A family-oriented approach to collaborative consultation. *Journal of Educational and Psychological Consultation, 1,* 169–187.

Fine, M. J. (1992). *Parent–teacher conferences: Resolving conflicts* [Video discussion guide]. Topeka, KS: Menninger Clinic.

Fine, M. J. (1995). Family–school intervention. In R. H. Mikesell, D-D. Lusterman, & S. H. McDaniel (Eds.), *Integrating family therapy: Handbook of family psychology and systems theory* (pp. 481–495). Washington, DC: American Psychological Association.

Friend, M., & Cook, L. (1992). *Interactions: Collaboration skills for school professionals.* New York: Longman.

Graden, J. L., & Bauer, A. M. (1992). Using a collaborative approach to support students and teachers in inclusive classrooms. In S. Stainback & W. Stainback (Eds.), *Curriculum considerations in inclusive classrooms: Facilitating learning for all students* (pp. 85–100). Baltimore: Paul H. Brookes.

Graden, J. L., Casey, A., & Christenson, S. L. (1985). Implementing a prereferral intervention system: Part I. The model. *Exceptional Children, 51,* 377–384.

Greenwood, C. R., Carta, J. J., Kamps, D., & Delquadri, J. (1993). *Ecobehavioral assessment systems software (EBASS): Observational instrumentation for school psychologists.* Kansas City, KS: Juniper Gardens Children's Project, University of Kansas.

Hendrickson, J. M. (1992). Assessing the student–instructional setting interface using an eco-behavioral observation system. *Preventing School Failure, 36*(3), 26–31.

Heron, T. E., & Heward, W. L. (1988). Ecological assessment: Implications for teachers of learning disabled students. *Learning Disability Quarterly, 11,* 224–232.

Kutsick, K. A., Gutkin, T. B., & Witt, J. C. (1991). The impact of treatment development process, intervention type, and problem severity on treatment acceptability as judged by classroom teachers. *Psychology in the Schools, 28,* 325–331.

Pugach, M. C., & Johnson, L. J. (1989a). The challenge of implementing collaboration between general and special education. *Exceptional Children, 56,* 232–235.

Pugach, M. C., & Johnson, L. J. (1989b). Prereferral interventions: Progress, problems, and challenges. *Exceptional Children, 56,* 217–226.

Rhodes, W. C., & Paul, J. L. (1978). *Emotionally disturbed and deviant children.* Englewood Cliffs, NJ: Prentice-Hall.

Robinson, E. L., & Fine, M. J. (1994). Developing collaborative home–school relationships. *Preventing School Failure, 39*(1), 9–15.

Sattler, J. M. (1990). *Assessment of children* (3rd ed.). San Diego: Jerome M. Sattler.

Schubert, M. A., Landers, M. F., Curtis, M. J., Anderson, T. E., & Curtis, V. (1984). Communication: One key to mainstreaming success. *The Exceptional Child, 31,* 46–53.

Sindelar, P. T., Griffin, C. C., Smith, S. W., & Watanabe, A. K. (1992). Prereferral intervention: Encouraging notes on preliminary findings. *The Elementary School Journal, 92,* 245–259.

Swap, S. (1984). Ecological approaches to working with families of disturbing children. In W. A. O'Conner & B. Lubin (Eds.), *Ecological approaches to clinical and community psychology* (pp. 107–144). New York: Wiley.

Thousand, J. S., & Villa, R. A. (1992). Collaborative teams: A powerful tool in school restructuring. In R. A. Villa, J. S. Thousand, W. Stainback, & S. Stainback (Eds.), *Restructuring for caring & effective education: An administrative guide to creating heterogeneous schools* (pp. 73–108). Baltimore: Paul H. Brookes.

Trickett, E. J., Leone, P. E., Fink, C. M., & Braaten, S. L. (1993). The perceived environment of special education classrooms for adolescents: A revision of The Classroom Environment Scale. *Exceptional Children, 59,* 411–420.

Wade, S. E., Welch, M., & Jensen, J. B. (1994). Teacher receptivity to collaboration: Levels of interest, types of concern, and school characteristics as variables contributing to successful implementation. *Journal of Educational and Psychological Consultation, 5,* 177–209.

Welch, M. (1994). Ecological assessment: A collaborative approach to planning instructional interventions. *Intervention in School and Clinic, 29,* 160–164, 183.

West, J. F., & Cannon, G. S. (1988). Essential collaborative consultation competencies for regular and special educators. *Journal of Learning Disabilities, 21,* 56–63, 28.

Ysseldyke, J., & Christenson, S. (1993). *The Instructional Environment System-II: A system to identify a student's instructional needs.* Longmont, CO: Sopris West.

IV

ASSESSMENT AND INTERVENTION WITH SCHOOLS

6

Assessment and Interventions With Schools

Eugene R. Moan
Ramona N. Mellott
Northern Arizona University

Students are faced with a vast array of situations occurring across many environments. There is a realization by educators, parents, and community leaders that education is not solely restricted to the school setting, but also takes place in other environments such as the home and the community. To design effective interventions that are both powerful and sustaining, it is necessary to include the child's other environments. Consequently, the relationship between the school, home, and community need to be cooperative and trusting if this process is intended to work (Putnam, 1987).

Schools play a significant role in the educational and social formation of young people. As such, schools must be responsive to demands both internal and external to the school environment if they are going to accomplish the challenging task of forming young persons into contributing members of society. Internal demands include factors within the school environment such as the age range of the student population, the racial and ethnic make-up of the student body, and the financial resources available to the school. External demands include expectations of the surrounding community, expectations of parents, and the requirements of regulatory groups and agencies. Understanding and working effectively with such a large number of contingency elements can be frustrating and difficult. These challenges can be seen, however, as opportunities to incorporate these ever present forces into a productive working coalition (Rutherford & Billig, 1995).

Because of their emphasis on the interface between individuals and the environments in which they function, ecological psychology models are particularly well suited to the task of assessing the school environment. Ecological assessment, in turn, leads to the development of interventions tailored to address the specific needs of the school by means of the unique resources available in the school and the surrounding community. *Ecological psychology* is a term used to describe an approach to understanding human behavior in a manner that differs significantly from the traditional linear causality perspective (Gladding, 1995). Behavior is, instead, seen as embedded within the context of a wide array of factors, each of which is important if one is to fully understand the resultant behavior. Ecological psychology is the synthesis of the works by a number of authors including Lewin (1951), Barker (1968), von Bertalanffy (1968), and Bronfenbrenner (1979).

According to ecological theory, the student and his or her multiple environments are viewed together rather than individually (Carroll, 1974). Behavior is determined by the interaction of individual and environmental characteristics (Apter, 1977; Hobbs, 1982). Students do not function in a "vacuum," rather the various environments play a major role in shaping their behaviors as well as their emotional and cognitive processes. Disturbance in a child's behavior is "seen as a mismatch between a child's abilities and the demands of his or her environment" (Conoley, 1988, p. 2). Thus, assessment and behavior change procedures "must address not only the behavior of the student, but also the behavior of others and the environmental variables associated with the behavior" (Evans & Evans, 1987, p. 9). Assessing the entire environment of the child will help facilitate interventions that focus on not only changing the behavior of the child, but, if necessary, changing the behaviors of others in the environments or some element of the environment affecting the problem behavior (Evans & Evans, 1987). According to Bateson (1971), changes in one aspect in the system or environment can lead to changes in other systems. The ultimate purpose is to maximize the individual student's adaptation to the various environments (Putnam, 1987).

Johnson, Swartz, and Martin (1995) delineated several factors that distinguish the ecological perspective. Integral to this approach is the idea that individuals do not exist in isolation, but rather they function within the context of an interrelated system of relationships (von Bertalanffy, 1968). These relationships are relatively stable and are arranged in an hierarchical order. A second characteristic of this approach is the assumption that individuals both influence their environment and are influenced by that same environment. This concept has been termed *circular causality* (Goldenberg & Goldenberg, 1991). A third assumption of the ecological approach is that the behavior of any individual is driven by both internal and external forces. Finally, the ecological perspective views behavior as individuals' attempts to maintain homeostasis within their environment (Thomas, 1992; Wicker, 1973).

THE EFFECTS OF CULTURE

Among the multitude of factors that influence behavior, culture plays a significant role. According to Webster (1989), culture is "the customary beliefs, social forms and material traits of a racial, religious, or social group" (p. 314). Social scientists use the term *culture* to refer to "the shared beliefs, assumptions, values, understandings, images, and symbols (including language) that guide people's thinking, feeling, and behaving" (Hurvitz & Straus, 1991, p. 18). Understanding the cultural context in which people live provides a critical frame of reference for assessing their thoughts, feelings, and behaviors. Behaviors and actions considered to be normal in one culture may be viewed as undesirable or even pathological in another context. Cultural understanding assists the observer in determining the behaviors in need of intervention and also promotes the development of culturally appropriate treatment approaches.

Several authors (Corey, 1991; Gladding, 1995; Ivey, Ivey, & Simek-Morgan, 1993; Sue & Sue, 1990; Tseng & Hsu, 1991) emphasized the need for culturally appropriate means of working with culturally different populations. Many methods of assessment and intervention are based on the values, traditions, and customs of a limited ethnic or socioeconomic strata of society. Such work can result in cultural encapsulation (Wrenn, 1962); that is, a tendency to label such viewpoints as *desirable* or *normal*. Interpretations drawn from information gathered under such conditions are subject to question. It is imperative that researchers evaluate their own cultural assumptions and how these assumptions may shape their interpretations of observed behaviors. When working with groups that are culturally different from their own, researchers must take great care to sensitize themselves to the relevant cultural factors that may influence the behaviors they are observing. Ecological approaches provide a strong framework for the inclusion of these factors.

ECOLOGICAL ASSESSMENT

Applying ecological theory to assessment has a number of implications. Hilton stated that the utilization of a systems viewpoint is essential when there is an acceptance of an ecological orientation. The assessment and intervention process has to be coordinated across the various environments. Emphasis is not placed solely on the child, but on the entire system surrounding the child. For an ecological assessment to be effective, data needs to be gathered from a greater variety of sources than those used in traditional assessment approaches (Hilton, 1987).

Teacher training programs are included among the fields in which an ecological perspective would be useful. These programs would be enhanced by the inclusion of an ecological perspective, especially for those who work with behaviorally disordered students. Young, Gable, and Hendrickson (1989) surveyed students in undergraduate and graduate teacher training programs across the nation and found that some elements of ecological approaches are being employed; however, the training emphasis is on classroom-based areas. Specifically, less than one third (between 14% and 29%) of the training hours are devoted to the application of biophysical, family, and community factors.

As such, it appears that an ecological perspective offers a more comprehensive and accurate view of a child's problem. An ecological assessment involves determining "how well the child's behavior matches environmental conditions and expectations and deciding which behaviors, settings, and conditions to target" (Evans & Evans, 1990, p. 49). The ecological approach includes assessment of three primary ecosystems—the home, school, and community (Hobbs, 1966). Communities may be further subdivided into subsystems such as the church, community centers, and neighborhood peers (Cantrell & Cantrell, 1985). The goal of the assessment is to plan interventions, not to diagnose and classify (Conoley, 1987). To this end, each subsystem should be assessed in considerable detail so as to facilitate the coordination of services and resources as well as to design effective interventions. Needs assessment surveys, assessment of the strengths and weaknesses of each subsystem, and identification of already existing resources in each environment are among the factors that need to be identified and included in the subsequent intervention strategies.

Aside from its use as a framework for understanding the actions of individuals, ecological psychology provides the basis for assessing behavior at various levels within a hierarchy. The same characteristics described in the preceding paragraphs can also be used as a framework for describing the function of groups and organizations. Schools are an example of an organizational unit to which the ecological approach has been applied (Bechtel, 1982; Conoley & Conoley, 1988; Felsenthal, 1982; Welch, 1994).

Ecological Assessment of Schools

Schools can be conceptualized as organizational units embedded within a hierarchy of other systems. These systems may be called superordinate or macrosystems. Schools are also made up of a collection of subsystems which are subordinate to, and incorporated within, the overall structure of the school. These systems are referred to as microsystems. Figure 6.1 depicts these interacting relationships.

Discussion of the ecological assessment of schools begins at the microsystems level. Within every school, a number of subgroups interact on a continual basis to form the school ecosystem or environment. Obvious systems subsumed within the overall school structure are the teaching staff, the principal and other school administrators, counselors, support staff such as librarians and nurses, teacher's aids, and the students themselves. Less obvious, but also integral to the school's functioning and climate, are the custodial staff, school cafeteria staff, maintenance workers, volunteering parents, and other adults serving as mentors or in a variety of other roles. Assessment of these subsystems is an important step toward changing and enhancing the school environment.

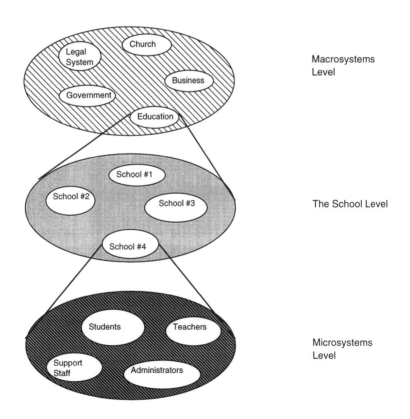

FIG. 6.1. The organizational hierarchy of a school system..

Assessment Procedures

Ecological assessment focuses on describing the behavior(s), settings, and conditions of concern (Evans & Evans, 1990). Evans and Evans recommended that the following be addressed during an ecological assessment process: (a) information on which behaviors are most disturbing, disruptive, or dangerous; (b) frequency of these behaviors, as well as antecedent and consequent events surrounding these behaviors; (c) the links to environmental variables; (d) which of these behaviors and environmental variables can be changed; (e) expectations of the settings involved; and (f) knowledge that will help clinicians know that they have succeeded in making changes. Carroll (1974) proposed six major steps in the ecological assessment process that include setting goals, developing a conceptual framework, implementing the assessment plan, evaluating results, formulating hypotheses, and, finally, planning the intervention.

Assessment of the school environment begins with an on-site visit with the school principal or other top administrators. The purposes of this initial contact are to develop administrative support and cooperation, as well as to identify key informants who can provide additional information about the school. Such people are considered key informants because they are aware of the policies, practices, and effectiveness of the past and current programs, and they are aware of the training needs of the school's staff, or the current problems and practices of students in the school (Nielsen, 1994). Key informants, in addition to the principal, may include other administrators, teachers, counselors, tutors, parents, school board members, school psychologists, nurses, librarians, and other professional staff members.

The process of utilizing multiple sources of information allows for triangulation of the data obtained (Berg, 1989). Triangulation corroborates the individual findings across information sources and increases the generalizability of the findings (Marshall & Rossman, 1989). The results of this assessment will yield a clear picture of what has been called the school culture and student climate (McWhirter, McWhirter, McWhirter, & McWhirter, 1993).

Assessment methods at this point are nearly exclusively comprised of interviews, surveys, and other self-report instruments. In true ecological fashion, the responses obtained influence the nature and direction of additional lines of inquiry. Additional information may be obtained through the use of checklists, behavior rating scales, ecomaps, force field analysis, and other means.

An understanding of the school's subsystems and environment is necessary but provides only a partial picture of the school. Each school is also part of other systems which include the communities in which the school exists and the families of the students.

Ecological Assessment of Families and Communities

Because education is not solely restricted to the school setting and takes place in other environments (Putnam, 1987), it is necessary to include the child's other environments such as the home and community in the assessment process. Assessing the entire environment will help facilitate interventions that focus not only on changing the child's behavior, but also on changing, if necessary, the behaviors of others in the environments or some element of the environment that is influencing the problem behavior (Evans & Evans, 1987).

Two critical systems that must be assessed in order to understand the functioning of children within school settings are the families from which these children come and the surrounding community in which these families live. Among the factors within the family that need to be considered are the size and structure of the family; ability of the family to provide basic needs such as food, clothing, and shelter; physical and mental health of the family members; cultural values held by the family; and the family's view of its own strengths and weaknesses. Within the surrounding community, factors that are useful to incorporate into the assessment process include economic resources for providing community services (e.g., police, fire protection), existence of other community support systems such as recreational facilities and social service agencies, ethnic and cultural standards of the community, and the nature of the relationship between the school and the community.

Assessment of these factors can be done in a number of ways. Telephone surveys can be conducted with a sample of the target population. A larger sample can often be reached through a survey conducted by mail; however, response to mail surveys can be quite low. Another data collection procedure that may be utilized is conducting personal interviews with all or part of the population of interest. This method is considerably more time consuming and labor intensive, but often results in a higher response rate and more complete response to the survey questions.

Assessment Procedures

The following are different assessment methods that have an ecological perspective and that provide useful information on family and community factors in the assessment process.

Checklists and Rating Scales.   Behavior checklists and rating scales, in the context of ecological assessment, are useful in measuring parent opinions of their child and the frequency of certain behaviors. They provide an objective means of measurement and attempt to quantify, to some extent, the identified behavior. Behavior checklists are usually found to be efficient in terms of cost, effort, and time and provide a fairly comprehensive picture of problems that may often go undetected during testing, interviews, and observation (Kratochwill & Sheridan, 1990). These checklists and rating scales can be used to measure the impact that family and other relevant environments have on the individual child. Checklists and rating scales differ in terms of response formats. Checklists often employ two types of responses, a yes–no format or a list of potential responses in which any combination may be checked (Welch, 1994). Some examples of relevant checklists to use with parents are the Child Behavior Checklist (Achenbach, 1991), Becker Adjective Checklist (Patterson, Reid, Jones, & Conger, 1975), Revised Behavior Problem Checklist (Quay & Peterson, 1983), and the Parent Daily Report (Patterson et al., 1975). Evans and Evans (1990) provided an ecological checklist to determine settings and conditions that may influence the target behavior including physiological factors; physical factors such as the home, school, and classroom; and psychosocial factors.

Rating scales are typically considered to be qualitative in nature, as they generally require a respondent to rank opinions or types of behaviors within some range of responses (Welch, 1994). An example includes five categories ranging from *strongly agree* to *strongly disagree*. These qualitative responses can be translated into numerical scores that can be used to derive means and other standardized scores. The Unrevealed Differences Questionnaire–Revised (URD–R) (Henggeler & Tavormina, 1980) is an instrumental and expressive discussion exercise administered to parents and adolescents to examine two dimensions of family relations: positive communication and conflict–hostility. Families are presented with nine situations, each with three to six alternative responses, and instructed to arrive at a family ranking of the alternative choices. Conflict hostility scores reflect the negative dyadic (e.g., marital, adolescent–mother, adolescent–father) interchanges that serve to inhibit intrafamilial communication. Positive communication scores indicate the rate of supportive statements and explicit exchange of information between the student and other family members that facilitate intrafamilial communication.

Hypotheses concerning family functioning and environment can be obtained by using instruments such as the Family Adaptability and Cohesion Evaluation Scales (FACES III; Olsen, Portner, & Lavee, 1991), the Family

Environment Scale (FES; Moos & Moos, 1974), and the Family Pre-Counseling Inventory (Stuart & Stuart, 1975). The Short Marital Adjustment Test (Locke & Wallace, 1959) can be used to assess marital satisfaction. This test can also be used in studies of the association between marital satisfaction and child adjustment (Emery, 1982). Perceived stressors within the family can be assessed with the 72-item Family Inventory of Life Events and Changes (McCubbin, Patterson, & Wilson, 1985). Family satisfaction can be assessed by using the Family Satisfaction Scale that is a 14-item scale measuring cohesion and adaptability (Olsen et al., 1991). Parental childrearing beliefs can be assessed with the Parent Belief Survey (Luster, 1985). Quality of the home environment can be assessed with the Parental Home Assessment Index (Poresky, 1989).

Ecomaps. The ecomap is a simple and useful assessment, goal setting, and monitoring instrument (Newbrough, Walker, & Abril, 1978). The ecomap can be used graphically to identify each system in which the individual child is involved. Some of these may include the family, religious organization, YMCA, neighborhood peers, and probation officer. How each of these systems interact with the identified child and contributes to the problem is important. The information obtained via an ecomap is used to set goals.

Family Life Space Ecological Model. Mostwin (1981) recommended the use of the Family Life Space Ecological Model in the diagnosis of the family situation in which the individual is an integral part. This approach is similar to the ecological model in that it believes that the network of persons and events interacting together create the unique universe of a person's existence.

In the initial diagnostic session, a configuration of the symbolic representation of the Family Life Space is created. The procedure usually involves the therapist drawing a circle on the blackboard, and the family members each separately and together deciding on who should be included in the circle and who should be kept on the outside. In general, the Family Circle consists of all those individuals who are related by blood, marriage, or adoption or who are living together in the same house. The ecological environment, a symbolic, powerful territory of meanings structured with *facts* is depicted around the circle through small squares representing institutions that have particular significance in the life of the family, and triangles for the psychological facts that pertain to meaningful, often stressful events connected to the life of the family (Mostwin, 1981). Psychological facts are classified into four independent strata that include the following: (a) events related to change, (b) events connected to stress, (c) social characteristics with an emotional component (e.g., poverty, race, etc.), and (d) biological problems with emotional components.

The drawing of the circle becomes a focal point of attention for the family and encourages family involvement in the treatment process. Initially, the diagnostic process focuses on the outside, on the environment, and progressively moves to the middle of the family circle, with an overview of the total situation always maintained (Mostwin, 1981).

Ecological Inventory.   The Ecological Inventory provides an assessment of individuals' various activities within the levels of their environment (Orelove & Sobsey, 1987). In this inventory, environments are grouped into major functional areas. These areas are then broken down into specific environments in each domain. These specific environments are then divided into more specific subenvironments. Activities that are associated with each subenvironment are identified and, finally, skills or critical job functions for each of the activities are specified. As these inventories can be extremely long and time consuming, one possible solution lies in limiting the number of areas and domains to be sampled.

Ecobehavioral Analysis.   Ecobehavioral analysis can be used in various settings in which the child is a participant including the home. This is an approach that describes the ecology of the environments and examines the interactions that occur between the ecology and the student behaviors (Greenwood & Carta, 1987). One of the goals of ecobehavioral analysis is to determine those behaviors of the student that are related to a promising outcome (Carta, Atwater, Schwartz, & Miller, 1990). An important feature of ecobehavioral assessment is that ecological factors are recorded with similar frequency and priority as student behaviors (Greenwood, Carta, Kamps, & Arreaga-Mayer, 1990). In addition, environmental factors are assessed at the interval level of measurement rather than at the ordinal level of measurement, thus allowing for the use of parametric statistical techniques for analyzing the data obtained.

Naturalistic Research.   Naturalistic research is based on behavior setting theory by Roger Barker (1968). Behavior setting theory seems to have substantial potential for understanding the way behavior actually occurs in the natural habitat. The two most common methods for studying individual behavior are chronologs (Scott, 1980) and specimen records (Barker & Wright, 1971; Wright, 1967). Chronologs and specimen records are running narrative records of all of a given individual's behavior at the molar level

(Scott, 1980). The observer simply records everything that the individual says and does and everything that is said and done to the individual. Context for behavior, as well as the behavior of others in the environment, is also recorded. This method has definite advantages when working with the family and the community. Observations can be made of the child's interactions with the family and with specific systems in the community, especially in relation to the problem behavior.

Interviews. Because children grow up in a family system, their behavior is affected to the extent that home and school systems overlap and interface with each other. The utilization of a systemic approach when working with a child is advantageous and can assist the systems to function in a manner that is beneficial to the child (Fine & Holt, 1983). Observing the interaction and the communication patterns of the family is important in a systems approach. Although interviewing can be a time-consuming process, information gathered through these means can be potentially more useful than test data, and can provide information that may have been omitted in case records and files (Bulgren & Knackendoffel, 1986). Interviews are particularly useful since the consultant can observe the family interaction and formulate hypotheses regarding family dynamics (Fine & Holt, 1983). Additionally, the type of communication that exists within the family can be assessed. A joint interview with all concerned family members can shed light on the problem as well as provide possible solutions to the problem. The psychologist may pay close attention to the communication processes within the family system and focus on the familial functioning as it occurs. Using observations of the communication process in conjunction with objective instruments, such as those previously described, increases the probability of the examiner gaining knowledge of the dynamic flow of family events revealed during the family interviews (Green, Fine, & Tollefson, 1988). Moreover, information gathered through interviews can assist the professional in tailoring interventions to the specific needs of the child in relation to the family.

Summary. Assessment methods utilized in the ecological approach for gaining information about the population to be studied are varied. They include both quantitative and qualitative methods. Furthermore, they are derived from theoretical orientations ranging from psychology, sociology, and cultural anthropology. Integrating and synthesizing this information into a comprehensive picture of the school, which is the subject of study, becomes the basis for planning interventions to address the needs that emerged during the assessment process.

Planning Interventions

After the initial data has been gathered, it must be analyzed and interpreted. This process should include a summary of the findings, both in terms of the strengths of the environment and the problems which exist within the environment. At this point, it is often helpful to return to the group from which the data was obtained in order to verify the accuracy of the data by checking to see if the group agrees with the initial findings, and, if agreement exists, to have the group rank the items in terms of their relative impact on the school's environment and functioning level.

When the strengths and problems have been identified and prioritized, the process of planning interventions can begin. A thorough review of the literature pertaining to the identified problems is a good starting point for obtaining useful suggestions for planning an intervention program. Identified resources may include specific programs for addressing the problem issues that emerged, existing resources such as printed materials, audio, and video, and organizations that focus their resources on the issues identified. The literature review is also helpful in establishing a conceptual framework for developing the intervention plan. The intervention plan should be reasonably expected to reduce the impact of the identified problems in a manner consistent with the culture and values of the family, school, and surrounding community. It is most likely to be successful if the plan incorporates and utilizes the strengths identified as already existing within the environment.

After the intervention plan is developed, it should be reviewed again by the sampled group in order to verify the acceptability of the intervention plan and to solicit the support of the group for implementation of the intervention procedures. Once the intervention plan is implemented, ongoing evaluation of the plan's impact on the target behaviors must be conducted. The results of this continual data gathering and evaluation becomes, in turn, the basis for planning future interventions or for moving toward a program designed to maintain the benefits produced by the interventions.

APPLICATION OF ECOLOGICAL
PSYCHOLOGICAL PRINCIPLES

As is evident, the importance of including a variety of systems in the assessment process of schools within communities cannot be ignored. The integration is by no means an easy task, and, for an effective intervention to follow, school personnel, students, their families, and key individuals in the community need to be involved in the assessment process. The triangulation of information from the various sources will enhance the probability that the communities are accurately assessed and that their unique cultural and contextual factors are considered. The following is a case example which illustrates the application of the ecological psychological principles to the assessment of a problem that is definitely a part of our schools—substance abuse. Alcohol and substance abuse problems are of particular concern in schools in Native American reservation communities. Students in these schools tend to begin using substances at an earlier age and use alcohol and drugs more frequently than students in similar age groups in nonreservation schools (U.S. Indian Health Service, 1987). The example further delineates how information from the assessment was used to tailor the intervention to the needs of those participating in the project.

Case Study

According to the U.S. Indian Health Service (1982), alcoholism is the most urgent problem facing Native Americans. The hospital discharge rate for alcohol-related diagnosis is about three times the U.S. national rate. Native American children begin to use drugs at earlier ages (U.S. Indian Health Service, 1987) and more extensively (Finley, 1989) than peers. Bobo, Gilchrist, Cvetkovich, Trimble, and Schinke (1988) reported that 12% of the students surveyed had begun drinking regularly by their ninth birthday and that 10% reported smoking marijuana at that same age. Loretto, Beauvais, and Oetting (1988) found that the patterns and incidence of drug use among Native American youth were very similar to national trends, but that reservation Indian youth used drugs more heavily than other U.S. youth. Creating drug-free schools on reservations is a priority. Project ASSIST was formed during the 1992-1993 academic year, after funding was received from the Drug-Free Schools and Communities Counselor Training Grants Program of the U.S. Department of Education (Martin, Mellott, & Moan, 1992). The purpose of the grant was to establish Student Assistance Programs (SAPs) in reservation-based schools. The SAP model was chosen because there was documentation indicating that it is an effective intervention strategy to help drug users and abusers in treatment and prevention (Palmer & Paisley, 1991).

Based on the ecological perspective, the SAP model emerged in the late 1970s and was patterned after the successful Employee Assistance Programs that had demonstrated success in business and industry. SAPs were first initiated in high schools, but soon came to be used in middle schools and elementary schools (Nielsen, 1994). These programs attempted to empower school staff by providing administrators, teachers, counselors, and support staff opportunities to assist children who may be experiencing substance abuse or other psychological problems (Anderson, 1988; Milgram, 1989; Moore & Forster, 1993; Svendsen & Griffin, 1986). Effective SAPs require a commitment by a wide variety of school personnel to involve themselves in the well-being of students. "Staff can serve in a variety of capacities in the SAP, ranging from the role of a teacher who completes the referral form identifying a child who is in need of the SAP's services to membership on a core team that makes the determination about the in-school and out-of-school treatment needs of the child" (Nielsen, 1994, p. 37). The core team is generally comprised of administrators, teachers, counselors, and support staff.

Prior to the establishment of SAPs in these schools, an assessment was conducted in order to obtain information relative to current practices of addressing substance abuse issues on school campuses and to identify the current availability and scope of drug abuse prevention activities in the schools. In order to conduct the assessment, a needs assessment survey instrument was developed. The existing professional literature was reviewed and cultural informants, representative of the major ethnocultural groups of the schools, were used extensively in all phases of the development of the survey. Once the survey was developed, trained interviewers visited the various schools and administered them through an interview format. Key personnel within the schools, such as administrators, teachers, students, and school counselors and psychologists, were interviewed. Again, keeping with the ecological psychology model, parents, persons from various community agencies, and tribal members were interviewed as well. Information obtained from this needs assessment determined the format of the training that followed. Additionally, volunteers were identified to participate in the training program.

After the participants received training in SAPs, they returned to their schools and were urged to establish similar such programs. Follow along assistance was provided for 1 year as the various schools worked toward establishing these programs. The study recognized that the results of the research and the outcomes of the interventions and follow-up were enhanced by a collaboration with the communities under study (Nielsen, 1994). Project ASSIST further demonstrated that, through training and follow-up procedures, communities can become empowered and address their future concerns by utilizing resources within the community. One of the conclusions was that future efforts might include training other personnel at the same schools in the SAP system to create support for the implementation of the program. Often, having only one person aware of what SAPs entail resulted in current participants having to convince other personnel of the need. By providing multiperson training, schools could have a core team in place to carry out SAP functions.

This idea created the impetus for a new grant submitted to the U.S. Department of Education (DOE) for funding to enhance further efforts toward creating drug-free environments in Project ASSIST reservation secondary schools by expanding the number of trained personnel (Martin, Mellott, Moan, & Farris, 1994). Specifically, this new grant targeted the administrative, library and educational information, and health systems personnel. It also focused on providing training to develop adult mentoring and peer helper services under the Student Assistance model.

The elements of parent and family involvement are an important aspect of a comprehensive approach to substance abuse problems among school children. These role models play a significant part in many children's social environment and contribute substantially to a child's experimentation with drugs (Horan & Straus, 1987). The behavior of parents is a powerful influence on their children's behavior in both positive and negative directions. On the negative side, some parents provide poor role models and even personally induct their children into the drug and alcohol culture (National Institute on Drug Abuse, 1983). Students deprived of supportive relationships are often poorly socialized to adult roles and are unable to make the contacts and networks necessary for educational and career success. Thus, providing adult mentors for students at risk can help compensate for inadequate or dysfunctional socialization. Adult mentors are generally persons from the community who are willing to personally involve themselves in the lives of young people by serving as role models for them. Adult mentors create opportunities for students to move successfully into new areas of socialization, education, and vocation (Ascher, 1988). Mentoring has helped students to mediate the relationship between stress and adjustment and to negotiate their life path and overcome personal social and institutional barriers (Flaxman, 1988).

Similar to adult mentoring, peers can serve as role models for other students. Peer influence is even more powerful during adolescence. Peer helper programs necessarily require the participation of the student population and school personnel (Jason & Rhodes, 1989). In peer helper programs, students work with other students (Jacobs, Masson, & Vass, 1976). Peer helpers, then, are students who provide a "caring source of support and information among a community of students" (Painter, 1989, p. 1). Peer helpers also serve as role models and reinforce positive behaviors (Lee,

Bryant, Noonan, & Plionis, 1987). Peer programs have been found to be effective and have proven to have an important role in drug abuse prevention programs (Bangart-Drowns, 1988; Tobler, 1986).

Prior to the establishment of these programs in Project ASSIST schools, a needs assessment was conducted and a questionnaire was developed assessing the potential usefulness of peer helping and adult mentoring programs (Selvey, Eggert, & Martin, 1995). The process for developing this survey was similar to the one described in the first phase of the project. The current professional literature was reviewed and factors that appeared to contribute to the success of peer counseling and adult mentoring programs were recorded. Factors that were considered to be similar were clustered together. As before, a meeting was held with key members from various Native American tribes. Additional factors emerged and were recorded as a result of the cultural informant meeting. Factor structures from the cultural informant meeting and the literature review were combined to create a survey for assessing the needs of the schools. The survey was mailed to the cultural informants and changes made as a result of their feedback.

Reservation-based schools were visited during which time interviews were conducted with key persons. Again, utilizing the ecological model, a variety of persons representing various elements of the school environment were interviewed: students, teachers, parents, administrators, school board members, and community liaisons. Participant comments that went beyond the scope of the survey were also solicited from each interviewee in order to enhance the completeness of the information gathered. The information obtained from these participants influenced the focus of training that was provided in setting up peer helper programs and adult mentoring services. A small number of changes were made to address program aspects that might be considered rude or intrusive in the cultural context of the participants in the Project ASSIST schools. One change made involved emphasis on the use of silence and the pace of verbal exchanges in the communication process.

Needs assessments for the second round of grant-funded activities were conducted in schools on each of the Indian reservations within the state of Arizona. The needs assessment data was then used to develop a comprehensive adult mentoring and peer counseling training programs. Additionally, direct training was provided to more than 125 peer counselors who were primarily Native Americans. Additional activities in Project ASSIST during 1996-1997 will include follow-up visits to the schools, further training assistance and support as requested by the schools, and ongoing evaluation of the impact of the programs.

An outline of the steps in the ecological assessment and intervention planning process in schools follows:

- Identify the problem to be examined.
- Review the current professional literature on the topic.
- Develop an assessment procedure based on information from the literature.
- Have knowledgeable persons review the procedure and provide additional input.
- Identify key informants and others who will be assessed.
- Conduct the assessment.
- Analyze the results and compare these to the literature.
- Develop interventions based on the needs identified in the assessment.
- Have knowledgeable persons review the proposed interventions and provide input.
- Conduct the intervention.
- Evaluate the impact of the intervention on the identified problem.
- Re-assess and plan further interventions as needed.

CONCLUSION

Children spend a large portion of their time in the school environment. Consequently, schools are expected to educate students to meet the demands that will be placed upon them in later life, including further academic training. Additionally, schools have the responsibility for developing, within students, skills that will be beneficial to them in the larger context of family and community life. In order for schools to be optimally effective, comprehensive ecological assessment of the school environment is necessary. Such assessment facilitates the enhancement of the school environment by identifying available resources and maximizing their use. Ecological assessment also serves as a guide for the development of intervention strategies which may be needed to address specific problems identified in the assessment process.

Schools exist within the context of the communities they serve and are comprised of students from families with highly variable and unique backgrounds. Understanding the needs of the individual children becomes the foundation for understanding the needs of the school. The cultural background of the students and the cultural standards of the community are integral components of the assessment process. A number of procedures, both of a quantitative and qualitative nature, are available to aid in the assessment of the school. From the results obtained in the assessment process, and with the continued cooperation of the participants, effective interventions can be developed for addressing the needs of the student population.

REFERENCES

Achenbach, T. M. (1991). *Manual for the Child Behavior Checklist/4–18 and 1991 Profile.* Burlington: University of Vermont Department of Psychiatry.

Anderson, G. L. (1988). *When chemicals come to school: The student assistance program model.* Greenfield, WI: Community Recovery Press.

Apter, S. J. (1977). Application of ecological theory: Toward a community special education model. *Exceptional Children, 43,* 366–373.

Ascher, C. (1988). *The mentoring of disadvantaged youth* (Rep. No. RI8806 2013) Washington Office of Educational Research and Improvement. (ERIC Document Reproduction Service No. ED306326).

Bangert-Drowns, R. (1988). The effects of school–based substance abuse education. *Journal of Drug Education, 18,* 243–264.

Barker, R. G. (1968). *Ecological psychology.* Stanford, CA: Stanford University Press.

Barker, R. G., & Wright, H. F. (1971). *Midwest and its children.* Hamden, CT: Archon Books.

Bateson, G. (1971). The cybernetics of "self": A theory of alcoholism. *Psychiatry, 34,* 1–18.

Bechtel, R. B. (1982). Contributions of ecological psychology to the evaluation of environments. *International Review of Applied Psychology, 31,* 153–167.

Berg, B. L. (1989). *Qualitative research methods for the social sciences.* Boston, MA: Harvard University Press.

Bobo, J. K., Gilchrist, L. D., Cvetkovich, G. T., Trimble, J. E., & Schinke, S. P. (1988). Cross-cultural service delivery to minority communities. *Journal of Community Psychology, 16,* 263–271.

Bronfenbrenner, U. (1979). *The ecology of human development.* Cambridge, MA: Harvard University Press.

Bulgren, J. A., & Knackendoffel, A. (1986). Ecological assessment: An overview. Section II: Methods and Procedures for instructional assessment. *The Pointer, 30*(2), 23–30.

Cantrell, C. M., & Cantrell, R. P. (1985). Assessment of the natural environment. *Education and Treatment of Children, 8,* 275–295.

Carroll, A. W. (1974). The classroom as an ecosystem. *Focus on Exceptional Children, 6,* 1–11.

Carta, J. J., Atwater, J. B., Schwartz, H. S., & Miller, P. A. (1990). Applications of ecobehavioral analysis to the study of transitions across early education settings. *Education and Treatment of Children, 13,* 298–315.

Conoley, J. C. (1987). Schools and families: Theoretical and practical bridges. *Professional School Psychology, 2,* 191–203.

Conoley, J. C. (1988). Positive classroom ecology. *Behavior in Our Schools, 2*(2), 2–7.

Conoley, J. C., & Conoley, C. W. (1988). Useful theories in school–based consultation. *Remedial and Special Education, 9*(6), 14–20.

Corey, G. (1991). *Theory and practice of counseling and psychotherapy* (4th ed.). Pacific Grove, CA: Brooks/Cole.

Emery, R. E. (1982). Interparental conflict and the children of discord and divorce. *Psychological Bulletin, 92,* 310–330.

Evans, S. S., & Evans, W. H. (1987). Behavior change and ecological model. *The Pointer, 31*(3), 9–12.

Evans, W. H., & Evans, S. S. (1990). Ecological assessment guidelines. *Diagnostique, 16,* 49–51.

Felsenthal, H. (1982). *Factors influencing school effectiveness: An ecological analysis of an "effective" school.* Paper presented at the annual meeting of the American Research Association, New York.

Fine, M. J., & Holt, P. (1983). Intervening with school problems: A family systems perspective. *Psychology in the Schools, 20*(1), 59–66.

Finley, B. (1989). Social network differences in alcohol use and related behaviors among Indian and non-Indian students, grades 6–12. *American Indian Culture and Research Journal, 13,* 33–48.

Flaxman, E. (1988). *Youth mentoring: Programs and practices.* (Report No. RI88062013). Washington Office of Educational Research and Improvement. (ERIC Document Reproduction Service No. ED308257).

Gladding, S. T. (1995). *Family therapy: History, theory, and practice.* Englewood Cliffs, NJ: Prentice-Hall.

Goldenberg, I., & Goldenberg, H. (1991). *Family therapy: An overview.* Pacific Grove, CA: Brooks/Cole.

Green, K., Fine, M. J., & Tollefson, N. (1988). Family systems characteristics and underachieving gifted adolescent males. *Gifted Child Quarterly, 32,* 267–272.

Greenwood, C. R., & Carta, J. J. (1987). An ecobehavioral analysis of instruction within special education. *Focus on Exceptional Children, 19,* 1–12.

Greenwood, C. R., Carta, J. J., Kamps, D., & Arreaga-Mayer, C. (1990). Ecobehavioral analysis of classroom interaction. In S. Schroeder (Ed.), *Ecobehavioral analysis and developmental disabilities: The twenty-first century.* New York: Springer-Verlag.

Henggeler, S. W., & Tavormina, J. B. (1980). Social class and race differences in family interaction: Pathological, normative, or confounding methodological factors? *Journal of Genetic Psychology, 137,* 211–222.

Hilton, A. (1987). Using ecological strategies when working with young children. *The Pointer, 31*(3), 52–55.

Hobbs, N. (1966). Helping disturbed children: Psychological and ecological strategies. *American Psychologist, 21,* 1105–1115.

Hobbs, N. (1982). *The troubled and troubling child.* San Francisco: Jossey-Bass.

Horan, J. J., & Straus, L. K. (1987). Substance abuse. In M. Hersen & V. B. Van Hasselt (Eds.), *Behavior therapy with children and adolescents: A clinical approach* (pp. 440–464). New York: Wiley.

Hurvitz, N., & Straus, R. A. (1991). *Marriage and family therapy: A sociocognitive approach.* New York: Haworth Press.

Ivey, A. E., Ivey, M. B., & Simek-Morgan, L. (1993). *Counseling and psychotherapy: A multi-cultural perspective.* Needham Heights, MA: Allyn & Bacon.

Jacobs, E., Masson, R., & Vass, M. (1976). Peer helpers: An easy way to get started. *Elementary School Guidance and Counseling, 11,* 68–71.

Jason, L., & Rhodes, J. (1989). Children helping children. *Journal of Primary Prevention, 9,* 203–212.

Johnson, M. J., Swartz, J. L., & Martin, W. E., Jr. (1995). Application of psychological theories for career development with Native Americans. In F. T. L. Leong (Ed.), *Career development and vocational behavior among ethnic minorities* (pp. 103–133). Mahwah, NJ: Lawrence Erlbaum Associates.

Kratochwill, T. R., & Sheridan, S. M. (1990). Advances in behavioral assessment. In T. B. Gutkin & C. R. Reynolds (Eds.), *The handbook of school psychology* (2nd ed., pp. 328–364). New York: Wiley.

Lee, S., Bryant, S., Noonan, N., & Plionis, E. (1987). Keeping youth in school: A public-private collaboration. *Children Today, 16*(4), 15–20.

Lewin, K. (1951). *Field theory in social science.* New York: Harper & Row.

Locke, H. J., & Wallace, K. M. (1959). Short marital adjustment and prediction tests: Their reliability and validity. *Marriage and Family Living, 21,* 251–255.

Loretto, G., Beauvais, F., & Oetting, E. (1988). The primary cost of drug abuse: What Indian youth have to pay for drugs. *American Indian and Alaska Native Mental Health Research, 2*(1), 21–32.

Luster, L. (1985). *Influences on maternal behavior: Child-rearing beliefs, social support, and infant temperament.* Unpublished doctoral dissertation, Cornell University, Ithaca, NY.

Marshall, C., & Rossman, G. B. (1989). *Designing qualitative research.* Newbury Park, CA: Sage.

Martin, W. E., Jr., Mellott, R. N., Moan, E. R., & Farris, K. K. (1994). *Expanding trained personnel to build integrated systems toward drug free reservation school environments.* Unpublished federal grant application, Northern Arizona University, Flagstaff.

Martin, W. E., Jr., Mellott, R. N., & Moan, E. R. (1992). *Training counselors and psychologists to establish student assistance programs for drug abuse prevention in high schools on American Indian reservations.* Unpublished federal grant application, Northern Arizona University, Flagstaff.

McCubbin, H. L., Patterson, J. M., & Wilson, L. (1985). Family inventory of life events and changes. In D. H. Olson, H. I. McCubbin, H. Barnes, A. Larsen, M. Moxen, & M. Wilson (Eds.), *Family inventories used in a national survey of families across the family life cycle* (pp. 82–119). St. Paul: Family Social Science, University of Minnesota.

McWhirter, A. M., McWhirter, B. T., McWhirter, E. H., & McWhirter, J. J. (1993). *At-risk youth: A comprehensive response*. Pacific Grove, CA: Brooks/Cole.

Milgram, G. G. (1989). Impact of a student assistance program. *Journal of Drug Education, 19,* 327–335.

Moore, D. D., & Forster, J. R. (1993). Student assistance programs: New approaches for reduced adolescent substance abuse. *Journal of Counseling and Development, 71,* 329–330.

Moos, R. H., & Moos, B. S. (1974). *Family Environment Scale.* Palo Alto, CA: Consulting Psychologists Press.

Mostwin, D. (1981). Life space ecological model of family treatment. *International Journal of Family Psychiatry, 2*(1–2), 75–94.

National Institute on Drug Abuse. (1983). *Parents, peers, and pot II: Parents in action.* (DHHS Publication No. ADM 83–1290). Washington, DC: U.S. Government Printing Office.

Newbrough, J. R., Walker, L., & Abril, S. (1978, April). *Workshop on ecological assessment.* Paper presented at the annual meeting of the National Association of School Psychologists, New York.

Nielsen, S. (1994). *An ecological assessment of the school–based substance psychological services for Native American Youth.* Unpublished doctoral dissertation, Northern Arizona University, Flagstaff.

Olsen, D. H., Portner, J., & Lavee, Y. (1991). *Family adaptability and Cohesion Evaluation Scales (FACES III).* St. Paul: Family Social Science, University of Minnesota.

Orelove, F. P., & Sobsey, D. (1987). *Educating children with multiple disabilities: A transdisciplinary approach.* Baltimore: Paul H. Brookes.

Painter, C. (1989). *Friends helping friends: A manual for peer counselors.* Minneapolis: Educational Media Corporation.

Palmer, J. H., & Paisley, P. O. (1991). Student Assistance Programs: A response to substance abuse. *The School Counselor, 38,* 287–293.

Patterson, G. R., Reid, J. B., Jones, R. R., & Conger, R. E. (1975). *A social learning approach to family intervention, Vol. 1: Families with aggressive children.* Eugene, OR: Castalia.

Poresky, R. H. (1989). Parental home assessment index: Internal and inter-parent reliability and construct validity. *Educational and Psychological Measurement, 49,* 993–998.

Putnam, M. L. (1987). Effective interventions for mildly handicapped adolescents in the home and the community. *The Pointer, 31*(3), 19–24.

Quay, H. C., & Peterson, D. R. (1987). *Manual for the Revised Behavior Problem Checklist.* Coral Gables, FL: University of Miami.

Rutherford, B., & Billig, S. H. (1995). Eight lessons of parent, family, and community involvement in the middle grades. *Phi Delta Kappan, 77*(1), 64–68.

Scott, M. M. (1980). Ecological theory and methods for research in special education. *The Journal of Special Education, 14,* 279–294.

Selvey, C. A., Eggert, J. E., & Martin, W. E., Jr. (1995). *Project ASSIST needs survey.* Unpublished instrument, Northern Arizona University, Flagstaff.

Stuart, R. B., & Stuart, F. (1975). *Family Pre-Counseling Inventory.* Champaign, IL: Research Press.

Sue, D. W., & Sue, D. (1990). *Counseling the culturally different* (2nd ed.). New York: Wiley.

Svendsen, R., & Griffin, T. (1986). *The student assistance program: How it works* (rev.). Hazelden, MN: Hazelden Foundation.

Thomas, M. B. (1992). *An introduction to marital and family therapy: Counseling toward healthier family systems across the life span.* New York: Macmillan.

Tobler, N. S. (1986). Meta-analysis of 143 adolescent drug prevention programs: Quantitative outcomes results of program participants compared to a control or comparison group. *Journal of Drug Issues, 16,* 537–568.

Tseng, W. S., & Hsu, J. (1991). *Culture and family.* Binghamton, NY: Haworth.

U. S. Indian Health Service. (1982). *Analysis of fiscal year 1981 IHS and U. S. hospital discharge rates by age and primary diagnosis.* Washington, DC: U. S. Government Printing Office.

U. S. Indian Health Service. (1987). *School/community-based alcoholism/substance abuse prevention survey.* Washington, DC: DHHS, Public Health Service, Health Resources and Services Administration.

von Bertalanffy, L. (1968). *General systems theory.* New York: Braziller.

Webster's ninth new collegiate dictionary. (1989). Springfield, MA: Merriam–Webster.

Welch, M. (1994). Ecological assessment: A collaborative approach to planning instructional interventions. *Interventions in School and Clinic, 29,* 160–164, 183.

Wicker, A. W. (1973). Undermanning theory and research: Implications for the study of psychological and behavioral effects of excess human population. *Representative Research in Social Psychology, 4,* 185–206.

Wrenn, C. G. (1962). The culturally-encapsulated counselor. *Harvard Educational Review, 32,* 444–449.

Wright, H. F. (1967). *Recording and analyzing child behavior.* New York: Harper & Row.

Young, C. C., Gable, R. A., & Hendrickson, J. M. (1989). An ecological perspective to training teachers of the behaviorally disordered: Where are we now? *Behavioral Disorders, 15*(1), 16–20.

7

Developing an Ecological Mind-Set on School–Community Collaboration

Edison J. Trickett
University of Maryland, College Park

This chapter outlines an ecological framework from which to view the increasingly important issue of how schools and the communities in which they are embedded can develop collaborative partnerships. The urgency of the collaboration concept comes from many forces concerned about the current and future functioning of schools as agents of education and socialization. Crowson and Boyd (1993), for example, suggested that "four interconnected movements—toward increased parental involvement in school governance, instructional partnerships, school-to-community 'outreach,' and children's service coordination—are reconfiguring school–community relations" (p. 140). Legal requirements relating to the entitlement of a free and appropriate education for special needs children (Brantlinger, 1991) focus additional attention on the importance of school–parent collaborations.

Underlying these many efforts is the implicit, if not explicit, understanding that the school is part of an *educational ecosystem* that constitutes "an embryonic collaborative network for the conduct of education in each community" (Goodlad, 1984, p. 350). As described by Jones (1992), Goodlad envisioned three broad goals schools can serve: (a) improving the quality and general effectiveness of existing institutions; (b) developing an understanding of education as a communitywide rather than school-based activity; and (c) developing new configurations of educational institutions including both the traditional ones and those of the media, business and industry, and cultural agencies. In viewing the school as part of an educational ecosystem, Goodlad drew attention to the various ways in which schools and communities may become interdependent partners in the education of children and youth. Such a vision rests on the elaboration of perspectives that can guide and inform practitioners, researchers, and citizens in creating the kinds of interdependencies that can serve as resources for the schools and the communities involved.

The remainder of the chapter outlines one conceptual approach to this task: an ecological metaphor for the development of school–community collaboration. First, the contours of an ecological perspective are presented, followed by specific topics illustrating the implications of an ecological mind-set for the development of school–community collaborations.

AN ECOLOGICAL PERSPECTIVE
AND SCHOOL–COMMUNITY COLLABORATION

In recent years, the concept of ecology as a metaphor for understanding behavior in context has gained currency in both education and psychology. Goodlad's use of the term *educational ecosystem* highlights the importance of seeing the school as embedded in a variety of other relations with external settings and communities relevant to the educational and socialization goals of the school. Within psychology, scholars such as Moos (1974, 1979), Barker (1968), and Bronfenbrenner (1979), have described alternative ecological perspectives. Although differing in emphasis and concepts, each focuses attention on the importance of understanding the social contexts of behavior and the notion that the environment can be conceptualized at differing levels of analysis, each of which influences individual behavior. With respect to the school, for example, Moos and Trickett (1979) presented extensive data not only on how school classrooms differ in various types of schools, but also on the relative contribution of variables at differing levels of the ecological environment to classroom climate. Thus, not only is classroom climate predicted by select teacher and student variables, but also by subject matter and organizational characteristics such as class size, school ideology (Trickett, McConahay, Phillips, & Ginter, 1985), and rural versus urban location (Trickett, 1978).

Although the frameworks of these scholars created invaluable paradigms for conceptualizing the array of ecological influences on individual behavior, none was explicitly designed with intervention goals in mind. The task of developing school–community collaboration may benefit from an ecological perspective that has, over time, attempted to apply an ecological mind-set to intervention as well as basic research. One perspective devoted to this integration is the ecological metaphor developed by Kelly and his colleagues in community psychology (Kelly, 1968, 1970, 1979, 1986; Kelly & Hess, 1986). This ecological perspective has been applied to both research and intervention in schools (Trickett, 1986; Trickett & Birman, 1989; Trickett, Kelly, & Todd, 1972; Trickett, Kelly, & Vincent, 1985; Trickett & Schmid, 1993).

The ecological metaphor is based on principles of field biology, in which the entire biological community is the object of study. Later sections of this chapter discuss four specific ecological processes that, taken together, provide ways of conceptualizing the ecological context of behavior. First, however, it is useful to outline three important assumptions that provide the spirit of an ecological mind-set for the development of school-community collaborations. They are the fundamental importance of environmental assessment, the development of a collaborative style, and the value of creating collaborations that mutually empower those participating in them. Taken together, these assumptions create a mind-set that is community focused, concerned about creating authentic relationships and programs, and evolutionary in that early collaborations are seen as the building blocks for later ones. Elsewhere (Trickett & Birman, 1989; Trickett, Kelly, et al., 1985; Trickett & Schmid, 1993), these assumptions have been linked to interventions in schools per se. Here, the intent is to focus them on school-community collaborations.

The Fundamental Importance of Environmental Assessment

Emphasis within an ecological perspective is placed on environmental assessment because successful collaboration rests on knowledge of the communities involved. Developing such knowledge requires frameworks for characterizing the community, processes for gathering relevant knowledge, and an ability to put oneself in the place of the other in the service of understanding diverse views, hopes, and dreams. Such an emphasis also puts a premium on spending time on information gathering and relationship building—two tasks seemingly at odds with the everyday demands of school personnel (Adelman & Taylor, 1993; Epstein & Dauber, 1991).

Developing a Collaborative Intervention Style

Ecologically based collaboration between school and community rests on the development of working reciprocal relationships. Such relationships increase the possibility that diverse perspectives will be listened to and that a shared sense of purpose can be developed. To accomplish such goals, it should be acknowledged that the kinds of expertise brought to the project by school and community representatives are equally valid although different in nature. The assertion is that the kind of relationship developed in the collaboration mediates its success, the degree to which valid information about problems is exchanged (Argyris, 1980), and the possibility that the collaboration can survive the test of time.

Creating an Empowering Intervention

Emphasis on environmental assessment provides knowledge about the community; a collaborative style provides a sense of working together around a problem or goal. Such accomplishments are indeed important to strive for in school–community collaboration. However, an ecological perspective incorporates an additional goal: How to structure current collaborative efforts so that they become enduring resources for the school and community over time. The concept of empowerment is central here. Although specific examples are given later, the empowerment concept involves the development of local skills, the activation and utilization of individual and community resources, and the sharing of power in the development of the collaboration. Such a goal rests on, but goes beyond, the image of collaboration per se.

With this set of assumptions and goals in mind, let us now turn to a description of the four ecological processes central to the ecological metaphor. They are applied to three topics reflecting the assessment, collaboration, and empowerment assumptions just described. They are (a) the community as an ecological context, (b) processes for developing and carrying out school–community collaborations, and (c) parent involvement programs as examples of efforts at empowerment.

THE IMPORTANCE OF ENVIRONMENTAL ASSESSMENT: COMMUNITY AS AN ECOLOGICAL CONTEXT

The first assumption just mentioned is the centrality of environmental assessment as a prelude to developing specific programs. The ecological metaphor offers four ecological processes that can guide this assessment: adaptation, cycling of resources, interdependence, and succession. Each is briefly described and linked to the assessment of the community as an ecological context.

Adaptation

From an ecological perspective, behavior is seen within a coping and adaptation framework. That is, individuals and groups adopt strategies, values, norms, and coping styles that are seen as useful in adapting to the world in which they live. Applied to communities, the adaptation principle signals the search for a broad understanding of what the community is like, the kinds of skills, behaviors, and norms it embodies, the opportunities for growth it provides, and the processes it uses to conduct its business.

There are multiple ways of describing communities, each of which adds richness to an understanding of how to develop collaborations. McKeown, Rubinstein, and Kelly (1987), for example, suggested that it is important to view communities in terms of the kinds of social processes used to accomplish such tasks as diffusing information, enforcing norms around appropriate child behavior, and mobilizing in times of crisis. They reminded us that each community has within it varied subcommunities. Nettles (1991) made the important point that most efforts at collaboration on behalf of disadvantaged students are conceptually narrow and do not integrate how communities and other ecologies affect disadvantaged students at school. She cited community structure, community climate or culture, and community processes for fostering citizen involvement as important ways of conceptualizing the community concept. Community structures include not only the formal and informal political and social networks, but the number and kind of community behavior settings (Barker, 1968) such as churches, playgrounds, community centers, and neighborhood organizations that aid the development of the community more generally.

Differences in community norms affect the possibilities for school–community collaboration. For example, Stevenson (1994) commented on the distrust in African-American communities around AIDS prevention efforts. Here, the minority distrust of science theme is elaborated, including a long-standing history of scientific racism and a cultural history of interrace relations in which Whites have merged race and sexuality very deeply in their images of Blacks. This author suggested the intervention implication of creating programs which build on, rather than undermine, the cultural integrity of the community. Luhan (1993) made a similar point about respecting cultural integrity in her description of the adaptation of the Taos Pueblo in Taos, New Mexico to the influx of tourists. This Native American community developed procedures and norms intended to protect the integrity of the cultural traditions valued by the community from the tourists whose economic resources they valued. While not focusing on collaboration per se, such work is useful as a reminder of communities' power as cultural entities whose stance toward so-called outsiders is critical to the fate of collaboration.

Although the concept of *community is* itself multifaceted, each of these differentiations provide concepts for community assessment. The adaptation principle suggests the importance of understanding how community structures, norms, and processes differ across communities. Such community differences are expected to require different kinds of collaboration around different issues. For example, research on the impact of the farm crisis on families in rural areas (Caudill, 1993; Van Hook, 1990) suggested that such deeply held community values as self-reliance, patriarchy, extended family influence, and religious fundamentalism affect family dynamics and student coping in the schools. Of particular concern is the adolescent norm of not sharing problems or family circumstances with nonfamily adults. These norms carry implications for the functioning of school personnel and mental health professionals in attempting to help these students and their families.

With respect to race, Ogbu (1991) discussed how the historical encounter of Blacks with individual and institutional racism has resulted in certain instrumental coping responses or survival strategies in school, particularly among inner-city Blacks and those who maintain a strong identification with the Black community. These strategies, intended to reduce the instrumental exploitation by the dominant culture, constitute an alternative cultural frame of reference that rests on ambivalence or opposition to a White cultural frame of reference, hence the pejorative connotations of "acting White." This dynamic is different in source and in kind from that reported in rural areas, suggesting that differing kinds of collaborative efforts around different issues may be useful in these culturally diverse communities.

The adaptation principle, then, suggests the overall importance of developing an understanding of the community as a prelude to the development of collaboration. This perspective was echoed by Steuart (1993) in his suggestion that the first intervention task is to conduct a crude analysis of the relevant population in terms of identity clustering to see if community boards and other gatekeepers represent the differing clusters in the community. However, the assessment task is broader than this. It should, in addition, provide a guide to local issues, settings, and political constituencies. The following three additional ecological processes further specify this assessment task and its implications for the development of collaborations.

Cycling of Resources

The cycling of resources principle is a critical focus of environmental assessment of the community more generally, for it directs attention to how resources are defined in differing communities, how they are distributed among different segments of the population, and how they may be nurtured to support collaborative work. From this perspective, both community and school are seen as potential pools of talent, energy, ideas, and supportive structures which need to be identified, appreciated, and developed. Elsewhere (Trickett et al., 1985; Trickett & Schmid, 1993), resources have been differentiated in terms of people, settings, and events.

The Resourcefulness of People: Manifest and Latent. A resource perspective on individuals includes both personal qualities and institutional roles relevant to school–community collaborations. Personal qualities may include knowledge of the community norms and dynamics, energy to devote to collaboration, and a commitment to improve the school as a resource for students and the community. Within the community, parents are perhaps the group most obviously connected to the school, and their involvement as resources is highlighted later in the chapter. However, others have institutional roles that make them resources for collaborations. For example, McAdoo and Crawford (1990) discussed not only the historical role of the Black church as a community resource, but also its special current emphasis on developing child-care programs. These programs, which complement activities relevant to schools, suggest the church to be one kind of community resource with both knowledge of community child-related needs and credibility. Similar comments apply to the centrality of the church in select refugee and immigrant communities, such as those of the Russian Pentecostals (Birman, 1994). Other institutions, such as community development agencies or neighborhood associations, also provide insider knowledge and talent.

It is important to acknowledge that every community has both manifest and latent resources. In addition to the more visible citizens who have risen to a place of influence in the community are many whose talents are not being engaged. Thus, one aspect of community assessment involves the search for individuals who have not yet emerged as visible resources. Creating relationships with citizens and occasions for utilizing such talent becomes an important collaboration-related task. The same, of course, applies to individuals in the school whose roles or personal styles have precluded an awareness of their commitments. In one school with a number of international students (Trickett & Birman, 1989), for example, unbeknownst to most of the administrators, the school librarian had developed an elaborate program to acquaint international students with the library. This individual, once identified, became one of many resources in a school development project involving the adaptation of international students.

Community Settings and Events as Resources.   The earlier comments on the role of the church highlight the importance of assessing community resources in terms of settings as well as individuals. Although the specific settings of relevance would be expected to vary from community to community and project to project, the importance of developing an awareness of and relationships with community settings is central to school–community collaboration. Such an awareness will clarify how the emerging collaboration can build on, rather than duplicate or undermine, existing community efforts. In like manner, community events, celebrations, or coping with local tragedy provide opportunities to learn about core community values, meet citizens out of role, and become known as someone concerned about the community.

In discussing the role of settings as resources, it should also be acknowledged that the school per se is a community resource. Dempsey and Noblit (1993) provided a poignant example of the school as a community resource. They depicted a reconstructive history of a school serving a primarily African-American community that was closed in the service of school desegregation. Because of the history of community ownership of the school, close relations had developed among parents and school personnel with childrearing seen as a community responsibility. The school connected members of the community to each other through parent participation in school events and home visits by teachers. "The closing of Rougemont was the end of social organization, the end of home visits. Nobody knew what anyone else was doing. You didn't see people the way you did" (p. 336).

The authors mentioned other unintended side effects of desegregation, such as the disproportionate burden on African Americans for busing, the closing of African-American schools, and the firing of African-American teachers. However, their closing comments underscore some of the many potential values of school–community collaboration. "In these stories (of reconstructing the narratives of the school closing) are what remains of a culture that equated education with emancipation, that valued schools as cultural entities, and that built communities with schools. In better understanding the cultural consequences of school desegregation for African Americans, we may come to understand what we all need in our communities and from our schools" (Dempsey & Noblit, 1993, p. 339).

The Principle of Interdependence

The interdependence principle focuses on the interconnections among differing components of the community and their implications for the schools. With respect to the interdependence of component parts of the community, the assessment process is geared to understanding how any efforts at collaboration may reverberate throughout different segments of the community. For example, Preston, Baranowski, and Higganbotham (1988–1989) talked about the process of orchestrating community intervention methods to "maximize the efficient diffusion of the targeted behaviors throughout the community" (p. 12). They affirmed the importance of environmental assessment, stating that successful diffusion rests on a knowledge of beliefs and values of the community in question, the social strata of the community, and two kinds of diffusion systems—centralized (hierarchical, top-down) and decentralized (social network, horizontal). They asserted that the process of successful diffusion differs in centralized and decentralized communities. "When the diffusion system is centralized, the point of origination of the new idea is critical to the dissemination process" (p. 16), but this is less critical in decentralized communities. Thus, the nature of the interdependencies in the community affects the course and success of the intervention.

The interdependence of community factors and the school includes numerous issues around which school–community collaboration may be useful. For example, the increase in students from different countries has rippled throughout many aspects of the schools, ranging from changes in the curriculum to issues of student placement to the hiring of bicultural or multicultural staff. Garcia (1992), for example, discussed some of the implications of multiculturalism for communicative competence in the classroom. The interdependence of home culture and school is portrayed in terms of the differing linguistic communities in which the child must learn to function. "Because classroom communication involves 'the language of curriculum, the language of control, and the language of personal identity' (Cazden, 1988, p. 3), cultural discontinuities between home and school can result in lost teaching and learning opportunities, as well as incorrect assessment of children's capabilities" (p. 60). Coping with such pervasive cultural changes has resulted in the development of many collaborative school–community programs tailored to the specific cultural circumstances of the new arrivals (National Coalition of Advocates for Students, 1991).

In addition to differences in cultural background, students bring other community experiences to school as well. Schmitz (1992) pointed out some of the many implications of community effects which children in public housing bring through the school door. Citing the high level of crime, drugs, and violence in neighborhoods with public housing projects, he suggested that a frequent adaptive strategy is to keep children home, thus increasing social isolation as well as an inability to concentrate on school work. Furthermore, such fears do not stop when the children or youth enter school. Indeed, "many youngsters worry that injury will come to the family while the child is away" (p. 42).

These examples of school–community interdependence are meant to increase concern with understanding how the community fits together and how the school's curriculum, norms, and policies mesh with the differing cultures and contexts that students bring to the school experience. Such an assessment is critical to understanding both the topics and processes around which school–community collaboration may be developed.

The Succession Principle

The succession principle, in field biology, refers to the processes through which biological communities evolve and change over time. As prior ecological conditions change, old forms of adaptation become less useful and new forms emerge in response to these changing conditions. Thus, one implication of the succession principle is to develop historical knowledge about communities, schools, and, most specifically, the community-school relationship. The prior principles of adaptation, resources, and interdependence provide an ecological mind-set for exploring the development of the community and the sociocultural histories of the varied groups it includes. It means appreciating the old political alliances, the ways in which the community has learned to process school-related initiatives, and learning the bases of the often found suspicion of school initiatives by segments of the community (Cochran & Dean, 1991). Such a perspective locates any current initiative in the context of historical relations and community sentiments and structures. While not intended to stifle efforts at change, it suggests an appreciation for those times when resistance to change seems to be unreasonable from the perspective of one party, but absolutely rational from the perspective of the other.

Previously cited papers provide examples of the power of history in affecting the issue of school–community collaboration. As such, the development of mistrust of science in the Black community around AIDS-related work (Stevenson, 1994), Ogbu's (1991) description of the contextual rationale for minority coping responses to the school experience, and Caudill's (1993) overview of the long-standing values held by citizens in rural areas represent both the pervasiveness and power of history. Less emphasized in the literature, although equally important, is the value of assessing the school in such historical terms as well; schools experience cycles of growth and decline, energy and malaise, and involvement with varied educational movements which are sometimes recalled as fads in retrospect. This cumulative history too exerts an influence over what is deemed possible, useful, and authentic in developing collaborations.

In addition to history, however, the succession principle includes a future orientation focusing on both the anticipation of future changes and hopes for a better tomorrow. Elsewhere (Trickett & Schmid, 1993), we used the phrase "coping and hoping" to describe the anticipatory aspect of the succession principle. Coping refers to those structures, ways of gathering information, and social settings where planning for the future occurs. Hoping refers to the kinds of futures deemed important as goals. It includes thinking about the kinds of settings that might be created to resolve current problems, ways to build on current projects or relationships for more comprehensive future initiatives, and efforts intended to anticipate how the school might change as its population or resources shift. Vincent (1986) provided an interesting example of the value of such anticipatory planning in her description of the merging of two schools into one. In this instance, an active principal identified relevant key individuals in the two schools and created an anticipatory planning process for acquainting teachers in the two schools with each other. These meetings were structured through an empowering process that created further momentum for a successful, though stressful, transition.

THE IMPORTANCE OF ATTENDING TO PROCESS IN DEVELOPING SCHOOL–COMMUNITY COLLABORATION

Preceding sections offered ways of developing an ecological mind-set for community assessment. Such knowledge is critical in understanding what kinds of collaborations may be useful and what community and school resources are available. However, less has been said about how to develop such collaborations. In this section, the ecological metaphor frames a discussion of how processes for carrying out the collaboration can help create empowering and enduring programs and relationships between school and community.

Adaptation and Coupling with the Community

With respect to the development of school–community collaborations, the broadest implication of the adaptation principle is what we have called elsewhere "coupling with the host environment" (Trickett, Kelly, et al., 1985; Trickett & Schmid, 1993). The spirit of an ecological mind-set focuses on adapting the program to the community rather than vice versa, "presented on the community's terms ... (and paying) attention to the importance of fitting ... activities to the common cycle of community life" (McKeown et al., 1987, p. 52). Doing so includes both the development of knowledge about the community and the creation of inclusionary processes relevant to the specific content of the collaboration.

Stockdill, Duhon-Sells, Olsen, and Patton (1992) provided one example of such a process. These authors described the Supporting Diversity in Schools (SDS) Program involving schools and community groups working with and comprised of Native Americans, African Americans, Hmong, Cambodians, and Hispanics. The goals of the program articulate well the spirit of the ecological mind-set:

> (1) helping to build curricula and school environments that are free of cultural and racial privilege; (2) helping school system staff learn from communities and families whose cultures are different from their own, and helping them apply their skills and knowledge; (3) affirming and strengthening the role of community organizations as cultural bridges between school and parents of color; and (4) affirming families of color as needed experts and resources regarding their children and their culture. (p. 21)

They emphasized the importance of developing processes for achieving shared goals among collaborating parties, and highlighted the relationship among collaborators as central to the overall success of the program. Under such conditions, collaborations cannot help but reflect processes and goals respectful of the community constituencies involved (see also D'Andrea, 1994).

Resource Conservation and Development as a Process Goal

In specifying resources in terms of people, settings, and events as part of the assessment process, attention is drawn to the identification of both existing and latent resources. However, once identified, processes relevant to their use and development are important to consider. Key aspects of the ecological perspective here focus on how to develop collaborations in a way that conserves existing resources and develops new ones related to the goals of the collaboration. The emphasis on conservation is intended to highlight the importance of creating processes that do not drain participants in the service of helping others. Programs of good intent that promote burnout for participants are seen as maladaptive over the long run. Here, then, the concept of coupling includes an appreciation of how the resources necessary to conduct the collaboration are anticipated and built into its structure. The emphasis on development of new resources includes not only active efforts to seek out the untapped energies of previously uninvolved citizens and school personnel; it also includes the value of creating new social settings that can promote the goals of the collaboration.

Although both the identification of individuals and the creation of settings are important in this regard, the process of creating settings deserves special mention because it is far more complex than first meets the eye (see Goldenberg, 1970; Sarason, 1972; Trickett, 1991). Sarason, for example, cited the formative role of unexamined assumptions in carrying out such undertakings. One such assumption is labeled "the myth of unlimited resources," or the unexamined hope that the new program can be accomplished with existing resources, an issue that haunts many well-intentioned efforts. Although Sarason's message involves the importance of understanding the often implicit assumptions underlying the creation of new settings or programs, the critical process issue here is that new settings such as collaborations are inevitably created in such a way that the long-range consequences of initial formative decisions and assumptions will not be well anticipated. Thus, processes for ongoing self-reflection seem important to build into collaborations.

In conceptualizing the differing ways in which assumptions and early decisions affect the development of settings for collaborations, case studies of collaboration offer great heuristic promise. For example, Pink (1992) provided insight into issues of community collaboration in describing parent participation in school governance in the restructuring of Chicago's public schools. He emphasized the influence on the collaboration of the unarticulated but powerful political agendas of varied participating groups. McCarty (1989) provided a vivid portrait of an educational reform experiment on a Navaho reservation. The Rough Rock demonstration school was designed as the first to be overseen by a locally elected, all Native American governing board. However, the idea for the school came not from the community but from the self-help ideology of the Great society in the 1960s which tied the evolution of the school to external forces and funding. As these forces changed focus over time, so did the autonomy of the school to set its own agenda, a conclusion not clearly foreseen in the beginning. Gruber and Trickett (1986) described the paradoxes of an effort to create an empowering governance structure in an inner-city public school. Here, issues of access to resources relevant to educational decision making, the ecology of the lives of parents, and differential expertise among parents, students, and teachers diluted the good intentions of school personnel about developing a truly empowering governance process.

Creating new settings as resources for collaboration that can endure over time represents a critical task in the larger picture of school–community collaboration. However, as these examples indicate, how to construct such settings represents a complex intellectual issue and social agenda for school–community collaboration.

Interdependence and Collaboration: Creating Settings for Information Exchange, Monitoring, and Assessment of Side Effects

The emphasis of the interdependence principle on the connections among various aspects of social systems suggests that change in one part of the system reverberates through other parts. The interdependence principle reminds us that collaborations "are never simple two-way transactions between a 'community' and a 'program,' but always necessarily involve other 'communities of interest,' whether funding sources, professional communities, or political groups" (McKeown et al., 1987, p. 52). Because of the interconnectedness of these varied groups and the complex set of influences, subtle pressures, and diverse agendas involved, it is important to develop settings to recognize and cope with the multiple voices and world views involved directly and indirectly in the collaboration. Such different views may be expressed in terms of cultural dimensions (Harry, 1992; Stockdill et al., 1992) or political agendas (Carlson, 1990), or may simply reflect differential knowledge about how schools operate (Delgado-Gaitan, 1993; Graue, 1993). However, as Stockdill and colleagues pointed out, when attempting to create a working group of culturally diverse individuals, an early step should be to focus on the development of shared goals. Such a process should itself constitute a goal and not be taken as a given.

Another implication of the interdependence principle for collaborative endeavors involves the inevitability of side effects of any collaboration. Such effects may result in unanticipated benefits, such as the improved image of the school in the community when a parent involvement program is launched (Comer & Haynes, 1991). More frequent in the literature, however, are examples of unanticipated consequences which cause problems in other parts of the system (Webb, Wilson, Corbett, & Mordecai, 1993).

Because of the inevitability of nonshared understandings and unanticipated side effects, school–community collaborations are aided by creating structures to share information and monitor the effects of the collaboration not only on participants but on the larger school and community. Such structures may include advisory boards (Kelly, 1979; Trickett & Gibson, 1980), regularly scheduled monitoring meetings with relevant school and community personnel, or frequent updating newsletters, depending on the ecologies of the schools and communities involved. For example, written communications are expected to be of limited use in some language minority communities (Harry, 1992), whereas face-to face meetings intended to explain to parents how schools work may be more useful in disseminating information (Delgado-Gaitan, 1993).

One extended example is provided by Trickett (1976), who reported on a project designed to assess parental interest in differing types of educational alternatives for their children in the public schools. The project was organized such that each of the neighborhoods participating in the project had its own representative to an overall advisory group. The project created two positions for project historians, one representing the university and one the community. Their task was to track the process of the project, meet with each other regularly to assess how both researchers and citizens were perceiving the effort, and prepare reports for university personnel and the different neighborhood advisory groups to share the information. This process served the knowledge and trust-building needs of the project well.

Succession and Collaboration: Examining the Past and Planning for the Future

School–community collaborations take place in the context of long-standing relationships between the school and citizens, parents, and community organizations. Explicit efforts to evaluate, or re-evaluate, the historical triumphs and pitfalls in these relationships over time is central to carrying out current collaborations. Such an effort promotes a self-critical and reflective stance about what has and has not worked historically; It provides an important agenda of discussion among parties involved in the collaboration, placing it in the context of the historical relationship of school to community. Kelly, Azelton, Burzette, and Mock (1993) discussed the creation of social settings that support diversity and focused on the value of settings that serve as places of reflection among those participating in a shared experience. The spirit of such a setting is what is intended here, although the emphasis is on past collaborations and other aspects of school–community relationships.

Such an undertaking, however, is predicated on the idea of collaboration as an ongoing process of commitment over time, not one confined to a particular project or program. Thus the ecological "trick" is to view any particular collaboration as a foundation on which to build future collaborations. Elsewhere (Trickett & Birman, 1989), we outlined one way of attempting to translate a particular program into a long-range resource for the school. Inherent in this perspective is the notion of enduring collaborative relationships that may be directed over time to differing kinds of issues and populations. The networks developed in one collaboration may shift, both in terms of community members and school personnel, but the continuity of institutional commitment remains.

The potential payoffs from such tenacity are numerous, beginning with the accrual of trust and goodwill in the community. Also important is the development, over time, of a knowledge of school and community resources that promote additive and integrative collaborations across areas of institutional and community concern. A longitudinal time perspective enhances the chances of creating programs that integrate rather than fragment and of finding opportunities for new collaborations as mutual knowledge and trust develop. It further serves as an antidote for the unfortunate history of cynicism about the possibility for change resulting from both school and community experience with one-shot research projects and short-term programs that end when the money runs out or the school board ideology shifts. The spirit of the ecological metaphor is one of going for the long haul over the quick fix.

PARENT INVOLVEMENT IN SCHOOLS: EMPOWERMENT AND ECOLOGY IN SCHOOL–COMMUNITY COLLABORATIONS

The area of parent involvement in schools illustrates how collaborations can serve the goal of empowerment, the third overarching aspect of the ecological metaphor discussed at the beginning of the chapter. Further, it shows ways in which the local ecology of parents and schools shapes the nature and potential of parent involvement efforts.

Whereas the image of collaboration is an important aspect of the ecological metaphor, the empowerment concept focuses on the value of collaborations that emphasize increasing parental choice and influence over the school-related aspects of their children's education. The empowerment concept is increasingly cited as central to educational reform, more generally (Crowson & Boyd, 1993; Pink, 1992), and the improvement of home–school relationships, in particular (Cochran & Dean, 1991; Comer & Haynes, 1991). Zimmerman (1995) defined *empowerment* in terms of processes in which

> people create or are given opportunities to control their own destiny and influence the decisions that affect their lives. They are a series of experiences in which individuals learn to: see a closer correspondence between their goals and a sense of how to achieve them; gain greater access to and control over resources; and where people, organizations, and communities gain mastery over their lives. Efforts to gain control, access to resources, and a critical understanding of one's sociopolitical context are fundamental aspects of empowering processes. (p. 583)

The term *parental involvement* is itself multifaceted, covering a wide range of activities and goals. Epstein and Dauber (1991) developed a useful typology that specifies five levels of home–school interdependence and a sixth level focusing on parent connections with community organizations with a role in providing services relevant to children and youth. The five levels of home–school interdependence provide a rough empowerment scale in terms of type of involvement, with Level 1 focusing on the provision of a nurturing home environment in which learning can take place and Level 5 dealing with involvement in governance and advocacy related to the school.

Typologies, although providing a framework for general conceptualization of alternatives, do not by themselves help understand the specific terrain in which any particular parent involvement program is designed and implemented. Ecological variation among both schools and parent groups affect what kind of parent involvement is both likely and desirable. With respect to schools, for example, Epstein and Dauber (1991), in a study of inner-city elementary and middle schools, found that teacher stereotypes of parents decreased with increased parent–teacher contact. They also found that parent involvement was greater in schools with self-contained classrooms than schools where the students switched teachers during the day. Comer and Haynes (1991) discussed another aspect of school variation that they believe affects parent involvement programs: the degree to which the school environment is bureaucratic and inflexible. They asserted that such programs are more likely to flourish when coupled with a school with a collaborative organizational structure.

Yet, parents living in different communities also differ in their prefer-ences and opportunities for involvement. Graue (1993) presented a compel-ling ethnographic picture of how parents constructed their parental roles in two communities differing in economic resources, local notions of home–school relations, and informational networks. She conducted partici-pant observations in two schools, one serving a rural, ethnically diverse, working-class population with a close-knit, small town feel, the other a primarily white bedroom community of commuting professionals. Thus, in the poorer, more diverse, rural community both parents were more likely to work outside the home, making school visits and volunteering less likely. They were more likely to segment the roles of parents and school, relying on the school to be the expert in matters educational and viewing no news from the school as good news. Here, parents never discussed the issue of school readiness, sending their children to school at the prescribed age. In the whiter and richer community, "being a good mother was being a data gatherer" (p. 484) about the school, and parents both felt and acted empow-ered in involving themselves in the school as volunteers and holding the school accountable for decisions. Here, the issue of school readiness was central to parental discourse, and children were often kept out of school because parents deemed them not ready.

The conclusions drawn by Graue (1993) about the contrasting home–school relations in the two communities clarify the importance of appreciating local ecology when considering parental involvement. Ap-proaches to parent involvement focusing on activities designed to increase parental presence in schooling are "blind to the social nature of parenting, the cultural meanings that are foundational to interaction among community members. It treats both parents and school people as unidimensional and ignores the pull of gender and social resources on activities and interactions" (p. 487). To design programs sensitive to local ecology, "we need to know more about the influences that shape the roles that parents take in schools, from the negotiations that occur in homes to the institutional structures and values that enhance or impede relationships. Both micro- and macroana-lyses are needed to avoid the policy-in-a-vacuum approach that has muddled our knowledge of interactions between parents and educational personnel" (p. 488).

Further data on dimensions of ecological importance for parent–school involvement come from literature discussing the dilemmas facing immi-grant parents in their efforts to adapt to this country and concurrently aid in their children's education. Such potential barriers as limited English profi-ciency, especially in the context of illiteracy in one's native language, can not only prevent the reading of school notices and invitations to school events (Commins, 1992), but such written outreach efforts have also been reported as having an unintended alienating effect (Harry, 1992). Furthermore, the survival needs reported by Graue in the rural community are equally powerful in many inner-city immigrant communities, where, as Ascher (1988) noted, "the daily struggle to survive may at times make it impossible for parents to reach out to an educational institution that cannot provide for its immediate needs" (p. 111). Cultural differences may, in addition, result in mistrust or misunderstanding between immigrant parents and schools. With respect to Latino parents, for example, MacPherson (1993) suggested that limited parent–school contact has fueled educators' perceptions that parents do not value education, and Plata (1989) found that parents may limit their contact with the schools because of "the cumulative effect of encounters with insensitive teachers, misdirected school curriculum, and the school's unbenefitting rules" (p. 87). In addition, Harry's ethnography of Puerto Rican parents of children in special education classes suggested that deference to authority disguised the real opinions of parents about the school in school interactions and that parents, although deferent to the school in terms of decisions, did not trust the school to make the best decisions as they involved their children. Here, deference was misinterpreted as indifference by school personnel.

Such examples only scratch the surface of the complex interactions that can relate to school efforts to empower parents through parent involvement. However, examples of programs that illustrate ways of grappling with these issues are available. We now turn to these.

CONTRASTING APPROACHES TO PARENT–SCHOOL INVOLVEMENT: THE COMER SCHOOL DEVELOPMENT PROGRAM AND THE COMITE DE PADRES LATINOS

Varied parent involvement programs are described in the literature (e.g., Brantlinger, 1991; Cochran & Dean, 1991; D'Andrea, 1994; Jones, 1992; Price, Cioci, Penner, & Trautlein, 1993; Stockdill et al., 1992). Two programs representing contrasting strategies and located in culturally diverse communities are selected here. The Comer program (Anson, Cook, Habib, Grady, Haynes, & Comer, 1991; Comer & Haynes, 1991) rests on the assertion that "for parent involvement programs to be successful, they should be part of a contextually focused school improvement process designed to create positive relationships that support children's total development" (Comer & Haynes, 1991, p. 271). It represents an "attempt to counteract the loosening of ties between school and community which has occurred over time as well as dealing with some of the residuals of the breakup of the African American family" (Anson et al., 1991, p. 59).

Emphasis is placed on changing the ecology of the school through a process called the School Development Program. This program is based on the creation of three additive structures: an inclusionary governance mechanism that includes all stakeholders, an interdisciplinary mental health team, and a parent program. Process guidelines include a no-fault problem-solving approach, consensus decision making, and a collaborative management approach that is inclusionary without paralyzing the school principal. The parent program includes different levels of potential parental involvement, and focuses on such tasks as planning events to improve school climate, taking advantage of historical events and holidays to celebrate diversity, and working with school personnel to develop a shared sense of direction (Anson et al., 1991). Included in the program are many of the implications of the ecological metaphor, including the valuing of parents as critical and distinctive resources and the development of social settings to deal with conflicts and their resolution. Importantly, the developers of this program pointed out that the ecology of schools affects both the timing and the nature of the specific activities generated by this overall approach to school improvement through parent involvement.

The *Comite de Padres Latinos* (Committee for Latin Parents), represented a different strategy for parent involvement which emerged out of the collaboration of a researcher, a school system, and a Latino community (Delgado-Gaitan, 1993). Here, an *ethnography of empowerment* approach was used to develop an insider perspective on literacy abilities and goals in Latino households. As part of this process, the researcher solicited parent input and insight about their literacy patterns in the home and in relation to the school. This process not only uncovered a variety of ways which parents fostered literacy that were unknown to the school, but also surfaced anger and frustration about parent experience in school interactions, including not having anyone in the school with whom they could communicate in Spanish. The researcher role changed to one of interventionist by collaborating with a father in organizing a parent group to initiate contact with the school around parent–school communication. Delgado-Gaitan painted a complex process portrait of the evolution of the parent group, their struggles with issues of differential acculturation of themselves and their own children, and the efforts made to recruit advocates from the school with whom to collaborate. The group also became a place for critical reflection on their common history of school interaction, shared feelings of isolation, and the debilitating effects of group stereotypes on their energy to interact with the school. Such reflection engendered confidence, hope, and efforts to seek changes at the school and district levels.

The contrasting programs suggest the value of regarding parent involvement as a multifaceted, differentiated concept that may succeed in different ways in different places and with different groups of parents. Both of these programs made palpable differences in the parent communities and the schools, and both represented efforts rooted in the particular circumstances of the communities involved. An ecological mind-set is nowhere better exemplified than in these two different programs, each emerging from and intending to affect different cultural and community contexts.

PARENT INVOLVEMENT AND THE STRUCTURE OF SCHOOLS: A FINAL COMMENT

The literature on parent involvement in schools contains two recurrent themes: (a) to accomplish meaningful involvement, schools must change in ways that allow existing roles to be expanded and new roles to be created for school system personnel, and (b) the current structure of schools makes such changes difficult to enact. Such conclusions apply to the wide range of school–community collaborations. Indeed, many of the authors cited throughout this chapter called for a rethinking of roles across disciplines and ecologies. The Comer project (Comer & Haynes, 1991), for example, outlines some of these new roles, as does the Cooperative Communication Between Home and School Program described by Cochran and Dean (1991). The majority of these recommendations call for roles emphasizing less the direct service and more the coordination and development of resources in the school and community to facilitate positive parental involvement in their children's schools (Adelman & Taylor, 1993; Pink, 1992; Steuart, 1993). Thus, the importance of community assessment and resource identification is becoming increasingly central to the development of such programs and needs to be reflected in both roles and training (Kraemer & Epps, 1991). The multiplicity of forms that parent involvement efforts have taken, however, and the varied goals they are designed to serve suggests that different roles for different goals should be the ecological image is emphasized.

However, these same authors lamented the difficulties in changing school policies, structures, and practices to accomplish these goals. Epstein and

Dauber (1991) asserted that most school programs and practices make difficult the good intentions of teachers to support parent involvement. Adelman and Taylor (1993), in describing a new role focusing on resource development, staff development, and enhancing community resource usefulness, said that "the above suggestion, of course, flies in the face of prevailing practice and training" (p. 37). Such a recurrent concern among those with long histories of working in varied schools suggests that programs or initiatives intending to increase parent involvement in particular, but also school–community collaboration in general, need to be as ecologically responsive to an understanding of the school environment as to the community in which the school is located.

The ecological perspective underlying this chapter has been applied to both assessment of schools and intervention in them (Kelly, 1979; Kelly & Hess, 1986; Trickett & Birman, 1989; Trickett & Schmid, 1993) and provides a complementary picture to the one painted in the current chapter. It suggests the value of creating ecological knowledge based on careful case studies and research efforts that clarify how the local ecologies of schools and communities come together in school–community collaborations. Such knowledge should inform the processes by which collaborations may be developed as well as provide a way of choosing which kinds make the most local sense. In such efforts, the ecological mind-set outlined in this chapter will hopefully be useful as a heuristic for maximizing the long-range value of school–community collaborations and as a resource for both.

REFERENCES

Adelman, H. S., & Taylor, L. (1993). School–based mental health: Toward a comprehensive approach. *Journal for Mental Health Administration, 20,* 12–45.

Anson, A. R., Cook, T. D., Habib, F., Grady, M. K., Haynes, N., & Comer, J. P. (1991). The Comer School Development Program: A theoretical analysis. *Urban Education, 26,* 56–82.

Argyris, C. (1980). *Intervention theory and method: A behavioral science view.* Reading, MA: Addison–Wesley.

Ascher, C. (1988). Improving the school–home connection for poor and minority urban students. *Urban Review, 22,* 109–123.

Barker, R. G. (1968). *Ecological psychology.* Stanford, CA: Stanford University Press.

Birman, D. (1994). *Mental health needs of Evangelical Christian refugees from the former Soviet Union.* Refugee Mental Health Branch, Center for Mental Health Services, Substance Abuse and Mental Health Services Administration, Rockville, MD.

Brantlinger, E. (1991). Home–school partnerships that benefit children with special needs. *Elementary School Journal, 91,* 249–259.

Bronfenbrenner, U. (1979). *The ecology of human development: Experiments by nature and design.* Cambridge, MA: Harvard University Press.

Carlson, C. E. (1990). HIPP: A comprehensive school-based substance abuse program with cooperative community involvement. *Journal of Primary Prevention, 10,* 289–302.

Caudill, M. H. (1993). School social work services in rural Appalachian systems: Identifying and closing the gaps. *Social Work in Education, 15,* 179–185.

Cazden, C. B. (1988). *Classroom discourse: The language of teaching and learning.* Portsmouth, NH: Heinemann.

Cochran, M., & Dean, C. (1991). Home–school relations and the empowerment process. *Elementary School Journal, 91,* 261–269.

Comer, J. P., & Haynes, N. M. (1991). Parent involvement in schools: An ecological approach. *Elementary School Journal, 91,* 271–277.

Commins, N. (1992). Parents and public schools: The experience of four Mexican-American immigrant families. *Equity and Choice, 8,* 40–45.

Crowson, R. L., & Boyd, W. L. (1993). Coordinated services for children: Designing arks for storms and seas unknown. *American Journal of Education, 101,* 140–179.

D'Andrea, M. (1994). The Family Development Project: A comprehensive mental health counseling program for pregnant adolescents. *Journal of Mental Health Counseling, 16,* 184–195.

Delgado–Gaitan, C. (1993). Researching change and changing the researcher. *Harvard Educational Review, 63,* 389–411.

Dempsey, V., & Noblit, G. W. (1993). Cultural ignorance and school desegregation: Reconstructing a silenced narrative. *Educational Policy, 7,* 318–339.

Epstein, J. L., & Dauber, S. L. (1991). School programs and school practices of parent involvement in inner-city elementary and middle schools. *Elementary School Journal, 91,* 289–305.

Garcia, G. E. (1992). Ethnography and classroom communication: Taking an "emic" perspective. *Topics in Language Disorders, 12,* 54–66.

Goldenberg, I. I. (1970). *Build me a mountain: Youth, poverty, and the creation of new settings.* Cambridge, MA: MIT Press.

Goodlad, J. A. (1984). *A place called school: Prospects for the future.* New York: McGraw-Hill.

Graue, M. E. (1993). Social networks and home–school relations. *Educational Policy, 7,* 466–490.

Gruber, J., & Trickett, E. J. (1986). Can we empower others? The paradox of empowerment in the governing of an alternative public school. *American Journal of Community Psychology, 15,* 353–371.

Harry, B. (1992). An ethnographic study of cross-cultural communication with Puerto Rican-American families in the special education system. *American Educational Research Journal, 29,* 471–494.

Jones, B. A. (1992). Collaboration: The case for indigenous community-based organization support of dropout prevention programming and implementation. *Journal of Negro Education, 61,* 496–508.

Kelly, J. G. (1968). Towards an ecological conception of preventive interventions. In J. W. Carter (Ed.), *Research contributions from psychology to community mental health* (pp. 76–100). New York: Behavioral Publications.

Kelly, J. G. (1970). Antidotes for arrogance: Training for a community psychology. *American Psychologist, 25,* 524–531.

Kelly, J. G. (1979). *Adolescent boys in high school: A psychological study of coping and adaptation.* Hillsdale, NJ: Lawrence Erlbaum Associates.

Kelly, J. G. (1986). Content and process: An ecological view of the interdependence of practice and research. *American Journal of Community Psychology, 14,* 581–589.

Kelly, J. G., Azelton, L. S., Burzette, R. G., & Mock, L. O. (1993). Creating social settings for diversity: An ecological thesis. In E. J. Trickett, R. J. Watts, & D. Birman (Eds.), *Human diversity: Perspectives on people in context* (pp. 424–451). San Francisco: Jossey-Bass.

Kelly, J. G., & Hess, R. (1986). *The ecology of prevention: Illustrating mental health consultation.* New York: Haworth Press.

Kraemer, J. J., & Epps, S. (1991). Expanding professional opportunities and improving the quality of training: A look toward the next generation of school psychologists. *School Psychology Review, 20,* 452–461.

Luhan, C. C. (1993). A sociological view of tourism in an American Indian community: Maintaining cultural integrity at Taos Pueblo. *American Indian Culture and Research Journal, 17,* 101–120.

MacPherson, A. (1993). Parent–professional partnership: A review and discussion of issues. *Early Child Development and Child Care, 86,* 61–67.

McAdoo, H., & Crawford, V. (1990). The Black church and family support programs. *Prevention in Human Services, 9,* 193–203.

McCarty, T. L. (1989). School as community: The Rough Rock demonstration. *Harvard Educational Review, 59*, 484–503.

McKeown, T. C., Rubinstein, R. A., & Kelly, J. G. (1987). Anthropology, the meaning of community, and prevention. *Prevention in Human Services, 5*, 35–64.

Moos, R. H. (1974). *Evaluating treatment environments: A social ecological approach.* New York: Wiley.

Moos, R. H. (1979). *Evaluating educational environments.* San Francisco: Jossey-Bass.

Moos, R. H., & Trickett, E. J. (1979). Determinants of classroom environments. In R. H. Moos (Ed.), *Evaluating educational environments* (pp. 159–182). San Francisco: Jossey-Bass.

National Coalition of Advocates for Students. (1991). *The good common school.* Boston, MA: National Coalition of Advocates for Students.

Nettles, S. M. (1991). Community involvement and disadvantaged students: A review. *Review of Educational Research, 61*, 379–406.

Ogbu, J. U. (1991). Minority coping responses and school experience. *Journal of Psychohistory, 18*, 433–456.

Pink, W. T. (1992). The politics of reforming urban schools. *Education and Urban Society, 25*, 96–113.

Plata, M. (1989). Multicultural considerations in conferring with Hispanic parents. *Journal of Instructional Psychology, 16*, 85–90.

Preston, M. A., Baranowski, T., & Higganbotham, J. C. (1988–1989). Orchestrating the points of community intervention: Enhancing the diffusion process. *International Quarterly of Community Health Education, 9*, 11–34.

Price, R. H., Cioci, M., Penner, W., & Trautlein, B. (1993). Webs of influence: School and community programs that enhance adolescent health and education. *Teachers College Record, 94*, 487–521.

Sarason. S. B. (1972). *The creation of settings and the future societies.* San Francisco: Jossey-Bass.

Schmitz, S. (1992). Three strikes and you're out: Academic failure and the children of public housing. *Journal of Education, 174*, 41–65.

Steuart, G. W. (1993). Social and cultural perspectives: Community intervention and mental health. *Health Education Quarterly*, Supplement 1, S99–S111.

Stevenson, H. C. (1994). The psychology of sexual racism and AIDS: An ongoing saga of distrust and the "sexual other." *Journal of Black Studies, 25*, 62–80.

Stockdill, S. H., Duhon–Sells, R. M., Olsen, R. A., & Patton, M. Q. (1992). Voices in the design and evaluation of a multicultural education program: A developmental approach. *New Directions in Program Evaluation, 53*, 17–33.

Trickett, E. J. (1976). The community survey on educational options. In B. Burgess (Ed.), *Facts and figures: A layman's guide to conducting surveys* (pp. 123–132). Boston, MA: Institute for Responsive Education.

Trickett, E. J. (1978). Towards a social-ecological conception of adolescent socialization: Normative data on contrasting types of public schools. *Child Development, 49*, 408–414.

Trickett, E. J. (1986). Consultation as a preventive intervention: Comments on ecologically based case studies. *Prevention in Human Services, 4*(3–4), 187–204.

Trickett, E. J. (1991). *Living an idea: Empowerment and the evolution of an inner city alternative high school.* Cambridge, MA: Brookline Books.

Trickett, E. J., & Birman, D. (1989). Taking ecology seriously: A community development approach to individually-based interventions. In L. Bond & B. Compas (Eds.), *Primary prevention in the schools* (pp. 361–390). Hanover, NH: University of New England Press.

Trickett, E. J., & Gibson, M. J. (1980). *The Community Support Project: Final report on needs assessment and evaluation.* Unpublished manuscript, University of Maryland, College Park.

Trickett, E. J., Kelly, J. G., & Todd, D. M. (1972). The social environment of the high school: Guidelines for individual change and organizational development. In S. Golann & C. Eisdorfer (Eds.) *Handbook of community mental health* (pp. 331–406). New York: Appleton-Century-Crofts.

Trickett, E. J., Kelly, J. G., & Vincent, T. A. (1985). The spirit of ecological inquiry in community research. In E. Susskind & D. Klein (Eds.), *Community research: Methods, paradigms, and applications* (pp. 283–333). New York: Praeger.

Trickett, E. J., McConahay, J. B., Phillips, D., & Ginter, M. A. (1985). Natural experiments and the educational context: The environment and effects of an inner-city alternative public high school on students. *American Journal of Community Psychology, 13*, 617–643.

Trickett, E. J., & Schmid, K. D. (1993). The school as a social context. In P. H. Tolan & B. J. Cohler (Eds.), *Handbook of clinical research and practice with adolescents* (pp. 173–202). New York: Wiley.

Van Hook, M. P. (1990). Impact of the farm crisis on youth: School responses. *Social Work in Education, 12*, 166–176.

Vincent, T. A. (1986). Two into one: An ecological perspective on school consolidation. *Prevention in Human Services, 4*, 113–149.

Webb, J., Wilson, B., Corbett, D., & Mordecai, R. (1993). Understanding caring in context: Negotiating borders and barriers. *Urban Review, 25*, 25–45.

Zimmerman. M. A. (1995). Psychological empowerment: Issues and illustrations. *American Journal of Community Psychology, 23*, 581–600.

V

ASSESSMENT
AND INTERVENTION
WITH COMMUNITIES

8

School-to-Work Transition: Ecological Considerations for Career Development

Edna Mora Szymanski
University of Wisconsin–Madison

School-to-work transition is far more than an educational event. On the one hand, transition is part of the continuum of life-long career development (Szymanski, 1994). On the other hand, it is the focus of political discourse on the relation of education and the economy (Apple & Zenk, 1996). This chapter provides an overview of transition for an audience of educators and human service providers. To this end, the following topics are addressed: (a) historical, political, and economic context; (b) career development and transition; (c) goal and intervention considerations; (d) additional considerations for students with disabilities, children in poverty, and minorities; and (e) connecting assessment and interventions with career development.

HISTORICAL, POLITICAL, AND ECONOMIC CONTEXT

School-to-work transition has been a national concern in the United States for several decades (Smith & Rojewski, 1993). In the past, as well as the present, this concern has been reflected in legislation (e.g., the Smith Hughes Act of 1917 and the School-to-Work Opportunities Act of 1994). However, this focus on a linkage between school and work has also been the subject of serious question (Apple & Zenk, 1996; Kantor, 1988, 1994).

On the one hand, proponents of school-to-work legislation and programs have argued that a strong linkage between education and employment is vital for a competitive workforce (Carnevale, 1995). Many of these proponents place the blame for deficits in the workforce on the educational system. On the other hand, scholars have criticized the narrowness of this focus and its tendency to obscure structural problems in the labor market (Osterman, 1995). For example, according to Apple and Zenk (1996), "the assumption that we will find long-term answers to the dropout dilemma and to the realities of poverty and unemployment by keeping our attention within the schools is dangerously naive" (p. 70). Although a full analysis of the various views of school-to-work transition is beyond the scope of this chapter, it is clear that school-to-work transition is far more than an educational issue.

Despite the controversies, school-to-work programs have existed for decades. Consider, for example, the career education movement of the 1970s. Descriptions of its origin and goals (see Herr & Cramer, 1992) seem hauntingly similar to current school-to-work literature. In fact, some have termed this cyclical pattern new wine in old bottles (Halpern, 1992).

Lack of attention to the career development process may compound the problems of the school-to-work movement. School-to-work programs focus on the educational system and the high school years. However, transition is part of career development, which is a lifelong process that involves families (Super, 1990).

CAREER DEVELOPMENT AND TRANSITION

Two forces combine to make career development the cornerstone of transition. First, career development is the lifelong process of expressing oneself through work and other life roles. It begins at birth and extends well beyond completion of school (Super, 1990). Second, the changing nature of work and the labor market mean that job change is often a part of life. "As a result of the changes in the labor market, more people work, but fewer have full-time, full benefit jobs, fewer escape long spells of unemployment, fewer feel secure that they will have well-remunerated work tomorrow, and fewer can anticipate having a pension on which to retire" (Yelin, 1991, p. 88).

Over the years, different disciplines have developed a wide range of disconnected theories and constructs to explain career development (Schein, 1986). Although convergence of major theories has been investigated (Savickas & Lent, 1994), the individual theories remain and continue to inform research (Holland, 1994; Osipow, 1994). Some major theories and references are presented in Table 8.1.

TABLE 8.1
Selected Career Development Theories and References

Theory	Literature Citations
Person–Environment Fit including: Holland's typology Minnesota theory of work adjustment Trait and factor theory	Rounds and Tracey (1990) Holland (1985) Lofquist and Dawis (1991) Brown (1990)
Super's theory Developmental contextualism	Super (1990) Vondracek, Lerner, and Schulenberg (1986) Vondracek and Fouad (1994)
Krumboltz's theory	Mitchell and Krumboltz (1990)
Hershenson's theory	Hershenson (1981)
Sociocognitive approach	Hackett and Lent (1994)
Sociological theories	Rothman (1987)
Organizational career theory	Hall (1986, 1990)

Many of the theories are ecological in nature; that is, they address the relationship of the individual and environmental factors in a developmental context. Specifically, the theories acknowledge that "the developmental processes taking place in the immediate settings in which human beings life, such as family, school, peer group, and workplace, are profoundly affected by conditions and events in the broader context in which these settings are embedded" (Bronfenbrenner, 1988, p. x).

The theories use different terminologies and have different areas of focus. However, taken together, they address five types of factors (i.e., individual, context, mediating, work environment, outcome) that are interactive and build on each other in a developmental process through the life span (Szymanski, Hershenson, Enright, & Ettinger, 1996). The discussion of career development and transition is thus organized according to the five types of factors.

Individual Factors

Individual characteristics, which are traits and attributes, are important elements in most career development theories (Szymanski, Hershenson, Enright, et al., 1996). They include physical and mental abilities (Brown, 1990), gender and race (Fitzgerald & Betz, 1994), interests (Lofquist & Dawis, 1991), and the aspects of disabilities that are individual traits (e.g., physical or mental limitations).

Individual factors interact with all other factors over time. For example, race and gender interact with context. With other factors controlled, both race (Haveman & Wolfe, 1994) and gender (Reskin & Padvic, 1994) negatively impact occupational attainment and earnings, thus affecting socioeconomic status. Similarly, interests are not fixed traits; they are learned (Mitchell & Krumboltz, 1990). The context in which individuals grow up influences their learning experiences, which in turn influence interests as well as beliefs (see mediational factors).

The interaction of individual and contextual factors is particularly important to career development and thereby transition. It is during the preschool and school years, when interests and abilities are developing, that the limiting effects of the context in which children live can be particularly detrimental (Bronfenbrenner, 1988).

Context Factors

Context factors are aspects of individuals' situations that are external to them. They include socioeconomic status, opportunity structures, family, education, non-normative influences (e.g., war), and relevant legislation (Szymanski, Hershenson, Ettinger, & Enright, 1996). They have been recognized as important to occupational attainment by theorists in sociology (see, e.g., Rothman, 1987) and vocational psychology (see, e.g., Fitzgerald & Betz, 1994; Vondracek, Lerner, & Schulenberg, 1986).

Contextual factors have considerable influence on transition outcomes.

1. The background of the family (size, race, occupation and education status of parents, stability, and structure) in which children grow up has a significant independent influence on their ultimate occupational attainment. Parental schooling and occupational status are robust and persistently related to a wide variety of outcomes.
2. These background characteristics heavily influence the schooling and training attained by an individual; individual educational attainment also appears to have an independent effect on labor market attainments. (Haveman & Wolfe, 1994, p. 77)

Labor market-related factors can compound background influences. Changes in the labor market and in job structures (Ryan, 1996) will have immediate influences on transition as well as sustained impact for future generations. Fewer good jobs for current graduates are likely to influence their future opportunities as well as the opportunities of their children.

Mediating Factors

Mediating factors are individual, group, or societal beliefs that impact on the interaction of individuals and their environments (Szymanski, Hershenson, Enright, et al., 1996). Individual mediating factors include work personality (see Hershenson 1981; Loftquist & Dawis, 1991); self-efficacy, which is belief about one's ability to accomplish a specific task (Bandura, 1982; Hackett & Lent, 1994); outcome expectations (Hackett & Lent, 1994); and cultural and religious beliefs, such as acculturation (LaFromboise, Coleman, & Gerton, 1993) and racial identity (Rowe, Behrens, & Leach, 1995). Social mediating factors, such as discrimination, stereotypes, and castification (Trueba, Rodriguez, Zou, & Cintron, 1993), are societal beliefs that affect individual opportunities.

Beliefs are particularly potent determinants of human behavior. Specifically, "the belief systems of self and other ... [are] crucial to the scientific understanding and the social harnessing of the forces that shape human development" (Bronfenbrenner, 1988, p. xiv). Developmental (see Super, 1990), sociocognitive (see Hackett & Lent, 1994), and developmental contextualism (see Vondracek & Fouad, 1994) approaches to career development recognize the importance of belief structures and the developmental nature of their influence.

Influences of belief structures may be particularly salient for minority students planning for transition. It is suspected that limitations in opportunity structures (i.e., context factors), which often accompany minority status, fundamentally alter the beliefs that stimulate career development processes (Osipow & Littlejohn, 1995). If opportunities are not evident or discrimination is anticipated, then outcome expectations may be limited, and educational preparation may not be pursued (see Arbona, 1995; Fitzgerald & Betz, 1994).

Beliefs also impact on what types of transition interventions and goals are appropriate. For example, some African Americans and Native Americans may prefer group interventions, whereas some Asian Americans may perceive such approaches as invasions of privacy. Similarly, many racial and ethnic minority groups value family, community, and cooperation more than the common Euro-American goals of individualism, independence, and competitiveness (Betz & Fitzgerald, 1995).

Belief structure is influenced, but not determined by, race and ethnicity. Minority individuals demonstrate a wide range of identifications with majority culture and their culture of origin (LaFramboise et al., 1993). For example, although independent decision making may be a goal for some Native Americans, connection with family, tribe, and community may be more important to others (Johnson, Swartz, & Martin, 1995). Thus, it is important to discern individual beliefs and avoid stereotypes.

Work Environment Factors

Work environment factors are aspects of work environments that can directly influence the behavior of workers (Szymanski, Hershenson, Enright, et al., 1996). This group of factors includes the task requirements and reinforcement systems (Dawis, 1994; Lofquist & Dawis, 1991), the characteristics of workers in the environment as operationalized by Holland's (1985, 1994) modal work environments, organizational culture (Rothman, 1987), and physical characteristics of the work environment that may limit or promote access by people with disabilities.

Transition involves more than getting the first job. Students must have the necessary social skills to successfully adjust to the work environment. Furthermore, they should have sufficient understanding of their own needs and values to be able to identify and secure appropriate reinforcement (e.g., salary, advancement, interpersonal relationships) in their chosen work environment. Many of the skills needed for successful adjustment to work environments (e.g., social skills, self-assessment, delaying immediate reinforcement) develop throughout life, beginning in the preschool years.

Outcome Factors

Outcome factors are the behaviors or states that result from the interaction of the other five groups of factors over time (Szymanski, Hershenson, Enright, et al., 1996). They include satisfaction that individuals experience as a result of jobs and work environments meeting their needs, satisfactoriness that results from workers fulfilling job and work environment requirements (Lofquist & Dawis, 1991), the correspondence or match of individuals with work environments (Rounds & Tracey, 1990), organizational productivity (Hall, 1986, 1990), and job stress and strain (Landy, 1992).

The success or failure of transition interventions is apparent from the outcome factors. If transition preparation has been effective, graduates should be satisfied, productive workers. However, even if transition is successful, job stress may become a problem.

Unfortunately, job stress is prevalent, especially with the decrease in good, well paying jobs. It often accompanies jobs in which workers have little control. Similarly, high demand and monotony may contribute to stress. Interestingly, however, social support, on and off the job, appears to lessen the impact of job stress (Landy, 1992). Social and interpersonal skills are important in identifying and using social support. These skills, which develop early in life, should be considered in transition planning.

Consideration of context, individual, mediating, work environment, and outcome factors can facilitate understanding the relationship of school-to-work transition to career development. The next challenge, however, is to plan transition in a way that facilitates career development. Therefore, goals and interventions are addressed.

GOALS AND INTERVENTION CONSIDERATIONS

School-to-work transition is one road stop on the lifelong career development highway. Career related literature, therefore, provides important considerations for transition. These considerations are discussed according to the following topics: goals, planning processes, interventions, and the real world of work.

Goals

The goal of school-to-work transition is the same for all students, including those who go directly to work and those who go on to college. It is positive career development.

It is important to remember that career development is not just about jobs. It is about self-expression through work and other life roles (Super, 1990). "It includes early recognitions that adults work, fantasies about the kind of work one might do as an adult, preferences among the kind of work available, preparation for working, securing positions in the work force, combining work with the personal and situational changes of life, and reflecting on work after one has ceased to engage in it" (Myers & Cairo, 1992, p. 551).

Although context and mediating factors tend to impact on career development (Osipow & Littlejohn, 1995; Vondracek & Fouad, 1994), it is nonetheless a lifelong, cognitive, and developmental process (Hackett & Lent, 1994). Therefore, the goal of transition should not just be to get students into jobs. Rather it should be to provide students with the skills necessary to plan and implement satisfying career paths.

Planning Processes

A major caveat in transition planning relates to the sociocognitive nature of career development. A continuous interplay of self-efficacy, outcome expectations, and interests occurs throughout the lifetime. This process, which is similar for students who go to college and those who directly enter the workforce, is lifelong. It does not begin to stabilize until late adolescence or early adulthood (Lent, Brown, & Hackett, 1994). Thus, it is important to assist students in considering a range of goals throughout adolescence and adulthood rather than prematurely foreclosing in a specific career path (Blustein, 1992).

The sociocognitive and lifelong nature of career development means that planning is an absolutely vital component of all transition interventions. "Any particular career decision ... is merely a single instance in a lifetime of career choice points. Unless we plan to work with an increasingly dependent client again and again across the decades, *our professional responsibility is to assure that each person learns the* [career planning] *process*" (Mastie, 1994, p. 37).

Chance is a frequent influence in career development. Although it cannot be anticipated, good planning skills help individuals to positively capitalize on chance when it occurs (Cabral & Salomone, 1990).

Career planning is a skill that can be learned and practiced throughout life. It is an active process in which individuals take responsibility for (a) gathering and integrating information about themselves, occupations, and the labor market; (b) generating and evaluating alternatives; (c) making decisions and formulating plans of action; (d) implementing career plans; and (e) evaluating their results (Phillips, 1992; Szymanski, Hershenson, Ettinger, & Enright, 1996).

Effective transition programs must provide students with the basic planning skills for their current and future career decisions. Planning is more important now than ever due to the changing nature of the labor market and the probability that students will need to change jobs many times in the future (Ryan, 1996). Therefore, programs that place students into jobs without assuring that they have basic planning competencies may inadvertently impede the development of necessary life skills.

Interventions

A wide range of interventions are available to facilitate career development and transition. These are discussed according to the broad categories of planning; skill and experience; and beliefs, habits, and expectations.

Planning.   The planning realm includes the full range of career counseling and guidance activities, which should occur throughout the school
years (Herr & Cramer, 1992). Career counseling and guidance is supported
by tools that assist students in planning. These include career planning
systems (Taylor, 1988), assessment tools (Kapes, Mastie, & Whitfield,
1994), career classes and workshops (Isaacson & Brown, 1993), and career
portfolios (Ettinger, Conyers, Merz, & Koch, 1995).

Skill and Experience.   A variety of educational alternatives are in use
for school-to-work transition. These include apprenticeship; cooperative
education; school-based enterprises/entrepreneurship; internships and prac-
tica; community-based volunteerism; technical preparation; and simula-
tions, shops, and labs. After-school and part-time jobs are also important
(Smith & Rojewski, 1993).

Beliefs, Habits, and Expectations.   The contextual and mediational
factors of career development dictate additional types of transition interventions to promote eventual entry into work roles. This group, which may be
particularly important for people with disabilities and minorities, includes
chores at home and school (Victor, McCarthy, & Palmer, 1986), exposure
to working role models of same gender and race (Betz & Fitzgerald, 1995),
mentoring programs (Smith & Rojewski, 1993), and general exposure to
workers and work roles.

The Real World of Work

The real world of work is not an ideal place. Job stress, downsizing, and
decreasing numbers of good jobs are realities faced by students in transition
from school-to-work (Landy, 1992; Ryan, 1996). School-to-work transition
programs are not likely to change these trends (Apple & Zenk, 1996; Kantor,
1994).

It is important for transition programs to acknowledge the flawed nature
of the work world that students will enter. Students should be prepared to
survive in a complex economic environment in which jobs are not plentiful
and often not pleasant. In order to mitigate the potential negative effects of
jobs, a strong self-concept, planning skills, use of social support, positive
use of leisure time, and other life skills are important elements of transition
preparation.

ADDITIONAL CONSIDERATIONS FOR STUDENTS
WITH DISABILITIES, CHILDREN IN POVERTY,
AND MINORITIES

Students with disabilities, children living in poverty, and racial and ethnic minorities are heterogeneous groups of individuals. There is no special career development theory for these populations, nor should there be (Szymanski, Hershenson, Enright, et al., 1996). Although disability and ethnicity are individual characteristics, they do not determine an individual's career development. Similarly, although growing up in poverty often has negative impact, such effects are not guaranteed (Haveman & Wolfe, 1994). Nonetheless, the following issues warrant consideration: developmental concerns, societal beliefs, cultural appropriateness, and support services.

Developmental Concerns

Career development begins early in life. Work personality begins to develop in the preschool years and is influenced by family and early experiences (Hershenson, 1981). Disability can inhibit some of these early experiences (Anastasiow, 1986). For example, a disability might limit opportunities to play and learn interpersonal skills. In addition, children with disabilities might not be held fully responsible for chores at home or school, and thus might not learn responsibility (Szymanski, 1994). Similar early limitations may be present for children who grow up in poverty and violence.

Interests are learned (Mitchell & Krumbolz, 1990). Limited experiences associated with disability or poverty can restrict interest development. Similarly, the lack of same-race and same-gender role models (Betz & Fitzgerald, 1995) or role models with similar disabilities may impede outcome expectations and career self-efficacy.

The developmental concerns presented in this section suggest that transition planning must proceed with considerable caution, especially for students with disabilities, those raised in poverty, and minorities. Supplemental work experience or mentoring programs may be necessary to enable such students to widen their career options.

Societal Beliefs

Both people with disabilities and members of racial and ethnic minority groups are impacted by beliefs of others regarding their abilities and their place in society. Discrimination and stereotypes have long impeded the career mobility of racial and ethnic minorities (see Leong, 1995; Trueba et al., 1993) and people with disabilities (see Kiernan & Schalock, 1989; Weaver, 1991).

Discrimination and stereotypes can limit the availability of work. In addition, they can have limiting effects on individual outcome expectations. While not denying its real impact, transition planning should take an empowerment approach to identifying and mitigating the impact of discrimination and stereotypical thinking.

Cultural Appropriateness

Transition interventions must be culturally appropriate. This means that they must be grounded in the student's culture (Hawks & Muha, 1991) and use appropriate techniques (Betz & Fitzgerald, 1995). In addition, it is important not to assume that independence is a culturally valid goal for everyone. For students who identify primarily with collectivist beliefs (e.g., Asian, Native American), family and community interdependence may be more important than independence. Nonetheless, it is important to remember that ethnicity does not predict cultural beliefs.

Support Services

A variety of interventions are available to assist students with disabilities in school-to-work transition. Assistive technology (e.g., adaptive software, screen enlargers) and job accommodations (e.g., lowering a work table, restructuring the sequence of job tasks) can lessen the effect of the disability on job performance (Shane & Roberts, 1989; Szymanski, Hershenson, Ettinger, et al., 1996). Similarly, supported employment, which involves providing long-term instructional or other supports to assist students in job performance (Rusch, 1990), can enable students to perform jobs for which they might not otherwise qualify.

The provision of supports, whether through assistive technology, job accommodation, or supported employment, provides some unique challenges. It is important that the supports do not draw negative attention to the student. Therefore, supports should be designed to promote student rather than service-provider control, be as natural as possible in the work environment, and be least intrusive (Parker, Szymanski, & Hanley–Maxwell, 1989; Szymanski, Hershenson, Ettinger, et al., 1996).

Above all, it is important to consider all students in transition as individuals. If they have disabilities, live in poverty, or are racial or ethnic minorities, additional considerations may or may not apply. The considerations presented in this section only suggest possible concerns.

CONNECTING ASSESSMENT AND INTERVENTIONS WITH CAREER DEVELOPMENT

Transition interventions involve a wide range of possibilities. The connection of assessment and interventions requires the collection of information and development of hypotheses. As noted earlier, self assessment is a critical skill in career planning. Thus, the role of educational professionals is to facilitate self-assessment rather than to provide answers. Table 8.2 provides a description of assessment questions and possible interventions according to the five factors of the ecological model of career development; Table 8.3 describes application to four hypothetical students.

TABLE 8.2
School-to-Work Assessment Questions and Interventions According to the Five Factors of the Ecological Model of Career Development

Individual Factors	
Questions	*Possible Interventions*
What are current abilities, interests, and limitations?	Active student involvement in self-assessment
What values are considered important to career planning by the student and by the family?	Career portfolio
Has the student had sufficient experiences to foster interest development?	After school and summer work experience
How can individual abilities be enhanced?	Skill training
How can limitations be lessened?	Assistive technology, job accommodation

Context Factors	
Questions	*Possible Interventions*
How have family background and neighborhood influenced perception of opportunities and responsibilities?	Work role models, mentors, chores, work experience, community empowerment
How has the student's education facilitated or impeded realization of potential?	Remedial education
What are the financial incentives or disincentives perceived by the student and family as associated with work?	Inclusion of financial considerations in career planning

Mediating Factors

Questions	Possible Interventions
What do the student and family believe about the student's work related abilities?	Career counseling, successful work experiences
What outcomes do the student and family expect from transition related efforts?	Appropriate role models, mentors
What are the student's abilities in career planning?	Career classes and workshops, career counseling
What are the student's and family's cultural and religious beliefs that relate to education and work?	Culturally sensitive career planning, culturally sensitive career portfolios
How has the student been impacted by discrimination or stereotypes?	Advocacy

Work Environment Factors

Questions	Possible Interventions
What is the organizational culture of the target work environment? Does the student understand how to get along in such a culture?	Job analysis, social skills training
What are the tasks of the work environment?	Job analysis
What are the reinforcements?	Job analysis, planning for career advancement
How accessible is the environment for students with disabilities?	Assistive technology, job accommodation

Outcome Factors

Questions	Possible Interventions
How well do the student's skills and behaviors job meet the requirements of possible work environment?	Additional training, on-the-job training and socialization, social skills training
How well do the reinforcements of the work environment meet the student's needs?	Additional training for career advancement, possible job change
Does the student experience job related stress? How well is the student equipped to cope with job related stress?	Stress reduction techniques, wellness planning, encourage use of social support, leisure and lifestyle planning

Note. Adapted from Szymanski and Hershenson (in press). Copyright by Pro-Ed. Adapted with permission.

SUMMARY

School-to-work transition refers to a politically charged initiative related to debates about the connection between education and employment. In addition, the term refers to one aspect of the lifelong process of career development. The sections of this chapter addressed transition planning and intervention through consideration of a five-factor ecological model of career development.

There is little doubt that career development is influenced by individual, contextual, mediating, work environment, and outcome factors. When

TABLE 8.3
Application of Assessment Interventions to Four Hypothetical High School Juniors

Factors	Students			
	Maria	John	Jean	James
Individual				
Description	Latina, gifted in math and science	White, average student; uses wheelchair due to injuries from farm accident.	White, very social; moderate cognitive disability; difficulty learning new tasks and relating in new situations.	African-American, excellent student.
Potential interventions	Self-assessment, advanced courses.	Self-assessment; check to be sure that wheelchair is maximally functional; assess, and, if necessary, enhance independent living skills.	Self-assessment, functional curriculum, social skills instruction; assess, and, if necessary, enhance independent living skills.	Self-assessment, advanced courses.
Context				
Description	Large, relatively poor family, poor school district.	Lower middle-class farm family, oldest of four children; family had major crop lost in recent flood.	Only child in upper middle-class family; wealthy school district.	Oldest of two children; wealthy family, good schools.
Potential interventions	Check for exposure to adequate high school courses for college prep; consider enrichment or college access programs course work; consider family financial needs relating to student's contribution.	Assure course work is adequate for post secondary education; consider family financial needs relating to student's contribution.	No major contextual considerations.	No major contextual considerations.
Mediating				
Description	Some traditional and some majority culture beliefs; family expects her to help with chores and bills; no one in her family has gone to college; her family worries about the cost of education.	Had always planned to be a farmer, now interested in other agricultural occupations; still feels very self-conscious using wheelchair; family supports postsecondary education but worries about the cost.	Family hopes that Jean can work and live on her own some day; Jean wants a job working with people but knows she will need help to learn and keep a job.	Family has high expectations for occupational attainment; James' father, who is an important role model in his life, is a leader in the African-American community.

Factors	Students			
	Maria	John	Jean	James
Potential interventions	Individual and/or group counseling; career planning portfolio; financial aid counseling; exposure to ethnically similar, working women role models; career exploration; counseling with family if needed and desired.	Individual and/or group counseling; career planning portfolio; financial aid counseling; exposure to working role models with disabilities; career exploration; counseling with family if needed and desired.	Individual and/or group counseling; career planning portfolio; exposure to working role models with disabilities; career exploration; a variety of supervised work experiences; counseling with family if needed and desired.	Individual and or/group counseling; career planning portfolio; career exploration; counseling with family if needed and desired.
Environment				
Description and potential considerations	Maria and her family will only agree to college if it is close to home; what level of pay does Maria aspire to? What needs does she seek to meet in the work environment?	John is interested in an agricultural program; he needs a campus that is physically accessible and prefers to stay near home; what level of pay and needs does the work environment need to provide?	Jean and her family are concerned about her ability to understand the implicit and explicit requirements in work and living independently. They hope she will be able to receive services through a local supported employment agency.	James knows that students at some schools are not hospitable to African-American students. He also knows that he will need to be cognizant of the impact of race in the organizational culture of some potential employers.
Outcome				
Potential considerations	It will be important for Maria to retain the social support she currently has in order to be better able to deal with future job stress; healthy leisure activities also may guard against job stress.	Social support will also be important for John; because he has not yet developed healthy leisure habits, they should be encouraged.	Social support remains an important consideration for warding of potential job stress and detecting major work related problems; healthy leisure habits should be encouraged.	Social support and good leisure habits are important to mitigate the impact of potential job stress.

transition is considered through the lenses of these five factors, it is apparent that educational interventions should enlarge career possibilities and fortify students against the stresses that lay ahead. Indeed, the goal of transition services should be improved career development.

ACKNOWLEDGMENT

Preparation of this manuscript was supported, in part, by Grant H133B30052 from the National Institute on Disability and Rehabilitation Research of the U.S. Department of Education. However, the views expressed are those of the authors and not necessarily those of the funding agency.

REFERENCES

Apple, M. W., & Zenk, C. (1996). Is education to blame for our economic problems. In M. Apple (Ed.), *Cultural politics and education*. New York: Teachers College Press.

Anastasiow, N., J. (1986). *Development and disability: A psychobiological analysis for special educators*. Baltimore, MD: Paul H. Brookes.

Arbona, C. (1995). Theory and research on racial and ethnic minorities: Hispanic Americans. In F. T. L. Leong (Ed.), *Career development and vocational behavior of racial and ethnic minorities* (pp. 37–66). Mahwah, NJ: Lawrence Erlbaum Associates.

Bandura, A. (1982). Self-efficacy mechanism in human agency. *American Psychologist, 37*, 122–147.

Betz, N. E., & Fitzgerald, L. F. (1995). Career assessment and intervention with racial and ethnic minorities. In F. T. L. Leong (Ed.), *Career development and vocational behavior of racial and ethnic minorities* (pp. 263–279). Mahwah, NJ: Lawrence Erlbaum Associates.

Blustein, D. L. (1992). Applying current theory and research in career exploration to practice. The *Career Development Quarterly, 41*, 174–184.

Bronfenbrenner, U. (1988). *Foreword*. In A. R. Pence (Ed.), *Ecological research with children and families: From concepts to methodology* (pp. ix–xix). New York: Teachers College Press.

Brown, D. (1990). Trait and factor theory. In D. Brown, L. Brooks, & Associates (Eds.), *Career choice and development: Applying contemporary theories to practice* (2nd ed., pp. 13–36). San Francisco: Jossey-Bass.

Cabral, A. C., & Salomone, P. R. (1990). Chance and careers: Normative versus contextual development. *Career Development Quarterly, 39*, 5–17.

Carnevale, A. P. (1995). Enhancing skills in the new economy. In A. Howard (Ed.), *The changing nature of work* (pp. 238–251). San Francisco, CA: Jossey-Bass.

Dawis, R. V. (1994). The theory of work adjustment as convergent theory. In M. L. Savickas & R. W. Lent (Eds.), *Convergence in career development theories: Implications for science and practice* (pp. 33–43). Palo Alto, CA: CPP.

Ettinger, J., Conyers, L, Merz, M. A., & Koch, L. (1995). *Strategies and tools for counselors, educators, and employers* (RRTC Working Paper No. 3). Madison: University of Wisconsin–Madison, Rehabilitation Research and Training Center on Career Development and Advancement.

Fitzgerald, L. F., & Betz, N. E. (1994). Career development in cultural context: The role of gender, race, class, and sexual orientation. In M. L. Savickas & R. W. Lent (Eds.), *Convergence in career development theories: Implications for science and practice* (pp. 103–117). Palo Alto, CA: CPP.

Hackett, G., & Lent, R. W. (1994). Theoretical advances and current inquiry in career psychology. In S. D. Brown & R. W. Lent (Eds.), *Handbook of counseling psychology* (2nd ed., pp. 419–451). New York: Wiley.

Hall, D. T. (1986). Introduction: An overview of current career development theory, research, and practice. In D. T. Hall & Associates (Eds.), *Career development in organizations* (pp. 1–20). San Francisco: Jossey-Bass.

Hall, D. T. (1990). Career development theory in organizations. In D. Brown, L. Brooks, & Associates (Eds.), *Career choice and development: Applying contemporary theories to practice* (2nd ed., pp. 422–454). San Francisco: Jossey-Bass.

Halpern, A. (1992). Transition: Old wine in new bottles. *Exceptional Children, 58*, 202–211.

Haveman, R., & Wolfe, B. (1994). *Succeeding generations: In the effects of investments in children.* New York: Russell Sage Foundation.

Hawks, B. K., & Muha, D. (1991). Facilitating the career development of minorities: Doing it differently this time. *Career Development Quarterly, 39*, 251–260.

Herr, E. L., & Cramer, S. H. (1992). *Career guidance and counseling through the lifespan: Systematic approaches* (4th ed.). New York: Harper Collins.

Hershenson, D. B. (1981). Work adjustment, disability, and the three r's of vocational rehabilitation: A conceptual model. *Rehabilitation Counseling Bulletin, 25*, 91–97.

Holland, J. L. (1985). *Making vocational choices: A theory of vocational personalities and work environments* (2nd ed.). Englewood Cliffs, NJ: Prentice-Hall.

Holland, J. L. (1994). Separate but unequal is better. In M. L. Savickas & R. W. Lent (Eds.), *Convergence in career development theories: Implications for science and practice* (pp. 45–51). Palo Alto, CA: CPP.

Isaacson, L. E., & Brown, D. (1993). *Career information, career counseling, and career development* (5th ed.). Boston, MA: Allyn & Bacon.

Johnson, M. J., Swartz, J. L., & Martin, W. E., Jr. (1995). Application of psychological theories for career development with Native Americans. In F. T. L. Leong (Ed.), *Career development and vocational behavior of racial and ethnic minorities* (pp. 103–133). Mahwah, NJ: Lawrence Erlbaum.

Kantor, H. A. (1988). *Learning to earn: School, work, and vocational reform in California, 1880–1930.* Madison: University of Wisconsin Press.

Kantor, H. A. (1994). Managing the transition from school-to-work: The false promise of youth apprenticeship. *Teachers College Record, 95*, 442–461.

Kapes, J. T., Mastie, M. M., & Whitfield, E. A. (Eds.). (1994). *A counselor's guide to career assessment instruments* (3rd ed., pp. 31–40). Alexandria, VA: The National Career Development Association.

Kiernan, W. E., & Schalock, R. L. (Eds.). (1989). *Economics, industry, and disability: A look ahead.* Baltimore, MD: Paul H. Brookes.

LaFromboise, T., Coleman, H. L. K., & Gerton, J. (1993). Psychological impact of biculturalism: Evidence and theory. *Psychological Bulletin, 114*, 395–412.

Landy, F. J. (1992). Work design and stress. In G. P. Keita & S. L. Sauter (Eds.), *Work and well being: An agenda for the 1990s* (pp. 119–158). Washington, DC: American Psychological Association.

Lent, R. W., Brown, S. D., & Hackett, G. (1994). Toward a unifying social cognitive theory of career and academic interest, choice, and performance. *Journal of Vocational Behavior, 45*, 79–122.

Leong, F. T. L. (Ed.). (1995). *Career development and vocational behavior of racial and ethnic minorities.* Mahwah, NJ: Lawrence Erlbaum Associates.

Lofquist, L. H., & Dawis, R. V. (1991). *Essentials of person environment correspondence counseling.* Minneapolis: University of Minnesota Press.

Mastie, M. M. (1994). Using assessment instruments in career counseling: Career assessment as compass, credential, process and empowerment. In J. T. Kapes, M. M. Mastie, & E. A., Whitfield (Eds.), *A counselor's guide to career assessment instruments* (3rd ed., pp. 31–40). Alexandria, VA: The National Career Development Association.

Mitchell, L. K., & Krumboltz, J. D. (1990). Social learning approach to career decision making: Krumboltz's theory. In D. Brown, L. Brooks, & Associates (Eds.), *Career choice and development: Applying contemporary theories to practice* (2nd ed., pp. 145–196). San Francisco, CA: Jossey-Bass.

Myers, R. A., & Cairo, P. C. (1992). Counseling and career adjustment. In S. D. Brown & R. W. Lent (Eds.), *Handbook of counseling psychology* (2nd ed., pp. 549–580). New York: Wiley.

Osipow, S. H. (1994). Moving career theory into the twenty-first century. In M. L. Savickas & R. W. Lent (Eds.), *Convergence in career development theories: Implications for science and practice* (pp. 217–224). Palo Alto, CA: CPP.

Osipow, S. H., & Littlejohn, E. M. (1995). Toward a multicultural theory of career development: Prospects and dilemmas. In F. T. L. Leong (Ed.), *Career development and vocational behavior of racial and ethnic minorities* (pp. 251–261). Mahwah, NJ: Lawrence Erlbaum.

Osterman, P. (1995). The youth labor market: Skill deficiencies and public policy. In A. Howard (Ed.), *The changing nature of work* (pp. 211–237). San Francisco, CA: Jossey-Bass.

Parker, R. M., Szymanski, E. M., & Hanley-Maxwell, C. (1989). Ecological assessment in supported employment. *Journal of Applied Rehabilitation Counseling, 20*(3), 26–33.

Phillips, S. D. (1992). Career counseling: Choice and implementation. In S. D. Brown & R. W. Lent (Eds.), *Handbook of counseling psychology* (2nd ed., pp. 513–547). New York: Wiley.

Reskin, B., & Padvic, I. (1994). *Women and men at work.* Thousand Oaks, CA: Pine Forge.

Rothman, R. A. (1987). *Working: Sociological perspectives.* Englewood Cliffs, NJ: Prentice-Hall.

Rounds, J. B., & Tracey, T. J. (1990). From trait-and-factor to person-environment fit counseling: Theory and process. In W. B. Walsh & S. H. Osipow (Eds.), *Career counseling: Contemporary topics in vocational psychology* (pp. 1–44). Hillsdale, NJ: Lawrence Erlbaum Associates.

Rowe, W., Behrens, J. T., & Leach, M. M. (1995). Racial/ethnic identity and racial consciousness: Looking back and looking forward. In J. G. Ponterotto, J. M. Casas, L. A. Suzuki, & C. M. Alexander (Eds.), *Handbook of multicultural counseling* (pp. 218–235). Thousand Oaks, CA: Sage.

Rusch, F. R. (1990). *Supported employment: Models, methods, and issues.* Sycamore, IL: Sycamore.

Ryan, C. (1996). Work isn't what it used to be: Implications, recommendations, and strategies for vocational rehabilitation. *Journal of Rehabilitation, 61*(3), 12–20.

Savickas, M. L., & Lent, R. W. (Eds.). (1994). *Convergence in career development theories: Implications for science and practice.* Palo Alto, CA: CPP.

Schein, E. H. (1986). A critical look at current career development theory and research. In D. T. Hall & Associates (Eds.), *Career development in organizations* (pp. 310–331). San Francisco: Jossey-Bass.

Shane, H., & Roberts, G. (1989). Using applied technology to enhance work opportunities for persons with severe physical disabilities. In W. E. Kiernan & R. L. Schalock (Eds.), *Economics, industry, and disability: A look ahead* (pp. 127–140). Baltimore, MD: Paul Brookes.

Smith, C. L., & Rojewski, J. W. (1993). School-to-work transition: Alternatives for educational reform. *Youth and Society, 25*, 222–250.

Super, D. E. (1990). A life-span, life-space approach to career development. In D. Brown, L. Brooks, & Associates (Eds.), *Career choice and development: Applying contemporary theories to practice* (2nd ed., pp. 197–261). San Francisco, CA: Jossey-Bass.

Szymanski, E. M. (1994). Transition: Life-span, life-space considerations for empowerment. *Exceptional Children, 60*, 402–410.

Szymanski, E. M., & Hershenson, D. B. (in press). Career development of people with disabilities. In R. M. Parker & E. M. Szymanski (Eds.), *Rehabilitation counseling: Basics and beyond* (3rd ed.). Austin, TX: Pro-Ed.

Szymanski, E. M., Hershenson, D. B., Enright, M. S., & Ettinger, J. (1996). Career development theories, constructs, and research: Implications for people with disabilities. In E. M. Szymanski & R. M. Parker (Eds.), *Work and disability: Issues and strategies in career development and job placement* (pp. 79–126). Austin, TX: Pro-Ed.

Szymanski, E. M., Hershenson, D. B., Ettinger, J., & Enright, M. S. (1996). Career development interventions for people with disabilities. In E. M. Szymanski & R. M. Parker (Eds.), *Work and disability: Issues and strategies in career development and job placement* (pp. 255–276). Austin, TX: Pro-Ed.

Taylor, K. M. (1988). Advances in career-planning systems. In W. B. Walsh & S. H. Osipow (Eds.), *Career decision making* (pp. 137–211). Hillsdale, NJ: Lawrence Erlbaum Associates.

Trueba, H. T., Rodriguez, C., Zou, Y., & Cintron, J. (1993). *Healing multicultural America: Mexican immigrants rise to power in rural California.* London, UK: Falmer.

Victor, J., McCarthy, H., & Palmer, J. T. (1986). Career development of physically disabled youth. In E. L. Pan, S. Newman, T. Becker, & C. Vash (Eds.), *Annual review of rehabilitation* (Vol. 5, pp. 97–150). New York: Springer.

Vondracek, F. W., & Fouad, N. A. (1994). Developmental contextualism: An integrative framework for theory and practice. In M. L. Savickas & R. W. Lent (Eds.), *Convergence in career development: Implications for science and practice* (pp. 207–214). Palo Alto, CA: CPP.

Vondracek, F. W., Lerner, R. M., & Schulenberg, J. E. (1986). *Career development: A life-span developmental approach.* Hillsdale, NJ: Lawrence Erlbaum Associates.

Weaver, C. L. (1991). Incentives versus controls in federal disability policy. In C. L. Weaver (Ed.), *Disability and work: Incentives, rights, and opportunities* (pp. 3–17). Washington, DC: AEI.

Yelin, E. H. (1991). *Disability and the displaced worker.* New Brunswick, NJ: Rutgers University Press.

9

Reconnecting Schools
With Families
of Juvenile Offenders

Sonja K. Schoenwald
Scott W. Henggeler
Michael J. Brondino
John C. Donkervoet
Medical University of South Carolina

The consequences of criminal activity for juvenile offenders include costs to themselves, their families, their victims, and the broader community. Serious delinquency (as distinguished from status offenses such as truancy or incorrigibility) is interrelated with poor academic performance, school drop-out, substance use and abuse, precocious sexual activity, and future unemployment (Huizinga, Loeber & Thornberry, 1994). The youthful offender's educational and vocational development is interrupted, if not forfeited entirely, when incarceration occurs, as are opportunities to obtain employment (Farrington, 1987). Costs to the victim and victim's family include property damage, physical injury, pain and suffering, and negative psychological effects. Delinquency also impacts social and institutional contexts in which youths and families who are neither victims nor perpetrators participate. Delinquent behavior may, for example, compromise the quality of the classroom learning environment (Zigler, Taussig, & Black, 1992). Monetary and social costs to the community include the high expenses associated with arrest and incarceration, repairs to public property, and the loss of a potentially productive, tax-paying citizen. Moreover, youths who engage in serious antisocial behavior consume much of the resources of public service systems (e.g., juvenile justice, child mental health, child welfare, special education).

Attenuating or preventing further criminal activity in delinquent youths would benefit the youths, their families, their potential victims, and the communities in which they live. The bulk of the evidence from delinquency treatment research, however, indicates that traditional counseling and case-work, special school classes, and tutoring programs are not effective, and that deterrence fear-based programs (e.g., shock incarceration, boot camps) may exacerbate delinquent behavior (Lipsey, 1992). Among the reasons for the ineffectiveness of most treatment approaches are that they focus on only one or two of the several known predictors of delinquency (Borduin, 1994; Henggeler, 1991; Mulvey, Arthur, & Reppucci, 1990; Romig, Cleland, & Romig, 1989; Zigler et al., 1992). Recent research findings regarding the causes and treatment of such serious antisocial behavior as delinquency and adolescent substance abuse clearly point to the need for ecologically based interventions. Therefore, this chapter examines the implications of this research for the development of effective ecological treatments for serious antisocial behavior. More specifically, we examine Multisystemic Therapy (MST; Henggeler & Borduin, 1990), an ecological approach that has proven effective with chronic and violent juveniles in several clinical trials (Santos, Henggeler, Burns, Arana, & Meisler, 1995), and highlight the MST approach to reconnecting families of juvenile offenders with schools, and vice versa.

RESEARCH ON DELINQUENCY: CASUAL MODELS AND TREATMENTS

Serious Behavior Problems Are Multidetermined

Research has demonstrated that virtually all types of serious clinical problems in youth are multidetermined (Belsky, 1993; Elliott, Huizinga, & Ageton, 1985; Henggeler, in press). The most compelling evidence that antisocial behavior, such as delinquency and adolescent substance abuse, is multidetermined utilizes causal modeling methodologies to examine the relationships between multiple variables. Data analyses falling under the heading of causal modeling (e.g., path analysis, structural equation modeling) can be used to test various complex and theory-driven models and hypotheses. While a discussion of the conditions under which causal inference may or may not be warranted (e.g., use of longitudinal vs. cross-sectional data, existence of logical and empirical bases for cause–effect inferences, viability of alternative inferences from the same analyses; see Hoyle & Smith, 1994) is beyond the scope of this chapter, the term *causal* does not necessarily imply conclusive evidence regarding cause and effect relationships. Causal modeling studies indicate whether, and to what extent, a theoretical model being tested is consistent with relationships observed in the data. With this caveat in mind, we summarize some of the evidence from causal modeling studies linking family, school, peer, and community characteristics to delinquent behavior.

Causal Modeling Studies.   Causal modeling literatures in the areas of delinquency (for a review, see Henggeler, 1991) and adolescent substance abuse (Brook, Nomura, & Cohen, 1989; Dishion, Reid, & Patterson, 1988; Oetting & Beauvais, 1987) indicate that characteristics of individual family members, family relations (low affection, high conflict), parenting practices (harsh or inconsistent discipline, poor monitoring), peer relations (association with deviant peers), school functioning (low family–school bonding, poor performance), and neighborhood functioning (disorganization, transience, criminal subculture) predict serious antisocial behavior in youth. Although researchers have applied various theoretical orientations (e.g., social learning theory; strain, control, and social learning theory combined) and measures of key constructs in specifying their models to cross-sectional (Patterson & Dishion, 1985; Simcha-Fagan & Schwartz, 1986) or longitudinal (Elliott et al., 1985) data, the resulting models provide convergent evidence regarding the interrelatedness of family, peer, school, and community factors in the development and maintenance of delinquent behavior.

Thus, for example, decreased parental monitoring was linked with increased association with delinquent peers and increases in delinquent behaviors (Patterson & Dishion, 1985), and increases in strains at home predicted subsequent decreases in family and school involvement (Elliott et al., 1985). More recently, Ary and colleagues (Ary et al., 1994) tested a general model of the development of adolescent problem behavior—defined as antisocial behavior, high risk sex, academic failure, and substance use—using longitudinal data. Findings showed that negative family interactions at Time 1 predicted inadequate parenting practices and peer deviance at Time 2, which directly predicted involvement in problem behavior at Time 3.

School effects were also important in each of the models. For example, Elliot and his colleagues (1985) found that increases in school strain (i.e., the discrepancy between students' academic goals and achievement of their goals) at Time 1 were associated with decreases in school achievement at Time 2. As with family strain, increased school strain contributed to greater involvement with delinquent peers, which led to increases in delinquent behavior. Similarly, a cross-sectional model (LaGrange & White, 1985) linked low commitment to education with low community organization and high delinquent behavior. Finally, a cross-sectional study (Patterson & Dishion, 1985) linked poor academic skills with increased delinquent behaviors. Association with deviant peers was a primary contributor to delinquency in all of the studies. More recently, a comparison of three alternative models that posited direct causal links between early disruptive behavior, poor academic achievement, and delinquent behavior indicated that disruptive behavior in the first grade directly predicted delinquent behavior in adolescence, while poor school achievement was not a necessary causal factor (Tremblay et al., 1992).

In general, the results of the modeling studies support the interconnectedness of family, school, peer, and community factors, although the evidence linking academic performance per se to delinquency has not been as consistent as the evidence linking child behavior and family–school relations to delinquency. In addition, reviewers of research on the lasting impact of early childhood intervention for at-risk youth have noted that the establishment of effective home–school linkages may be as important to school success (Seitz, 1990) and delinquency prevention as the provision of academic/cognitive enhancements (Seitz, 1990; Zigler et al., 1992).

Thus, evidence from longitudinal studies is consistent with previously articulated theories regarding the importance of parent–school bonding to child development, in general (Comer, 1980), and in preventing delinquency, specifically (Hawkins & Weis, 1985; Hirschi, 1969). Moreover, findings from intervention studies suggest that the positive effects of family–school linkage can be obtained regardless of parent's level of education and that such effects may be more longstanding than intensive in-school remediation efforts. Rodick and Henggeler (1980), for example, conducted a four-group randomized trial comparing standard reading, non-intervention, the SMART program (a school-based program to enhance reading comprehension), and an intervention modeled after Rev. Jesse Jackson's PUSH for Excellence program. In the latter intervention, a worker visited the family and asked the parent to restructure the home environment for 1 hour per evening to facilitate joint parent–child attention to homework and other school-related activities (e.g., preparation for a test). Following the agreement to restructure the home environment, the worker called the family periodically to provide encouragement and support. Results showed that although youth in both intervention programs (SMART and PUSH) made gains in reading comprehension relative to youth in the regular reading and nonintervention groups, the PUSH group maintained gains 6 months after the interventions ended, whereas the SMART group did not.

Treatment Research

In light of the consistent findings regarding the multiple predictors of serious antisocial behavior in youth, one would expect that effective treatment approaches should be complex, multi faceted, and ecologically valid (i.e., intervening directly in the pertinent systems; Whittaker, Schinke, & Glichrist, 1986). To date, however, the focus of most treatments of delinquency have targeted limited segments of the youth's ecology.

As noted in the introduction to this chapter, traditional approaches to the treatment of juvenile delinquents implemented in juvenile justice, mental health, and school settings (e.g., one-on-one counseling, tutoring) have failed to impact chronic or serious delinquent behavior (for reviews see Borduin, 1994; Lipsey, 1992; Mulvey et al., 1990). Treatments developed and validated in academic settings have not fared much better with serious antisocial behavior. Empirically driven, structured, and skill-oriented treatments such as behavioral parent training and cognitive-behavior therapy have shown promise with milder forms of antisocial behavior, but have failed to produce long-term effects with serious juvenile offenders (Bank, Marlowe, Reid, Patterson, & Weinrott, 1991; Guerra & Slaby, 1990; Weisz, Walter, Weiss, Fernandez, & Mikow, 1990).

Recently, innovative models of service delivery such as individualized care, intensive case management, therapeutic foster care, and a variety of family preservation services have been implemented with delinquents, but little empirical evidence supports their effectiveness with this population (Schoenwald, Scherer, & Brondino, in press). Similarly, few empirical data support the effectiveness of school-based prevention programs that target delinquency and substance abuse (see Henggeler, in press; Kumpfer, 1989). Even if such programs were found to be effective, juvenile offenders are less likely to be recipients of such services because they are often missing from schools due to truancy, suspension, expulsion, or drop-out.

Ecological Approaches. Whereas the literature on ecological approaches to the conceptualization of child behavior problems is rich in theory and description, there is comparatively little empirical work to validate specific ecological models of treatment (for a review see Munger, 1991). Although a variety of tools to assist in the ecological assessment of child behavior and ideas for intervention have been developed, none have been empirically validated with youth presenting serious behavior problems. Moreover, a unified school of thought regarding the defining characteristics of ecologically based treatments for children and families has yet to emerge among proponents of psychological ecology (Lewin, 1951, as cited in Munger, 1991), behavioral ecology (Willems, 1977), environmental psychology (Stokols, 1978), and social ecology (Bronfenbrenner, 1979).

The theory of social ecology posited by Bronfenbrenner (1979) has spawned a number of approaches to address problems and issues in the study of child development (Pence, 1988). The only such approach to demonstrate lasting effects on serious antisocial behavior is multisystemic therapy (MST).

MULTISYSTEMIC THERAPY

Predicated on socioecological (Bronfenbrenner, 1979) and family systems models of behavior, the MST approach targets for intervention the known correlates of delinquent behavior in the interconnected systems (family, peer, school, neighborhood) in which the youth is embedded. MST is an intensive, time-limited, home- and family-focused treatment approach that has demonstrated effectiveness in randomized trials with chronic and violent juvenile offenders and their families (Borduin et al., 1995; Henggeler, Melton, & Smith, 1992; Henggeler, Melton, Smith, Schoenwald, & Hanley, 1993; Scherer, Brondino, Henggeler, Melton, & Hanley, 1994). In these studies, MST has been equally effective with families of different cultural backgrounds (African American and Caucasian) and socioeconomic status. Current projects are examining the effectiveness of MST with diagnosed substance-abusing and substance-dependent juvenile offenders (Henggeler, Pickrel, & Brondino, 1995); with gang-affiliated juvenile offenders, many of whom are Hispanic (Thomas, 1994); and as an alternative for youth about to be hospitalized for homicidal, suicidal, and psychotic behavior (Henggeler & Rowland, in press). MST has also been effective with small samples of maltreating parents (Brunk, Henggeler, & Whelan, 1987) and adolescent sex offenders (Borduin, Henggeler, Blaske, & Stein, 1990). A summary of MST treatment principles and intervention strategies is presented next. For a more extensive discussion of these issues, and of the empirical and theoretical underpinnings of MST, see the clinically oriented volume that describes MST in detail (Henggeler & Borduin, 1990; Henggeler, Schoenwald, Borduin, Rowland, & Cunningham, in press). In addition, the Multisystemic Strategic Procedures Manual (Henggeler et al., 1994) presents specific guidelines for implementing MST for serious problems in youth.

Translating the Theory of Social Ecology Into a Treatment Model

Consistent with Bronfenbrenner's (1979) theory of social ecology, MST views individuals as being nested within a complex of interconnected systems that encompass individual (e.g., biological, cognitive), family, and extrafamilial (e.g., peer, school, neighborhood) factors. Behavior problems can be maintained by problematic transactions within or between any one or combination of these systems (e.g., family–school, family–peer, and peer–school mesosystems). Thus, MST shares with other ecological approaches the assumption that multiple aspects of people's ecology impacts their behavior, and vice versa. MST is a treatment model in which this assumption is operationally defined in terms of nine treatment principles. The treatment principles guide the development of case conceptualization and intervention strategies in accordance with what is known about the correlates and causes of serious antisocial behavior. Thus, MST directly targets for change those factors within the juvenile offender's family, peer, school, and neighborhood that are contributing to that juvenile's antisocial behavior (Henggeler & Borduin, 1990). Moreover, to optimize the ecological validity of interventions (Henggeler, Schoenwald, & Pickrel, 1995), MST is conducted directly in the natural ecologies (e.g., home, school, community) of the youth and family.

Model of Service Delivery. The provision of MST is consistent with the family preservation model of service delivery. Family preservation is based on the philosophy that the most effective and ethical route to helping children and youth is through helping their families. Thus, families are seen as valuable resources, even when they are characterized by serious and multiple needs. While the particular practice models that characterize family preservation programs vary in terms of treatment objectives, theoretical orientation, duration and intensity, critical service delivery characteristics are shared (Nelson & Landsman, 1992). These characteristics include low caseloads, delivery of services in community settings (e.g., home, school, neighborhood center), time-limited duration of treatment, 24 hours per day and 7 days per week availability of therapists, and provision of comprehensive services. With respect to MST, specifically, caseload size has averaged from four to six families per counselor, and duration of treatment has ranged from 3 to 5 months. Thus, a team of three counselors provides service for approximately 50 families each year. Depending on the stage of treatment and extant crises, sessions may be held every day or as infrequently as once a week. Emphasis is placed on the efficient use of treatment sessions, each typically lasting 30 to 75 minutes and concluding with the assignment of explicit tasks related to the identified goals.

MST Principles

Principles.   The MST principles are enumerated below. Detailed descriptions of these principles, and examples that illustrate the translation of the principles into specific intervention strategies are provided in the clinical volumes (Henggeler & Borduin, 1990; Henggeler et al., in press) and manual (Henggeler et al., 1994).

1. The primary purpose of assessment is to understand the fit between the identified problems and their broader systemic context.
2. Therapeutic contacts should emphasize the positive and should use systemic strengths as levers for change.
3. Interventions should be designed to promote responsible behavior and decrease irresponsible behavior among family members.
4. Interventions should be present-focused and action-oriented, targeting specific and well-defined problems.
5. Interventions should target sequences of behavior within and between multiple systems.
6. Interventions should be developmentally appropriate and fit the developmental needs of the youth.
7. Interventions should be designed to require daily or weekly effort by family members.
8. Intervention efficacy is evaluated continuously from multiple perspectives.
9. Interventions should be designed to promote treatment generalization and long-term maintenance of therapeutic change.

These principles inform therapists' efforts to set the stage for lasting therapeutic gains by focusing on the empowerment of families through the mobilization of indigenous child, family, and community resources. Thus, the overriding goal of MST is to empower parents (parent, and family, is broadly defined to include the adult, or adults, who serves as the youth's primary parent figure or guardian) with the skills and resources needed to independently address the inevitable difficulties that arise in rearing teenagers and to empower youth to cope with family, peer, school, and neighborhood problems.

Interventions. The choice of modality used to address a particular problem is based largely on the empirical literature on its efficacy. As such, MST interventions are usually adapted and integrated from pragmatic, problem-focused treatments that have at least some empirical support. These include strategic family therapy (Haley, 1976), structural family therapy (Minuchin, 1974), behavioral parent training (Munger, 1993), and cognitive behavior therapies (Kendall & Braswell, 1993). In addition, and as appropriate, biological contributors to identified problems are identified and psychopharmacological treatment is integrated with psychosocial treatment.

Initial therapy sessions identify the strengths and weaknesses of the adolescent, the family, and their transactions with extrafamilial systems (e.g., peers, friends, school teachers, principals, parents' workplace, social service agencies). The treatment plan is designed in collaboration with family members and is, therefore, family-driven rather than therapist-driven. Problems identified conjointly by family members and the therapist are explicitly targeted for change, and the strengths of each system are used to facilitate such change. Although specific strengths and weaknesses can vary widely from family to family, one or more of the aforementioned determinants of serious behavior problems are usually implicated in the identified problems. Within a context of support and skill building, the therapist places developmentally appropriate demands on the adolescent and family for responsible behavior. Treatment sessions focus on facilitating attainment of goals that were defined conjointly by family members and the therapist. As substantive progress is made toward meeting one goal, treatment sessions incorporate additional goals. In addition, treatment interventions have the flexibility to be relatively intense, in terms of both time in treatment (e.g., multiple sessions per week) and task orientation of treatment sessions (e.g., explicit goal setting and extensive homework assignments).

At the family level, adolescents presenting serious clinical problems and their parents frequently display high rates of conflict and low levels of affection. Similarly, parents or guardians frequently disagree regarding discipline strategies; and their own personal problems (e.g., substance abuse, depression, marital problems) often interfere with their ability to provide necessary parenting. Family interventions in MST often attempt to provide the parent(s) with the resources needed for effective parenting and for developing increased family structure and cohesion. Such interventions might include introducing systematic reward and discipline systems (e.g., Munger, 1993), prompting parents to communicate effectively with each other about adolescent problems, problem solving day-to-day conflicts, addressing marital problems that interfere with parenting practices, and developing social support networks in the parents' natural ecology (e.g., neighborhood, workplace, church, extended family, community organizations). The key to effective interventions, however, is determining and addressing the barriers to effective parenting. Although typical mental health services address parenting difficulties by providing structured parenting classes to enhance parental knowledge, such interventions rarely address the core barriers to effective parenting. In families of youth presenting serious clinical problems, the more substantive core barriers are likely to include parental substance abuse, parental psychopathology, low social support, high stress, marital (or adult relationship) conflict, and poverty. These barriers must be successfully resolved before enhanced parenting knowledge can be used to influence youth behavior.

At the peer level, a frequent goal of treatment for adolescents presenting serious clinical problems is to decrease their involvement with deviant and drug using peers, and to increase association with prosocial peers (e.g., through church youth groups, organized athletics, afterschool activities, employment). Consistent with MST principles, even peer interventions are usually designed to facilitate the capacity of the parent or caregiver to initiate and monitor changes in the youth's peer interactions over time (see Principle 9, regarding treatment generalization). Thus, interventions aimed at changing peer groups and peer interactions often consist of helping parents to actively support and encourage associations with nonproblem peers (e.g., meeting peers and their parents, monitoring peer activities, facilitating opportunities to meet prosocial peers, providing transportation, privileges for increased contact with prosocial peers) and to strongly discourage associations with deviant peers (e.g., applying significant sanctions). Likewise, with the assistance of the therapist, the parents develop strategies to monitor and promote the youth's school performance/vocational functioning. As discussed in the next section, typically included in this domain are strategies for helping parents to open and maintain positive communication lines with teachers, and restructure afterschool hours to promote academic efforts.

Finally, although the emphasis of treatment is on systemic change, there are also situations in which individual interventions can facilitate behavioral change in the adolescent or parents. Interventions in these situations generally focus on modifying the individual's social perspective-taking skills, belief system, and motivational system, and encouraging the youth to deal assertively with negative peer pressures. Similarly, individual interventions for parents may address issues such as parental depression and lack of positive social support for the parent.

Treatment is terminated when evidence from multiple sources (e.g., youth, parent, school, probation officer) indicates that: (a) the youth has no significant clinical problems and the family has been functioning reasonably well for at least 1 month; (b) the youth is making reasonable educational/vocational efforts; (c) the youth is involved with prosocial peers and is minimally involved with problem peers; and (d) the clinician and supervisor feel that the parent(s) have the knowledge, motivation, and resources needed for handling subsequent problems. Treatment may also be terminated when some of the preceding goals have been met, but treatment has reached a point of diminishing returns for therapy time invested.

MST: RECONNECTING SCHOOLS AND FAMILIES OF JUVENILE OFFENDERS

Assessment Within and Beyond the School Ecology

To understand the fit of the youth's behavior with school-related factors (Principle 1), the MST therapist seeks information regarding the ecology within the school setting and the interplay of school-related factors with the broader ecological context of the youth (e.g., home life, peer relations). The major areas assessed include: (a) the intellectual/academic abilities of the individual youth, (b) psychological factors influencing school behavior (e.g., anxiety, fear of failure, trauma-related symptoms), (c) learning environment (e.g., competencies, teaching styles, and interpersonal behavior of school personnel; physical and social characteristics of the classroom; physical characteristics of the school), (d) family factors (e.g., parental expectations for school attendance and performance, structuring home life to promote education), and (e) family–school linkage (e.g., quality and quantity of parental involvement with school personnel, parental support of teachers).

The MST approach to the assessment of school-related issues that contribute to the development or maintenance of a youth's behavior problems begins with the parent(s). Prior to the initiation of contact with the school, the MST therapist solicits parental perceptions of the five factors just enumerated. In addition, the therapist obtains the parent's perspective on the child's difficulties at school and solutions that have been attempted at school and at home. Next, the MST therapist obtains the perspectives of school personnel with respect to these issues. This information-gathering process may include the child's teacher(s), guidance counselors, coaches, and school staff who may have less regular contact with the adolescent (such as lunchroom monitors, administrators), and often involves therapist observation of the child in different settings. Information about behavioral variations that occur in different classrooms, parts of the day, or subjects, may help identify adults, peers, abilities, and interests that can be used to develop an effective plan for attenuating problem behavior.

Setting the Ecological Stage for Successful Intervention.   In the interest of establishing truly collaborative relationships with the key figures in all crucial systems in the youth's ecology, MST therapists are careful to respect the hierarchy and operating procedures of the school when initiating contact. Permission to visit the school and talk with teachers is sought from the school principal and other administrators whose decisions influence both school policies, in general, and the life of the referred child, specifically. Thus, for example, assistant principles often serve disciplinary functions in middle schools and high schools, and should be contacted if this is the case. When access to administrators, teachers, and coaches, for example, is approved, the MST therapist obtains information from as many sources as possible.

The MST therapist approaches the teacher as a fellow professional who has a great deal of expertise, particularly in the school environment. Thus, for example, meetings are scheduled at the teacher's convenience, and the therapist may take a "one-down" stance during such meetings (Henggeler & Borduin, 1990). Interventions should require a limited amount of the teacher's time and effort. Time-consuming interventions are not likely to be implemented consistently given the multiple, simultaneous demands of classroom teaching. When in-class interventions are critical to attaining MST treatment goals, it is essential that the teacher(s) participate fully in the development of the goals and parameters for the intervention. If teacher reluctance to participate is detected, the MST therapist seeks to understand and rectify the barriers to participation. These barriers may be a result of relative inexperience or lack of skill with the intervention, a history of negative experiences with externally imposed interventions developed by "experts," or a history of negative interactions with the child or the child's family. The respectful stance of the MST therapist, inclusion of the teacher in intervention planning, and minimization of teacher time and effort required to implement the intervention are often sufficient to overcome the first two barriers. Strategies for addressing problematic teacher–family interactions are discussed in the context of the case example presented subsequently. In many cases, emphasizing goals shared by the teacher, the family, and the therapist (e.g., decreasing disruptions in the classroom) facilitates teacher participation.

Case Illustration

In this section, a case example is used to facilitate discussion of issues related to the assessment and delivery of school-related interventions from an MST perspective.

Jason, a 15-year-old ninth grader, had failed the ninth grade for his second time when he was referred for MST. He displayed significant behavioral problems since the age of 12 and was suspended several times. Jason's troublesome behaviors at school included oppositional responses to teacher requests, refusal to follow through with schoolwork, verbal disruption of the classroom, repeated truancy, and occasional threats to teachers. Jason also fought with peers, and his best friends were a group of difficult children (i.e., children who would get in trouble for fighting, verbal abuse of the teacher, and oppositionality). Jason had recently been charged with vandalism.

Individual Factors. In assessing the fit between these behaviors and the total ecology (Principle 1), the therapist identified several aspects of Jason's educational experience that appeared to contribute to his troublesome behavior at school. A review of Jason's records (which included scores from intelligence and educational testing completed 2 years prior to referral) suggested that he possessed average intelligence and was able to maintain pace with his agemates. When educational testing data are not available, the MST therapist may recommend that testing be performed to rule out the possibility that significant intellectual deficits are interfering with academic performance and to identify areas in which the child may require additional assistance. The therapist also determined, during the course of family, individual, and school meetings, that Jason's academic performance problems did not appear to stem from some type of psychological difficulty (e.g., anxiety, fear of failure, trauma-related symptoms).

Classroom Factors. In talking with Jason's teachers, the therapist learned that Jason's behavior was somewhat manageable in some classrooms, and quite obstreperous in others. The therapist arranged to observe Jason in several classrooms, and observed that his behavior was most obnoxious in the presence of a group of students who egged each other into frivolity, inattention, and acting out. Jason's conflict with teachers occurred primarily when Jason was reprimanded for "cutting up" with his classmates.

Thus, the therapist identified a consistent correlate of Jason's obnoxious behavior with peers and teachers and, on the basis of this evidence, tentatively ruled out cognitive ability and psychological factors as major contributors to Jason's behavior problems.

Family–School Linkage. Next, the MST therapist began to develop an intervention plan with Jason's parents and pertinent school personnel. At this juncture, the therapist found that communications between Jason's parents and the school had become quite contentious. Consistent with the MST emphasis on empowering families and facilitating long-term generalization of treatment gains (Principle 9), the MST therapist tried to forge a family–school alliance rather than proceeding with intervention plans from the position of "go between." As often occurs, the process of re-establishing productive family–school communications was met with significant reluctance on both sides. Parent(s) and school personnel may perceive one another as responsible for the child's behavior problems; each may implicitly or explicitly demand, "Why can't *you* make this child behave, that's *your* job." Conflictual interactions can lead to active avoidance of parent–teacher interactions. Alternatively, parent–school contact occurs primarily around issues of discipline, suspension, or expulsion, which further reinforces a negative pattern of family–school interactions.

To establish or re-establish a family–school alliance, the MST therapist should be aware of common obstacles that may inhibit the development of positive family–school bonds. A history of conflictual parent–school interactions is only one such obstacle. Parents may avoid contacting the school because they had negative experiences in school themselves, feel intimidated by school officials, have difficulty understanding the language or jargon used in reports sent home or in meetings at school, face practical difficulties such as lack of transportation, child care, or leave time from work, or face personal difficulties that render social interaction difficult, such as anxiety or depression. Some parents, on the basis of information obtained only from their child, may also feel that the school is "wrong" and that the child/parent is "right."

The therapist seeks to understand the perspectives of the parents and school personnel, and armed with that understanding tailors strategies for overcoming the barriers to the particular family and family–school situation at hand. When parents feel intimidated or confused by school personnel, the therapist often plays a more active role in initial parent–school meetings by, for example, modeling courteous but assertive requests for clarification. The therapist quickly shifts the responsibility for such communications to the parent and school personnel, however, so as to facilitate the aims of long-term generalization and parental empowerment. When anger or attitudinal bias ("it's all your fault") on the part of either party (parent and/or school personnel) interferes with successful parent–school communication, interventions may include strategizing about what the parents will do if difficulties arise and role-playing possible scenarios to identify problematic topics and interactions and to practice reasonable responses to those scenarios. Similarly, the MST therapist may meet with school personnel who appear to avoid communication, exacerbate conflict, and exhibit attitudinal biases regarding a youth and family.

With Jason's father, the therapist developed a premeeting role-play that mimicked the (real-life) situation in which the father was accused of being a "bad parent" and given unsolicited advice on how to raise his children. Through consistent practice (i.e., three sessions, on subsequent days, lasting 1 hour each), Jason's father was increasingly able to complete the role-played scenarios without overt displays of anger. He participated in two strategy planning meetings with Jason's teachers that included the MST therapist. In the second meeting, the MST therapist consciously limited her participation to allow the parents and teacher to arrive at mutually desired solutions.

Over the course of these meetings, problem areas requiring attention at school and home were identified. Initially, two intervention strategies were implemented: One targeted the negative influence of antisocial peers on Jason's classroom behavior, and the other focused on linking Jason's behavior at school with consequences at home. With respect to the first, teachers presiding over classrooms in which Jason exhibited significant behavior problems negotiated seating arrangements so that Jason was detached from antisocial peers.

Connecting Behavior at School With Consequences at Home. A plan was developed in which Jason would receive significant consequences at home for his behavior at school. A positive report sent home by a teacher (i.e., lack of misbehavior and active participation) earned Jason a maximum of 30 minutes of Nintendo per evening. If Jason received a negative report, he was required to spend an additional 30 minutes studying and 30 minutes doing chores that evening. In addition to connecting consequences at home with behavior at school, the MST therapist worked directly with the family to identify barriers at home that might prevent Jason's completion of his homework. The therapist worked with the family to ensure that both a place and time for homework completion was provided during every evening. The family agreed that all televisions and radios would be turned off for the hour after dinner; this agreement presented a marked change for all family members (siblings included), as the family was accustomed to having the television on from morning until bedtime. In addition, his parents would read or work quietly during that time. In this way, distractions were minimized and Jason's parents demonstrated, concretely, the value they placed on their son's academic performance. As the therapist expected, on the basis of initial and ongoing assessment of Jason's family and the subsystems that comprised it, issues related to parental management of the siblings' displeasure about the television policy surfaced, as did differences between Jason's parents regarding the best way to manage the siblings during the quiet hour. In consultation with the parents, intervention strategies designed to increase inter-parental consistency and parental capacity to effectively manage sibling relations were implemented.

Initially, the family–school interventions were quite successful, as indicated by reports from teachers, parents, and Jason (see Principle 8). However, despite teacher consistency in keeping Jason and his problematic peers separated, Jason and the peers found new ways to act up in class. Together with the therapist, the parents decided that Jason's mother (she was not employed outside the home at the time) would attend school with Jason, sitting beside him in each class he had trouble. By the beginning of the third day, Jason's level of discomfort with this arrangement was so great that he agreed to attend to his responsibilities more consistently and began to do so. In addition, the therapist and Jason's parents began to explore interventions to decrease Jason's association with antisocial peers in school (interventions implemented earlier in treatment had successfully reduced his involvement with antisocial peers after school and on weekends).

CONCLUSION

The MST approach to reconnecting schools with families of juvenile offenders is informed both by social ecological theory and by empirical findings regarding the correlates and causes of serious antisocial behavior. An ongoing clinical trial of substance abusing/dependent adolescent offenders (Henggeler, Pickrel, & Brondino, 1995) is providing opportunities to examine the associations between improvements in family functioning, improvements in school–family linkage and school performance, and reductions in antisocial behavior. Given MST's success in sustaining reductions in recidivism and drug use and in improving family functioning

(Borduin et al., 1995; Henggeler et al., 1992; Henggeler et al., 1993), it is expected that these data will demonstrate positive and interrelated effects of MST interventions. Such interventions include, but extend beyond, the school ecology to address factors affecting family functioning, family–school linkages, and the peer and community contexts in which youth and families undertake educational pursuits.

ACKNOWLEDGMENT

Preparation of this manuscript was supported, in part, by National Institute on Drug Abuse Grant DA-08029 and by National Institute of Mental Health Grants MH-51852 and R24MH53558-01.

REFERENCES

Ary, D. V., Duncan, T. E., Biglan, A., Metzler, C. W., Noell, J. W., & Smolkowski, K. (1994, November). *A social context model of the development of adolescent problem behavior.* Paper presented at the annual convention of the Association for the Advancement of Behavior Therapy, San Diego, CA.

Bank, L., Marlowe, J. H., Reid, J. B., Patterson, G. R., & Weinrott, M. R. (1991). A comparative evaluation of parent-training interventions for families of chronic delinquents. *Journal of Abnormal Child Psychology, 19,* 15–33.

Belsky, J. (1993). Etiology of child maltreatment: A developmental-ecological analysis. *Psychological Bulletin, 114,* 413–434.

Borduin, C. M. (1994). Innovative models of treatment and service delivery in the juvenile justice system. *Journal of Clinical Child Psychology, 23(Suppl.),* 19–25.

Borduin, C. M., Henggeler, S. W., Blaske, D. M., & Stein, R. (1990). Multisystemic treatment of adolescent sexual offenders. *International Journal of Offender Therapy and Comparative Criminology, 34,* 105–113.

Borduin, C. M., Mann, B. J., Cone, L., Henggeler, S. W., Fucci, B. R., Blaske, D. M., & Williams, R. A. (1995). Multisystemic treatment of serious juvenile offenders: Long-term prevention of criminality and violence. *Journal of Consulting and Clinical Psychology, 63,* 569–578.

Bronfenbrenner, U. (1979). *The ecology of human development: Experiences by nature and design.* Cambridge, MA: Harvard University Press.

Brook, J. S., Nomura, C., & Cohen, P. (1989). A network of influences on adolescent drug involvement: Neighborhood, school, peer, and family. *Genetic, Social, and General Psychology Monographs, 115,* 125–145.

Brunk, M., Henggeler, S. W., & Whelan, J. P. (1987). A comparison of multisystemic therapy and parent training in the brief treatment of child abuse and neglect. *Journal of Consulting and Clinical Psychology, 55,* 311–318.

Comer, J. P. (1980). *School power.* New York: The Free Press.

Dishion, T. J., Reid, J. B., & Patterson, G. R. (1988). Empirical guidelines for a family intervention for adolescent drug use. *Journal of Chemical Dependency, 2,* 189–224.

Elliott, D. S., Huizinga, D., & Ageton, S. S. (1985). *Explaining delinquency and drug use.* Beverly Hills, CA: Sage.

Farrington, D. P. (1987). Early precursors of frequent offending. In J.Q. Wilson & G.C. Loury (Eds.), *From children to citizens: Vol. 3. Families, schools, and delinquency prevention* (pp. 27–50). New York: Springer Verlag.

Guerra, N. G., & Slaby, R. G. (1990). Cognitive mediators of aggression in adolescent offenders: 2. Intervention. *Developmental Psychology, 26,* 269–277.

Haley, J. (1976). *Problem-solving therapy.* San Francisco: Jossey-Bass.

Hawkins, J. D., & Weis, J. G. (1985). The social development model: An integrated approach to delinquency prevention. *Journal of Primary Prevention, 6,* 73–95.

Henggeler, S. W. (1991). Multidimensional causal models of delinquent behavior. In R. Cohen & A. Siegel (Eds.), *Context and development* (pp. 211 – 231). Hillsdale, NJ: Lawrence Erlbaum Associates.

Henggeler, S. W. (in press). The development of effective drug abuse services for youth. *Untitled volume developed by the Milbank Foundation and National Institutes of Drug Abuse (NIDA).* New York: Blackwells—North America.

Henggeler, S. W., & Borduin, C. M. (1990). *Family therapy and beyond: A multisystemic approach to treating the behavior problems of children and adolescents.* Pacific Grove, CA: Brooks/Cole.

Henggeler, S. W., Melton, G. B., & Smith, L. A. (1992). Family preservation using multisystemic therapy: An effective alternative to incarcerating serious juvenile offenders, *Journal of Consulting and Clinical Psychology, 60,* 953–961.

Henggeler, S. W., Melton, G. B., Smith, L. A., Schoenwald, S. K., & Hanley, J. (1993). Family preservation using multisystemic therapy: Long-term follow-up to a clinical trial with serious juvenile offenders. *Journal of Child and Family Studies, 2,* 283–293.

Henggeler, S. W., Pickrel, S. G., & Brondino, M. J. (1995). *Multisystemic therapy of substance abusing/dependent delinquents: Outcomes for drug use, criminality, and out-of-home placement at posttreatment and 6-month follow-up.* Manuscript submitted for publication.

Henggeler, S. W., & Rowland, M. D. (in press). Investigating alternatives to hospitalization of youth presenting psychiatric emergencies. *Emergency Psychiatry.*

Henggeler, S. W., Schoenwald, S. K., Borduin, C. M., Rowland, M. R., & Cunningham, P. B. (in press). *Multisystemic treatment for antisocial behavior in youth.* New York: Guilford.

Henggeler, S. W., Schoenwald, S. K., & Pickrel, S. G. (1995). Multisystemic therapy: Bridging the gap between university- and community-based treatment. *Journal of Consulting and Clinical Psychology, 63,* 709 – 717.

Henggeler, S. W., Schoenwald, S. K., Pickrel, S. G., Brondino, M. J., Borduin, C. M., & Hall, J. A. (1994). *Treatment manual for family preservation using multisystemic therapy.* Columbia: South Carolina Health and Human Services Finance Commission.

Hirschi, T. (1969). *Causes of delinquency.* Berkeley: University of California Press.

Hoyle, R. A., & Smith, G. T. (1994). Formulating clinical research hypotheses as structural equation models: A conceptual overview. *Journal of Consulting and Clinical Psychology, 62,* 429–440.

Huizinga, D., Loeber, R., & Thornberry, T. P. (1994). *Urban delinquency and substance abuse. Initial findings* (Office of Juvenile Justice and Delinquency Prevention; pp. 1–25). Washington, DC: U.S. Department of Justice.

Kendall, P. C., & Braswell, L. (1993). *Cognitive-behavioral therapy for impulsive children* (2nd ed.). New York: Guilford.

Kumpfer, K. L. (1989). Prevention of alcohol and drug abuse: A critical review of risk factors and prevention strategies. In D. E. Shaffer, I. Philips, & N. B. Enzer (Eds.), *Prevention of mental disorders, alcohol, and other drug use in children and adolescents* (pp. 309–371). Rockville, MD: U.S. Department of Health and Human Services, Office for Substance Abuse Prevention.

LaGrange, R. L., & White, H. R. (1985). Age differences in delinquency: A test of theory. *Criminology, 23,* 19–45.

Lipsey, M. W. (1992). Juvenile delinquency treatment: A meta-analytic inquiry into the variability of effects. In T. D. Cook, H. Cooper, D. S. Cordray, H. Hartman, L. V. Hedges, R. J. Light, T. A. Louis, & F. Mosteller (Eds.), *Meta-analysis for explanation: A casebook* (pp. 83–127). New York: Russell Sage.

Minuchin, S. (1974). *Families and family therapy.* Cambridge, MA: Harvard University Press.

Mulvey, E. P., Arthur, M. A., & Reppucci, N. D. (1990). *Review of programs for the prevention and treatment of delinquency.* Washington, DC: U.S. Government Printing Office, Office of Technology Assessment.

Munger, R. L. (1991). *Child mental health practice from the ecological perspective.* New York: University Press of America.

Munger, R. L. (1993). *Changing children's behavior quickly.* Lanham, MD: Madison Books.

Nelson, K. E., & Landsman, M. J. (1992). *Alternative models of family preservation: Family-based services in context.* Springfield, IL: Charles C. Thomas.

Oetting, E. R., & Beauvais, F. (1987). Peer cluster theory, socialization characteristics, and adolescent drug use: A path analysis. *Journal of Counseling Psychology, 34,* 205–213.

Patterson, G. R., & Dishion, T. M. (1985). Contributions of families and peers to delinquency. *Criminology, 23,* 63–79.

Pence, A. (Ed.). (1988). *Ecological research with children and families: From concepts to methodology.* New York: Teachers College Press.

Rodick, J. D., & Henggeler, S. W. (1980). The short-term and long-term amelioration of academic and motivational deficiencies among low-achieving inner-city adolescents. *Child Development, 51,* 1126–1132.

Romig, D. A., Cleland, C., & Romig, J. (1989). *Juvenile delinquency: Visionary approaches.* Columbus, OH: Merrill.

Santos, A. B., Henggeler, S. W., Burns, B. J., Arana, G. W., & Meisler, N. (1995). Research on field-based services: Models for reform in the delivery of mental health care in difficult clinical populations. *The American Journal of Psychiatry, 152*(8), 1111–1123.

Scherer, D. G., Brondino, M. J., Henggeler, S. W., Melton, G. B., & Hanley, J. H. (1994). Multisystemic family preservation with rural and minority families of serious adolescent offenders: Preliminary findings from a controlled clinical trial. *Journal of Emotional and Behavioral Disorders, 2,* 198–206.

Schoenwald, S. K., Scherer, D. G., & Brondino, M. J. (in press). Effective community-based treatments for serious juvenile offenders. In S.W. Henggeler & A.B. Santos (Eds.), *Innovative models of mental health treatment for "difficult to treat" populations.* Washington, DC: American Psychiatric Press.

Seitz, V. (1990). Intervention programs for impoverished children: A comparison of educational and family support models. *Annals of Child Development, 7,* 73–103.

Simcha-Fagan, O., & Schwartz, J. E. (1986). Neighborhood and delinquency: An assessment of contextual effects. *Criminology, 24,* 667–703.

Stokols, D. (1978). Environmental psychology. *Annual Review of Psychology, 29,* 253–295.

Thomas, C. R. (1994). *Island Youth Programs.* Galveston: University of Texas Medical Branch.

Tremblay, R. E., Masse, B., Perron, D., & Leblanc, M., Schwartzman, A. E., & Ledingham, J. E. (1992). Early disruptive behavior, poor school achievement, delinquent behavior, and delinquent personality: Longitudinal analyses. *Journal of Consulting and Clinical Psychology, 60,* 64–72.

Weisz, J. R., Walter, B. R., Weiss, B., Fernandez, G. A., & Mikow, V. A. (1990). Arrests among emotionally disturbed violent and assaultive individuals following minimal versus lengthy intervention through North Carolina's Willie M. Program. *Journal of Consulting and Clinical Psychology, 58,* 720–728.

Whittaker, J. K., Schinke, S. P., & Gilchrist, L. D. (1986). The ecological paradigm in child, youth, and family services: Implications for policy and practice. *Social Service Review, 60,* 483–503.

Willems, E. (1977). Behavioral ecology. In D. Stokols (Ed.), *Perspectives on environment and behavior* (pp. 39–68). New York: Plenum.

Zigler, E., Taussig, C., & Black, K. (1992). Early childhood intervention: A promising preventative for juvenile delinquency. *American Psychologist, 47,* 997–1006.

VI

CONCLUSION

10

Integrated Application of Applied Ecological Psychology in Schools Within Communities

William E. Martin, Jr.
Northern Arizona University
Jody L. Swartz
Northern Arizona University
University of Wisconsin–Superior

The process of fully understanding or changing a person's behavior involves many interacting influences. Applied ecological psychology attempts to account for these complex, person–environment outcomes. Consequently, there has been a sustained interest in ecological psychology within several social sciences for nearly a century. However, the question remains, has applied ecological psychology contributed in significant ways to improve children's lives within schools and communities?

Certainly, the applied ecological psychology orientation is intimately embedded within the kindred fields of community psychology, person–environment psychology, and, to a more distant extent, with environmental psychology.[1] Of these, community psychologists, perhaps, have come the closest to systematically delineating a consistent philosophy and methodology that embodies the applied ecological psychology approach. However, there has been progress in applying ecological psychology approaches in education, especially from the assiduous efforts of leaders like Apter (1977, 1982), Bronfenbrenner (1979, 1986, 1995), Hobbs (1966, 1975, 1982), Moos (1976, 1987), Rhodes (1967), Trickett (1976, 1978, 1984, 1986, 1991; Trickett, Kelly, & Vincent, 1985; Trickett & Schmid, 1993), and Fine (1985,

---

[1]Parenthetically, one might even argue that only community psychology has met the requirements of a real psychological specialty using criteria such as those promulgated by Robert I. Watson (cited in Benjamin, 1992): (a) societies to foster scholarly interchange (APA Division 27—Society for Community Research and Action: Division of Community Psychology), (b) a journal in which to publish the research (*American Journal of Community Psychology*), and (c) a graduate program for training.

1990, 1995). Nevertheless, there continues to be a great need to validate the effectiveness of applied ecological psychology paradigms that positively impact children in schools within communities.

The complexities associated with understanding child–school–community interactions over time can be so overwhelming that it becomes easier to faithfully acknowledge them while at the same time kindly ignoring them, only to proceed to focus on more unidimensional explanations of child behavior. Generally, school professionals often perceive ecological psychology assessment and intervention approaches as having substantial face validity with limited user-friendly practical application. Nevertheless, we cannot escape the reality that a child's behavior is a function of intricate interactions between the child's personal characteristics and various environmental influences. Moreover, Shaftel and Fine (chapter 5, this volume) emphasized that having an awareness of systems (micro, meso, exo, and macro) "and their interplay helps in conceptualizing the issues and possible interventions by avoiding the self-limiting viewpoint of a single problem source" (p. 96). Furthermore, Trickett (chapter 7, this volume) highlighted "the importance of seeing the school as embedded in a variety of other relations with external settings and communities relevant to the educational and socialization goals of the school" (p. 140).

Despite the ostensibly overwhelming complexities of the educational ecosystem on student behavior and the team-based effort necessary to develop and implement ecological assessment and intervention strategies, the preceding chapters demonstrated that applied ecological psychology approaches can be sensibly used by school professionals to implement systemic assessments and interventions. As a review, we highlight several of the authors' approaches organized according to the student, the classroom, the school, the community, and transitions, as well as provide concluding comments.

THE STUDENT

It is a given that to understand problem behavior, one must first gain information on the individual. Specifically, behavior does not exist in isolation from the individual. From an ecological perspective, individual factors extend beyond those of a biophysical and intrapersonal origin to encompass a vast array of characteristics from familial, social, and educational contexts. To this end, ecological assessment and intervention necessarily incorporate these individual factors into the problem conceptualization and development of treatment strategies. Gaddis and

Hatfield (chapter 2, this volume) identified the following factors affecting student behavior that should be considered when assessing student problem behavior: physiological factors (e.g., vision, hearing, pharmaceutical interventions, medical conditions), physical aspects of environment (e.g., classroom spatial density, seating arrangement, classroom lighting, noise), child temperament and goodness of fit, and influence of significant others in the environment (e.g., peers, teachers, aides, administrators).

In their discussion, the authors delineated a method and suggested instruments for conducting an assessment of these ecosystem factors. To further explicate the assessment process, the authors presented a case study that included a review of records, teacher and parent interviews, observational data, and rating scales that lead to the generation of hypotheses about factors contributing to problem behavior.

Whereas Gaddis and Hatfield presented an ecological assessment model for students with problem behavior, Conoley and Rotto (chapter 3, this volume) reviewed the elements of and considerations in planning ecological interventions. According to Conoley and Rotto, when considering that there are three possible avenues for change (i.e., change the student, the environment, or the expectations and demands placed on the student by others in the environment), we must remember that students are embedded within systems that may hold expectations beyond the present capabilities of the individual. Consequently, the problem is neither purely located within the individual or the environment, but is at a point between the two.

For students with serious behavioral problems, the importance of intervening at the systems level must be underscored. For example, Schoenwald, Henggeler, Brondino, and Donkervoet (chapter 9, this volume) provided a cogent discussion and case example of an efficacy-based intervention paradigm for youth exhibiting serious antisocial behavior. The authors reviewed the consistent empirical evidence for the multifaceted, multidetermined, and interrelated factors that serve to increase serious antisocial behavior and delinquency. As such, it would seem only logical that programs across the nation would use intervention strategies that follow these findings. However, this is not so according to the authors: "the focus of most treatments of delinquency have targeted limited segments of the youth's ecology" (p. 191).

Schoenwald et al. identified convergent evidence, through causal modeling and longitudinal studies, as to the interrelatedness of family, peer, school, and community factors in understanding serious antisocial behavior in youth. Specifically, they described the following six salient systemic areas that provide the foci for ecological assessments and interventions:

1. Characteristics of individual family members.
2. Family relations (e.g., low affection, high conflict).
3. Parenting practices (e.g., harsh or inconsistent discipline, poor monitoring).
4. Peer relations (e.g., association with deviant peers).
5. School functioning (e.g., low family–school bonding, poor performance).
6. Neighborhood functioning (e.g., disorganization, transience, criminal subculture).

According to the authors, these six areas provide the direction and basis for Multisystemic Therapy (MST), a socioecological and family systems intervention model. MST is an intensive, time-limited, home- and family-focused treatment approach that incorporates assessments of and interventions within problem situations at multiple systems levels. Although the primary emphasis is on the family system, school and community contexts are targeted when necessary. Certainly of all ecologically oriented treatment approaches, MST has the most solid empirical basis. The authors cited its effectiveness with chronic and violent juvenile offenders and their families (including various ethnocultural backgrounds); substance dependent youth; gang-affiliated juvenile offenders; youth exhibiting homicidal, suicidal, and psychotic behavior; and sex offenders.

THE CLASSROOM

In the same way that individual factors may be the target of assessment and intervention, we must remember that behavioral problems result from a discordance in the system, a point between the individual and the environment. For school-aged youth, further understanding of this discordance requires, first, careful examination of the classroom environment and, subsequently, collaboration with key individuals in the setting in devising and implementing interventions. McLellan and Sanchez (chapter 4, this volume) discussed six ecological assessment components on which teachers can focus for students within a classroom: child context, acculturation, home and school environment, temperament issues, academic achievement, and learning capacity.

According to the authors, strategies to assess these six areas include a developmental history, a cultural and contextual guide process, psychometric inventories, curriculum-based assessment, portfolio assessment, and dynamic assessment. In addition to discussion of assessment targets and associated strategies, McLellan and Sanchez provided a case study, which exemplifies their suggested approach to ecological assessment.

It is clear that ecological assessment requires a large amount of data and, correspondingly, a significant amount of effort for those involved in problem identification and intervention development. As such, Shaftel and Fine (chapter 5, this volume) suggested that effecting positive change in the classroom setting may require collaboration with other school or mental health personnel to assist the classroom teacher in both the assessment and intervention of learning and behavior problems. Accordingly, they proposed that, to achieve successful outcomes in collaborative consultation, both the teacher and the consultant must work together to identify the problem, analyze the problem, implement the plan, and evaluate the effect of the intervention on the targeted learning or behavior concern. In this model, Shaftel and Fine specified the following classroom factors to consider in an ecosystemic intervention: (a) factors that the teacher brings to the classroom, (b) factors that the child brings to the classroom, (c) physical organization of the classroom, (d) teacher management style, (e) curriculum and instructional materials, (f) use of auxiliary personnel, and (g) family–school factors.

According to Shaftel and Fine, assessment of these factors involves using multiple data sources that focus on the interactions between the student and the environment. Additionally, there is a recognition that behavior is situation specific and individual students have unique needs. Furthermore, Shaftel and Fine emphasized that ecological assessment is a dynamic process involving many techniques including checklists and rating scales; observational techniques; interviews; and obtaining information from student records, permanent products, and tests.

THE SCHOOL

Both the student and the classroom are embedded within the larger structure of the school, which directly and indirectly affects the individual's functioning. Conoley and Rotto (chapter 3, this volume) suggested that within the school context, there are four agents or targets of change that are integral to an ecological psychology intervention: the child, parent, teacher, and setting. Within this, they proposed that changes can occur along the following dimensions: setting/environment, skills/strategies, relationships, and instruction. These changes can occur by using academic, socioemotional, behavioral, and resource strategies.

Many possibilities for ecosystem assessments and interventions emerge from Conoley and Rotto's student system framework, but as the authors point out, "It is not hard to think of interventions, but it is hard to get others to cooperate" (p. 71, this volume). This rightly emphasizes the operational necessity for coordinated teams to implement effective ecological psychology strategies. Conoley and Rotto maintained that functions optimizing the effectiveness of team approaches include sharing information, identifying strengths and problems, engaging in group problem solving, using consensus decision making, giving and receiving feedback, and careful planning that includes specification of individual responsibilities and clearly defined evaluation criteria. Moreover, they proposed that team members must be sensitive to each other's unique goals or criteria for success and may need to adjust their behavior rather than solely focusing on changing the behavior of the child.

THE COMMUNITY

Whether the problem occurs with a particular student or a group of students, knowledge of the community can provide more comprehensive and salient information for use in assessment and intervention. According to Conoley and Rotto, when working with primarily the individual student, the importance of the community is not negated. Indeed, Conoley and Rotto posited that the following community elements are central to developing a comprehensive ecomap of the student system:

- School.
- Current family.
- Legal/judicial.
- Sports.
- Mental health treatment.
- Neighborhood.
- Medical history.
- Church group.
- Social services.
- Peer group.
- Extended family.
- Media.
- Absent family.

The authors suggested that these important student systems can be used to create an ecomap that can guide critical aspects of intervention planning.

In a similar vein, Moan and Mellott (chapter 6, this volume) went beyond the individual to examine the school context in their articulation of an organizational hierarchy in which schools, microsystems, and macrosystems interact to respond to school- and community-wide youth problems. In their hierarchy, microsystems are comprised of students, teachers, support staff, and administrators, while such establishments as the legal system, church, business, education, and government embody the macrosystem level.

Moan and Mellott outlined the following steps to conduct an ecological assessment and intervention that takes into consideration the potent reciprocal and continuous influence of the macrosystem–school–microsystem relationship:

1. Identify the problem to be examined.
2. Review the current literature on the topic.
3. Develop an assessment procedure based on information from the literature.
4. Have knowledgeable persons review the procedure and provide additional input.
5. Identify key informants and others who will be assessed.
6. Conduct the assessment.
7. Analyze the results and compare these to the literature.
8. Develop interventions based on the needs identified in the assessment.
9. Have knowledgeable persons review the proposed interventions and provide input.
10. Implement the intervention.
11. Evaluate the impact of the intervention on the identified problem.
12. Re-assess and plan further interventions as needed.

As is often the case, certain behavior problems can seem pandemic. Remediation and prevention of such school- and community wide problems necessarily requires effort from all involved systems. Similar to Moan and Mellott, Trickett (chapter 7, this volume) emphasized the need to engender a sense of collaboration between schools and communities. In doing this, he articulated four ecological processes that provide a framework to conceptualize the ecological context of behavior that is also applied to school–community collaborations:

- Adaptation—behavior within a coping and adaptation framework.
- Cycling of resources—how resources are defined, distributed, and nurtured.

- The principle of interdependence—interconnections among differing components of the community and their implications for schools.
- The succession principle—communities evolve and change over time (e.g., assumptions, processes, and interventions).

Trickett provided an impassioned discussion of parent involvement in schools as fertile examples of empowerment and ecology in school–community collaborations. In this, Trickett emphasized the importance of not only understanding the community as an ecological context through environmental assessment, but also attending to process in the development of optimal school–community collaborations. According to Trickett, such examples of cases where the spirit and structure of ecological assessment and intervention are evident can be found in the Comer School Development Program and the *Comite de Padres Latinos*.

TRANSITIONS

The importance of the school–community partnership is certainly evident when considering that ecological assessment and intervention extend beyond a focus on problem behavior to encompass preventative strategies involved in planning for transitions such as those from school to work. Ideally, schools are proactive in providing students with the skills necessary to plan for and implement satisfying career paths (Szymanski, chapter 8, this volume).

In her discussion of the school to work transition, Szymanski advanced a theoretical framework of five types of factors affecting the career development and transition process.

Individual factors are defined as traits and attributes and include physical and mental abilities, gender and race, interests, and aspects of disabilities that are individual traits such as physical or mental limitations.

Context factors are external aspects of individuals' situations and include socioeconomic status, opportunity structures, family, education, non-normative influences, and relevant legislation.

Mediating factors can be individual (e.g., work personality, self-efficacy, outcome expectations, acculturation, and racial identity) or social (e.g., discrimination, stereotypes, and castification).

Work environment factors include task requirements and reinforcement systems, worker characteristics, modal work environments and organizational culture, and physical characteristics of the work environment.

Outcome factors involve work satisfaction, work satisfactoriness, correspondence, organizational productivity, and job stress and strain.

Szymanski's five-factor ecological model of career development provides a useful guiding structure for collecting information and generating hypotheses while at the same time connecting assessment and intervention.

CONCLUSION

Philosophically, ecological psychology is grounded in a blend of two potent influences. Foremost, it is driven by impassioned ideals associated with social change while waist deep in struggle between the phenomenological and objective world of trying to understand the behavior of people interacting with environments. This blend of social activism and objective reality in contexts has generated many interesting philosophical and methodological dialogues among interventionists (see Tolan, Keys, Chertok, & Jason, 1990a). Unfortunately, the popular position that ecological psychology approaches are subjective (relativistic) versus objective (logical), constructivistic versus scientific, or qualitative versus quantitative have polarized and possibly even delayed the growth of the field. For example, reflecting a contextual and constructive stance, Tolan, Keys, Chertok, and Jason (1990b) stated, "The value of research knowledge, then, is its descriptive richness, explanatory utility, and conceptual robustness, rather than its situational independence, ability to prove a general fact, and generalizability of results" (p. 7). Although divergent views, such as this, have yielded positive effects of stimulating philosophical depth and innovative research methodology in ecological psychology, it is clear that, for ecological psychology as a field not to stagnate, continued evolution in areas of research and practice is imperative. We believe that the field needs to move forward to advocate for more inclusion of diverse and integrated paradigms. Moreover, we can seek, as research goals, both descriptive richness and generalizability of results. The work of Henggeler and his colleagues (e.g., Henggeler, 1991; Henggeler & Borduin, 1990; Henggeler, Melton, Smith, Schoenwald, & Hanley, 1993; Henggeler, Schoenwald, & Pickrel, 1995) exemplifies the effective integration of scientific and contextual/constructivistic methodology. They convincingly combined the use of clinical field trials, which include assessments, with interventions in the natural contexts of children (Follette, 1993). In a different but comparably integrative fashion, Trickett and his colleagues (Kelly, 1979, 1986; Kelly, Azelton, Burzette, & Mock, 1993; Trickett, McConahay, Phillips, & Ginter, 1985; Trickett, Kelly, & Todd, 1972; Trickett, Kelly, & Vincent, 1985; Trickett &

Schmid, 1993) endeavored to reflect the descriptive richness of educational ecosystems through use of case studies and research efforts that capitalize on the resources inherent in local ecologies and emphasize the benefits of collaborative efforts toward change.

As illustrated in Henggeler's and Trickett's contrasting applied ecological psychology approaches, we need to promote diverse and integrative paradigms that will enable the field to progress and assist educational ecosystems in optimizing their impact on those who move through their systems. At the same time, we need to sustain our passion for improving the lives of children as they interact with their environments. In essence, the school is far more than simply a source of academic information; for individuals, families, and communities, the school has the potential to serve as an organizing force in successful and ultimately worthwhile collaborations that capitalize on the embeddedness of these systems within the larger context of the macrosystem. It is hoped, then, that the previous chapters both provided the reader with a greater functional understanding of applied ecological psychology as well as suggested directions for further knowledge acquisition.

REFERENCES

Apter, S. J. (1977). Applications of ecological theory: Toward a community special education model for troubled children. *Exceptional Children, 43*, 366–373.

Apter, S. J. (1982). *Troubled children/Troubled systems.* New York: Pergamon Press.

Benjamin, L. T., Jr. (1992). Introduction to the special issue. *American Psychologist, 47*, 109.

Bronfenbrenner, U. (1979). *The ecology of human development.* Cambridge, MA: Harvard University Press.

Bronfenbrenner, U. (1986). Ecology of the family as a context for human development: Research perspectives. *Developmental Psychology, 22*, 723–742.

Bronfenbrenner, U. (1995). Developmental ecology through space and time: A future perspective. In P. Moen, G. H. Elder, Jr., & K. Luscher (Eds.), *Examining lives in context* (pp. 619–647). Washington, DC: American Psychological Association.

Fine, M. J. (1985). Intervention from systems ecological perspective. *Professional Psychology: Research and Practice, 16*, 262–270.

Fine, M. J. (1990). Facilitating home–school relationships: A family-oriented approach to collaborative consultation. *Journal of Educational and Psychological Consultation, 1*, 169–187.

Fine, M. J. (1995). Family–school intervention. In R. H. Mikesell, D.-D. Lusterman, & S. H. McDaniel (Eds.), *Integrating family therapy. Handbook of family psychology and systems theory* (pp. 481–495). Washington, DC: American Psychological Association.

Follette, V. (1993). An ecological approach to treatment. *The Scientist Practitioner, 3*(1), 10–17.

Henggeler, S. W. (1991). Multidimensional causal models of delinquent behavior. In R. Cohen & A. Siegel (Eds.), *Context and development* (pp. 211 – 231). Hillsdale, NJ: Lawrence Erlbaum Associates.

Henggeler, S. W., & Borduin, C. M. (1990). *Family therapy and beyond: A multisystemic approach to treating the behavior problems of children and adolescents.* Pacific Grove, CA: Brooks/Cole.

Henggeler, S. W., Melton, G. B., Smith, L. A., Schoenwald, S. K., & Hanley, J. (1993). Family preservation using multisystemic therapy: Long-term follow-up to a clinical trial with serious juvenile offenders. *Journal of Child and Family Studies, 2*, 283–293.

Henggeler, S. W., Schoenwald, S. K., & Pickrel, S. G. (1995). Multisystemic therapy: Bridging the gap between university- and community-based treatment. *Journal of Consulting and Clinical Psychology, 63,* 709–717.

Hobbs, N. (1966). Helping disturbed children: Psychological and ecological strategies. *American Psychologist, 21,* 1105–1115.

Hobbs, N. (1975). *The futures of children.* San Francisco: Jossey-Bass.

Hobbs, N. (1982). *The troubled and troubling child.* San Francisco: Jossey-Bass.

Kelly, J. G. (1979). 'Tain't what you do, it's the way you do it. *American Journal of Community Psychology, 7,* 239–413.

Kelly, J. G. (1986). Content and process: An ecological view of the interdependence of practice and research. *American Journal of Community Psychology, 14,* 581–589.

Kelly, J. G., Azelton, L. S., Burzette, R. G., & Mock, L. O. (1993). Creating social settings for diversity: An ecological thesis. In E. J. Trickett, R. J. Watts, & D. Birman (Eds.), *Human diversity: Perspectives on people in context* (pp. 424–451). San Francisco: Jossey-Bass.

Moos, R. H. (1976). *The human context: Environmental determinants of human behavior.* New York: Wiley.

Moos, R. H. (1987). Person–environment congruence, in work, school, and health care settings. *Journal of Vocational Behavior, 31,* 222–230.

Rhodes, W. C. (1967). The disturbing child: A problem of ecological management. *Exceptional Children, 33,* 449–455.

Tolan, P., Keys, C., Chertok, F., & Jason, L. (1990a). *Researching community psychology: Issues of theory and methods.* Washington, DC: American Psychological Association.

Tolan, P., Keys, C., Chertok, F., & Jason, L. (1990b). Conversing about theories, methods, and community research. In P. Tolan, C. Keys, F. Chertok, & L. Jason (Eds.), *Researching community psychology: Issues of theory and methods.* Washington, DC: American Psychological Association.

Trickett, E. J. (1976). The community survey on educational options. In B. Burgess (Ed.), *Facts and figures: A layman's guide to conducting surveys* (pp. 123–132). Boston, MA: Institute for Responsive Education.

Trickett, E. J. (1978). Towards a social-ecological conception of adolescent socialization: Normative data on contrasting types of public schools. *Child Development, 49,* 408–414.

Trickett, E. J. (1984). Towards a distinctive community psychology: An ecological metaphor for training and the conduct of research. *American Journal of Community Psychology, 12,* 261–279.

Trickett, E. J. (1986). Consultation as a preventive intervention: Comments on ecologically based case studies. *Prevention in Human Services, 4*(3–4), 187–204.

Trickett, E. J. (1991). *Living an idea: Empowerment and the evolution of an inner city alternative high school.* Cambridge, MA: Brookline Books.

Trickett, E. J., Kelly, J. G., & Todd, D. M. (1972). The social environment of the high school: Guidelines for individual change and organizational development. In S. Golann & C. Eisdorfer (Eds.), *Handbook of community mental health* (pp. 331–406). New York: Appleton-Century-Crofts.

Trickett, E. J., Kelly, J. G., & Vincent, T. A. (1985). The spirit of ecological inquiry in community research. In E. Susskind & D. Klein (Eds.), *Community research: Methods, paradigms, and applications* (pp. 283–333). New York: Praeger.

Trickett, E. J., McConahay, J. B., Phillips, D., & Ginter, M. A. (1985). Natural experiments and the educational context: The environment and effects of an inner-city alternative public high school on students. *American Journal of Community Psychology, 13,* 617–643.

Trickett, E. J., & Schmid, K. D. (1993). The school as a social context. In P. H. Tolan & B. J. Cohler (Eds.), *Handbook of clinical research and practice with adolescents* (pp. 173–202). New York: Wiley.

Future Directions: Specification, Validation, and Funding of Ecologically Based Interventions for Schools Within Communities

Scott W. Henggeler
Medical University of South Carolina

This afterword is written from the perspective of a health services researcher who develops and evaluates family- and community-based mental health services for youths who are truly at imminent risk of out-of-home placement and their multineed families. Clarification of this perspective is important because each of the authors in this volume probably has more experience *working* directly in school ecologies and greater knowledge of the corresponding literature than I have. I bring to the task, however, experience addressing the mental health needs of children and attempting to impact policy regarding how these needs are met by local, state, and federal service systems. Regarding clinical needs, schools are absolutely critical toward meeting long-term treatment goals of youths who are presenting grave emotional disturbance, drug abuse, or serious antisocial behavior. Schools provide opportunities to develop relationships with prosocial peers and the educational foundation that will largely determine the youth's future economic viability. Unfortunately, a primary goal of many of the schools that work with children with serious problems is to exclude them from school or to segregate them with other problem children. At the level of service systems, all system of care reforms view the school as a critical player at the table. Unfortunately, school decision makers rarely seem to come to the table and, when they do come, are often slow to accept responsibility for collaborating with other public entities that serve children and families. For example, I once attended a meeting of state commissioners of mental health, juvenile justice, and social welfare, or their representatives, convened to address the problem of school truancy. The department of education sent a mid-level manager who began the meeting by declaring, "If you want to do something about it, that's fine, but truancy is not the school's problem." My

221

recommendations for future research directions address issues of school insularity and lack of accountability.

THE FAMILY–SCHOOL MESOSYSTEM

Strategies for engaging families as collaborators in their children's education should be specified, replicated, and validated. Even among researchers who are conducting school-based intervention projects and among several authors of this volume, families are too readily dismissed as nonessential or uncooperative. As my colleague Dr. Phillippe Cunningham questions teachers and administrators who bemoan the lack of school involvement among parents of poor children, "What are the barriers that prevent parents from coming to school meetings?" The teachers and administrators answer, "conflicting work schedules, lack of transportation, no child care, anxiety." Dr. Cunningham next asks, "What do you do to try to get parents to come?" The teachers and administrators answer, "We send reminders home and have cookies at the meeting." Dr. Cunningham then asks, "How do your solutions address the parents' barriers?" Thus, there are good reasons why schools have had considerable difficulty engaging economically disadvantaged parents and parents of youths presenting serious problems as collaborators in the quest to achieve important social and educational outcomes. As described in this volume (e.g., Shaftel & Fine, p.103; Trickett, pp. 146, 155–160), however, several strategies and models have been used successfully to engage parents. These and other promising strategies should be fully specified and their effectiveness should be validated.

ECOLOGICAL INTERVENTIONS

In the final chapter of this volume, Drs. Martin and Swartz noted that ecological models have "substantial face validity with limited user-friendly practical application" (p. 210). In other words, the specification of ecological interventions is greatly lacking. This lack of specification pertains not only to ecological interventions conducted within school, but to broadly disseminated ecological models such as "Wraparound" as well. In the absence of strong specification, the valid replication of effective ecological intervention models will be near impossible. Moreover, as we continue to learn in our dissemination research with multisystemic therapy, substantive quality assurance measures must be integrated into treatment protocols and ongoing supervisory and consultative feedback is required to maintain the integrity of ecologically oriented interventions. The field cannot progress until promising models of intervention are delineated, validated, and cross validated. Moreover, I believe that the specific treatment strategies used in these models should not be eclectic. Eclecticism promotes the continued use of treatment strategies for children that have no empirical support, are more convenient for the practitioner than useful for the client, and, in fact, may do more harm than good. Rather, the treatment approaches used in ecological interventions should be those that have received at least some support in the research literature.

SCHOOLS WITHIN COMMUNITIES

Contrary to some prevailing opinions, resources that serve the mental health and preventive needs of children and adolescents are not lacking. Throughout the mental health, juvenile justice, and social welfare systems, astronomical amounts of fiscal resources are being spent on the mental health needs of children. Unfortunately, the vast majority of the funding is devoted to out-of-home placements that are expensive and have no demonstrated effectiveness (e.g., residential treatment, group homes, incarceration, hospitalization). The children in these placements have at least two commonalties: They would benefit from living in a supportive family context and from receiving a good education.

The current sad state of mental health services for children provides great opportunities for applying ecological psychology for schools within communities. As Drs. Martin and Swartz note in their concluding paragraph, "the school has the potential to serve as an organizing force in successful and ultimately worthwhile collaborations that capitalize on the embeddedness of these systems within the larger context of the macrosystem." Specifically, for example, schools can collaborate with child-serving agencies to bring children (and the funding linked with the children) home. As a major player at the table of system reform, schools can negotiate for the inclusion of secondary preventive and primary preventive school-based services in return for facilitating the reintegration of "deep-end" youths into academic environments. Successful reintegration of children from out-of-home placements provides considerable cost savings, and those savings can be redistributed to the types of effective programs (e.g., certain prevention programs) that are usually underfunded. Although this may seem a farfetched idea, numerous system reform efforts have demonstrated the viability of reintegration (e.g., Alaska Youth initiative, Annie E. Casey Foundation projects), and our research center is currently embarking on related projects in two states.

Author Index

A

Abril, S., 56, *72*, 125, *136*
Achenbach, T. M., 124, *134*
Adams, R. S., 33, *51*
Adelman, H. S., 141, 159, *160*
Ageton, S. S., 188, 189, *203*
Aguirre-Deandreis, A. I., 66, *71*
Algozzine, B., 31, 32, 35, 37, 42, *51*
Allen-Meares, P., 56, *71*
Anastasiow, N.J., 176, *182*
Anderson, C., 105, *112*
Anderson, G. L., 130, *134*
Anderson, T. E., 107, 109, 110, *114*
Anson, A. R., 157, 158, *160*
Apple, M. W., 167, 168, 175, *182*
Apter, S. J., 16, *23*, 55, 57, *71*, 98, 99, *112*, 118, *134*, 209, *218*
Arana, G. W., 188, *205*
Arbona, C., 171, *182*
Argyris, C., 142, *160*
Arreaga-Mayer, C., 126, *135*
Arthur, M. A., 188, 191, *204*
Ary, D. V., 189, *203*
Ascher, C., 131, *134*, 157, *160*
Atwater, J. B., 126, *134*
Augustyn, K., 18, *25*
Ausubel, D., 82, *93*
Axelrod, S., 33, *51*
Azar, B., 21, *23*
Azelton, L. S., 153, *161*, 217, *219*

B

Baer, D. W., 4, *23*
Balow, B., 31, 37, *53*
Bandura, A., 22, *23*, 79, 83, *93*, 171, *182*
Bangart-Drowns, R., 132, *134*

Bank, L., 191, *203*
Baranowski, T., 147, *162*
Barclay, J. R., 33, *51*
Barker, R. G., ix, *xi*, 6, 8, 9, 11, *23*, 55, 68, *71*, 118, 126, *134*, 140, 143, *160*
Barone, C., 66, 69, *71*
Barrett, D. M., 18, *23*
Bartlett, C. J., 10, *26*
Bates, J. E., 59, *71*
Bateson, G., 118, *134*
Bauer, A. M., 107, *113*
Beauvais, F., 129, *135*, 189, *205*
Bechtel, R. B., 120, *134*
Behrens, J. T., 171, *184*
Bell, K., 66, *71*
Belsky, J., 84, *93*, 188, *203*
Benedict, R., 97, *112*
Benjamin, L. T., 209, *218*
Bennett, D. S., 59, *71*
Berg, R. L., 122, *134*
Bergan, J. R., 108, *112*
Bernal, M. E., 83, *93*
Betz, N. E., 6, 8, *26*, 169, 170, 171, 175, 176, 177, *182*
Biddle, B. J., 33, *51*
Biglan, A., 189, *203*
Bijou, S. W., 4, *23*
Billig, S. H., 117, *136*
Billman, J., 33, *51*
Birch, H., 33, *53*, 55, *73*
Birman, D., 141, 145, 154, *160*, *162*
Black, J. B., 82, *94*
Black, K., 187, *205*
Blair, M., 66, *71*
Blaske, D. M., 192, *203*
Blustein, D. L., 174, *182*
Bobo, J. K., 129, *134*
Borduin, C. M., 9, *24*, 188, 191, 192, 193, 194, 198, *203*, *204*, 217, *218*
Boyd, W. L., 139, 155, *161*

225

Boyer, E. L., 68, *71*
Braaten, S. L., 18, *26*, 70, *73*, 104, *114*
Brady, M. P., 18, *25*
Brantlinger, E., 139, 157, *160*
Braswell, L., 195, *204*
Brody, G. H., 35, *51*
Brondino, M. J., 191, 192, 202, *204*, *205*
Bronfenbrenner, U., 3, 9, 11, 12, 13, 21, *23*, 77, 78, 79, *93*, 96, 111, *112*, *113*, 118, *134*, 140, *160*, 169, 170, 171, *182*, 192, 193, *203*, 209, *218*
Brook, J. S., 189, *203*
Brophy, J. E., 35, *51*, 68, *71*
Brown, A. L., 88, *93*
Brown, D., 169, 175, *182*, *183*
Brown, S. D., 174, *183*
Brunk, M., 192, *203*
Bryan, T. H., 35, *51*
Bryant, C., 70, *72*
Bryant, L. E., 65, *72*
Bryant, S., 132, *135*
Bulgren, J. A., 17, *23*, 101, 102, 104, 105, *113*, 127, *134*
Burden, R. L., 105, *113*
Burk, E., 33, *51*
Burns, B. J., 188, *205*
Burns, G. I., 39, *51*
Burzette, R. G., 153, *161*, 217, *219*
Buysse, V., 107, *113*

C

Cabral, A. C., 174, *182*
Cahen, L. S., 68, *72*
Cairns, B., 11, *23*
Cairns, R. B., 11, *23*
Cairo, P. C., 173, *183*
Caldwell, J., 33, *53*
Campione, J. C., 88, *93*
Cannon, G. S., 106, *114*
Cantrell, C. M., 120, *134*
Cantrell, M. L., 8, 18, *23*, 28, 65, *72*
Cantrell, R. P., 8, 18, *23*, 28, 65, *72*, 120, *134*
Carey, W. B., 87, *93*
Carlson, C. E., 152, *160*
Carlson, C. I., 8, 17, 18, *23*
Carnevale, A. P., 167, *182*
Carroll, A. W., 118, 122, *134*
Carta, J. J., 91, *93*, 104, *113*, 126, *134*, *135*
Casey, A., 107, *113*
Caudill, M. H., 144, 148, *161*

Cazden, C. B., 147, *161*
Ceci, S. J., 11, *23*
Chase, W. G., 83, *93*
Chertok, F., 217, *219*
Chess, S. A., 33, 34, 40, *51*, *53*, 55, *73*, 84, *94*, 98, 99, *113*
Chi, M. T., 83, *93*
Christenson, S. L., 4, 16, 17, *24*, 32, 40, *51*, *54*, 61, 70, *73*, 87, *94*, 104, 105, 107, 111, *113*, *114*
Cintron, J., 171, *184*
Cioci, M., 157, *162*
Cleland, C., 188, *205*
Clements, B. S., 102, *113*
Cochran, M., 148, 155, 157, 159, *161*
Cohen, P., 189, *203*
Cole, M., 15, *24*
Coleman, H. L. K., 171, *183*
Comer, J. P., 59, *72*, 152, 155, 157, 158, 159, *160*, *161*, 190, *203*
Commins, N., 157, *161*
Cone, L., 192, *203*
Conger, R. E., 124, *136*
Connors, L. J., 103, *113*
Conoley, C. W., 69, 71, *72*, 120, *134*
Conoley, J. C., 4, 16, 17, *24*, 55, 56, 57, 65, 68, 69, *71*, *72*, 99, 100, 104, *113*, 118, 120, *134*
Conyers, L., 175, *182*
Cook, L., 107, *113*
Cook, T. D., 157, 158, *160*
Corbett, D., 153, *163*
Corey, G., 119, *134*
Cramer, S. H., 168, 175, *183*
Crawford, V., 145, *161*
Crowson, R. L., 139, 155, *161*
Cuellar, J., 81, *93*
Cunningham, P. B., 9, 20, *26*, *204*
Curtis, V., 107, 109, 110, *114*
Curtis. M. J., 107, 109, 110, *114*
Cvetkovich, G. T., 129, *134*

D

D'Andrea, M., 150, 157, *161*
Daniels, J. A., 71, *72*
Dauber, S. L., 141, 155, 160, *161*
Davis, R. V., 5, 14, *24*, *25*, 169, 171, 172, *182*, *183*
Dean, C., 148, 155, 157, 159, *161*
DeBaryshe, B. D., 61, *72*
Delgado-Gaitan, C., 152, 153, 158, *161*

Delquadri, J. C., 66, 72, 91, *93*, 104, *113*
DeMatta, R., 3, 17, *25*
Dempsey, V., 146, *161*
Dewey, J., 83, *93*
Diamond, K. E., 13, 21, *24*
Dishion, T. J., 189, *203*
Dishion, T. M., 189, 190, *205*
DiVesta, F. J., 82, *93*
Doris, J., 31, *53*
Drew, K. D., 33, *52*
Duhon-Sells, R. M., 150, 152, 157, *162*
Duncan, T. E., 189, *203*
Dunn, C., 18, *26*

E

Edwards, T. J., 81, *93*
Eggert, J. E., 132, *136*
Ekehammer, B., 6, *24*
Eklund, S. J., 8, 17, 18, *23*
Elder, G. H., 13, *24*
Elliott, D. S., 188, 189, *203*
Elliott, S. N., 19, *26*
Emery, R. E., 125, *134*
Emmer, E. T., 102, *113*
Enright, M. S., 169, 170, 171, 172, 174, 176, 177, *184*
Epps, S., 159, *161*
Epstein, J. L., 103, *113*, 141, 155, 159, *161*
Ettinger, J., 169, 170, 171, 172, 174, 175, 176, 177, *182*, *184*
Evans, S. S., 4, 5, 16, 17, 19, *24*, 61, *72*, 101, 102, 104, 105, *113*, 118, 120, 122, 123, 124, *134*
Evans, W. H., 4, 5, 16, 17, 19, *24*, 61, *72*, 101, 102, 104, 105, *113*, 118, 120, 122, 123, 124, *134*
Evertson, C. M., 102, *113*
Eyberg, S. M., 38, 39, *52*, *53*

F

Farber, B. A., 37, *51*
Farley, F. H., 33, *51*
Farrington, D. P., 187, *203*
Farris, K. K., 131, *135*
Felcan, J., 35, *51*
Felner, R. D., 68, *72*
Felsenthal, H., 18, 20, *24*, *134*
Feltovich, P., 83, *93*

Fernandez, G. A., 191, *205*
Fernandez, T., 81, *94*
Filby, N. N., 68, *72*
Fine, M. J., 4, 9, *24*, 64, *72*, 103, 104, 105, 108, 110, *113*, *114*, 127, *135*, 209, *218*
Fink, C. M., 18, *26*, 70, *73*, 104, *114*
Finley, B., 129, *135*
Fish, M., 84, *93*
Fisher, M. L., 37, *54*
Fitzgerald, L. F., 169, 170, 171, 175, 176, 177, *182*
Flaherty, C. E., 37, *53*
Flaxman, E., 131, *135*
Follette, V., 217, *218*
Forehand, R., 35, *51*, *52*, *53*
Forster, J. R., 130, *136*
Fouad, N. A., 169, 171, 173, *184*
Fraser, B. J., 105, *113*
Friend, M., 107, *113*
Fucci, B. R., 192, *203*
Fuhrer, U., 6, *24*
Funderburk, B. W., 39, *52*

G

Gable, R. A., 4, 5, 17, 20, *24*, 27, 104, *113*, 120, *137*
Gaddis, L. R., 33, *52*
Galambos, N., 33, *52*
Garbarino, J., 86, 92, *93*
Garcia, G. E., 147, *161*
Garcia, M., 80, *93*
George, S., 33, *52*
Gerson, R., 57, *72*
Gerton, J., 171, *183*
Gettinger, M., 66, *72*
Gibson, M. J., 153, *162*
Gilchrist, L. D., 129, *134*, 191, *205*
Giles, H., 83, *93*
Ginter, M. A., 68, *72*, 140, 141, 145, 150, *162*, 217, *219*
Gladding, S. T., 118, 119, *135*
Glaser, R., 83, *93*
Glass, G. V., 68, *72*
Goetz, E. T., 82, *94*
Gold, Y., 44, *52*
Goldenberg, H., 118, *135*
Goldenberg, I. I., 118, *135*, 151, *161*
Goldstein, A. P., 68, *72*
Good, T. L., 35, *51*, 68, *72*
Goodlad, J., 68, *72*, 139, 140, *161*

Graden, J. L., 170, *113*
Grady, M. K., 157, 158, *160*
Graham, P., 33, *52*
Graue, M. E., 152, 156, 157, *161*
Green, K., 127, *135*
Greenwood, C. R., 66, 72, 91, *93*, 104, *113*, 126, *135*
Griest, D. L., 35, *52*, *53*
Griffin, C. C., 106, *114*
Griffin, T., 130, *136*
Gruber, J., 152, *161*
Guerra, N. G., 191, *204*
Gump, P. V., 6, 8, *23*, *24*, 55, 68, *71*, 72
Gutkin, T. B., 19, *26*, 107, *113*

H

Habib, F., 157, 158, *160*
Hackett, G., 169, 171, 173, 174, *182*, *183*
Haley, J., 195, *204*
Hall, D. T., 169, 172, *183*
Hall, J. A., 192, *204*
Hall, R. V., 33, *51*, 66, 72, 91, *93*
Halpern, A., 168, *183*
Hamilton, S. F., 65, 72
Hanley, J. H., 192, *204*, *205*, 217, *218*
Hanley-Maxwell, C., 177, *184*
Hanrahan, P., 13, 21, *24*
Harootunian, B., 68, 72
Harris, L. C., 81, *93*
Harry, B., 152, 153, 157, *161*
Harth, R., 58, *73*
Haveman, R., 170, 176, *183*
Hawkins, J. D., 190, *204*
Hawks, B. K., 177, *183*
Haynes, G., 4, 16, 19, *24*, 56, 72, 99, 100, 104, *113*
Haynes, N. M., 59, 72, 152, 155, 157, 158, 159, *160*, *161*
Heider, F., 79, *93*
Hembroke, H. A., 11, *23*
Hendrickson, J. M., 4, 5, 20, *24*, *27*, 104, *113*, 120, *137*
Henek, T., 35, *51*
Henggeler, S. W., 9, 19, 20, *24*, *26*, *135*, 188, 189, 190, 191, 192, 193, 194, 198, 202, *203*, *204*, *205*, 211, 212, 217, *218*, *219*
Heron, T. E., 102, 104, *113*
Herr, E. L., 168, 175, *183*
Hershenson, D. B., 169, 170, 171, 172, 174, 176, 177, 179, *183*, *184*

Hertzig, M., 33, *53*
Hervis, O., 81, *94*
Hess, R., 141, 160, *161*
Heward, W. L., 102, 104, *113*
Hewett, F. M., 3, 5, 16, *24*, 55, 72
Higganbotham, J. C., 147, *162*
Higgins, E. T., 80, *93*
Hilton, A., 5, *24*, 58, 72, 119, 120, *135*
Hirschi, T., 190, *204*
Hobbs, N., 2, 4, 16, *24*, *25*, 55, 57, *72*, 118, 120, *135*, 209, *219*
Holbrook, J., 33, *52*
Holland, J. L., 14, *25*, 168, 169, 172, 181, *183*
Holt, P., 127, *135*
Horan, J. J., 131, *135*
Howell, K. W., 41, *52*
Hoyle, R. A., 188, *204*
Hsu, J., 119, *136*
Huizinga, D., 187, 188, 189, *203*, *204*
Hurvitz, N., 119, *135*
Hwang, C., 18, *25*

I

Iglesias, A., 82, *94*
Isaacson, L. E., 175, *183*
Isabella, R. A., 84, *93*
Ivey, A. E., 119, *135*
Ivey, D. C., 71, 72
Ivey, M. B., 119, *135*
Iwanicki, E. F., 37, 44, *52*, *53*

J

Jackson, S. E., 35, 36, 37, 43, 44, *52*, *53*
Jacobs, E., 131, *135*
Jason, L., 131, *135*, 217, *219*
Jasso, R., 81, *93*
Jensen, J. B., 107, *114*
Johnson, G., 3, 17, *25*
Johnson, J., 3, 17, *25*
Johnson, L. J., 106, 107, *113*, *114*
Johnson, M. J., 4, *25*, 118, *135*, 172, *183*
Johnson, M. W., 87, *94*
Jones, B. A., 139, 157, *161*
Jones, R. R., 124, *136*

K

Kamphaus, R. W., 41, 42, *53*

Kamps, D., 104, *113*, 126, *135*
Kantor, H. A., 167, 175, *183*
Kantor, J. R., 5, *25*
Kapes, J. T., 175, *183*
Kaser, R., 17, *25*
Kaufman, A. S., 87, *93*
Kaufman, N. L., 87, *93*
Keiper, R. W., 37, *53*
Kelly, J. G., 9, 10, *25*, *26*, 141, 143, 150, 152, 153, 160, *161*, *162*, 209, 217, *219*
Kendall, P. C., 195, *204*
Kendler, T. S., 22, *25*
Keogh, B. K., 36, *52*
Kerr, M. M., 38, *52*
Keys, C., 217, *219*
Kiernan, W. E., 177, *183*
Knackendoffel, A., 17, *23*, 101, 102, 104, 105, *113*, 127, *134*
Knight, G. P., 83, *93*
Koch, L., 175, *182*
Koffka, F., 5, *25*
Korinek, L., 35, *51*
Korn, S., 33, 40, *53*
Kornblau, B. W., 36, *52*
Kraemer, J. J., 159, *161*
Kratochwill, T. R., 108, *112*, 124, *135*
Krumboltz, J. D., 169, 170, 176, *183*
Kuhn, T. S., ix, *xi*
Kumpfer, K. L., 191, *204*
Kurtines, W. M., 79, 81, *94*
Kutsick, K. A., 107, *113*

L

LaFromboise, T., 171, *183*
LaGrange, R. L., 189, *204*
Landerholm, E., 18, *25*
Landers, M. F., 107, 109, 110, *114*
Landsman, M. J., 193, *205*
Landy, F. J., 172, 173, 175, *183*
Lane, B. A., 56, *71*
Lavee, Y., 124, *136*
Leach, M. M., 171, *184*
Leblanc, M., 190, *205*
LeCompte, W. A., 4, *25*
Ledingham, J. E., 190, *205*
Lee, S., 131, *135*
Lent, R. W., 168, 169, 171, 173, 174, *182*, *183*, *184*
Leone, P. E., 18, *26*, 69, 70, *71*, *73*, 104, *114*
Leong, F. T. L., 177, *183*

Lerner, J. V., 33, 34, *52*
Lerner, R. M., 34, *52*, 169, 170, *185*
Lewin, K., 6, 7, 9, 11, *25*, 55, 72, 118, *135*
Linehan, S. A., 18, *25*
Lipsey, M. W., 188, 191, *204*
Littlejohn, E. M., 171, 173, *184*
Locke, H. J., 125, *135*
Loeber, R., 187, *204*
Lofquist, L. H., 14, *24*, *25*, 169, 171, 172, *182*, *183*
Loretto, G., 129, *135*
Lowenthal, B., 18, 20, *25*
Luhan, C. C., 143, *161*
Luria, A. R., 80, *93*
Luster, L., 125, *135*

M

McMahon, R. J., 35, *52*, *53*
MacPherson, A., 157, *161*
Mann, B. J., 192, *203*
Marlowe, J. H., 191, *203*
Marshall, C., 122, *135*
Martin, R. P., 33, 35, 39, 40, *52*, *53*, 87, *93*
Martin, W. E. Jr., 4, *25*, 86, *94*, 118, 129, 131, 132, *135*, *136*, 172, *183*
Maslach, C., 36, 43, 44, *52*
Masse, B., 190, *205*
Masson, R., 131, *135*
Mastie, M. M., 174, 175, *183*
Matute-Bianchi, M. E., 81, *93*
McAdoo, H., 145, *161*
McCarthy, H., 175, *184*
McCarty, T. L., 151, *162*
McConahay, J. B., 140, 141, 145, 150, *162*, 217, *219*
McCubbin, H., 125, *136*
McDevitt, S. C., 33, *51*, 87, *93*
McGoldrick, M., 57, *72*
McKee, W. T., 40, *53*
McKeown, T. C., 143, 150, 152, *162*
McWhirter, A. M., 122, *136*
McWhirter, B. T., 122, *136*
McWhirter, E. H., 122, *136*
McWhirter, J. J., 122, *136*
Meisler, N., 188, *205*
Mellott, R. N., 129, 131, *135*
Melton, G. B., 192, 203, *204*, *205*, 217, *218*
Merz, M. A., 175, *182*
Metzler, C. W., 189, *203*
Mikow, V. A., 191, *205*

Milgram, G. G., 130, *136*
Miller, P. A., 126, *134*
Minuchin, S., 195, *204*
Mischel, W., 17, *25*
Mitchell, L. K., 169, 170, 176, *183*
Moan, E. R., 129, 131, *135*
Mock, L. O., 153, *161*, 217, *219*
Montagna, D., 66, *72*
Moore, D. D., 130, *136*
Moos, B. S., 18, *25*, 125, *136*
Moos, R. H., 5, 8, 9, 10, 18, 21, *25*, *26*, 67, *73*,
    125, *136*, 140, *162*, 209, *219*
Mordecai, R., 153, *163*
Moseley, M., 33, *52*
Mostwin, D., 125, 126, *136*
Muha, D., 177, *183*
Mulvey, E. P., 188, 191, *204*
Munger, R. L., 191, 192, 195, *204*
Murday, D., 8, 9, *26*
Murray, H. A., 13, *26*
Muscott, H. S., 19, *26*, 58, *72*
Myers, R. A., 173, *183*

N

Nagle, R. J., 20, *26*, 33, *52*, *53*
National Coalition of Advocates for Students,
    147, *162*
National Institute on Drug Abuse, 131, *136*
Nelson, K. E., 193, *205*
Nelson, R., 66, *71*
Nettles, S. M., 143, *162*
Newbrough, J. R., 56, *72*, 125, *136*
Nielsen, S., 122, 129, 130, *136*
Noblit, G. W., 146, *161*
Noell, J. W., 189, *203*
Nomura, C., 189, *203*
Noonan, N., 132, *135*

O

Oetting, E. R., 129, *135*, 189, *205*
Ogbu, J. U., 81, *93*, 144, 148, *162*
Olmedo, E. L., 81, *93*
Olsen, D. H., 124, 125, *136*
Olsen, R. A., 150, 152, 157, *162*
Orelove, F. P., 126, *136*
Osipow, S. H., 168, 171, 173, *183*, *184*
Osterman, P., 168, *184*

Owens, S. M., 39, *51*

P

Padula-Hall, M. A., 71, *72*
Padvic, I., 170, *184*
Paget, K. D., 20, *26*, 33, *52*, *53*
Painter, C., 131, *136*
Paisley, P. O., 129, *136*
Palmer, D. J., 82, *94*
Palmer, J. H., 129, *136*
Palmer, J. T., 175, *184*
Parker, R. M., 18, *26*, 177, *184*
Parsons, F. D., 5, *26*
Parsons, J. E., 80, *93*
Patterson, G. R., 61, *72*, 124, *136*, 189, 190, 191,
    203, *205*
Patterson, J. M., 125, *136*
Patton, M. Q., 150, 152, 157, *162*
Paul, J. L., 99, *114*
Payton, D. S., 71, *72*
Pena, E., 82, *94*
Pence, A., 192, *205*
Penner, W., 157, *162*
Perez-Vidal, A., 81, *94*
Perron, D., 190, *205*
Peterson, D. R., 42, *53*, 124, *136*
Phillips, D., 140, 141, 145, 150, *162*, 217, *219*
Phillips, S. D., 174, *184*
Phinney, J. S., 81, *94*
Pickrel, S. G., 9, 20, *24*, *26*, 192, 193, 202, *204*,
    217, *219*
Pierce, P. P., 107, *113*
Pink, W. T., 151, 155, 159, *162*
Plake, B., 80, 81, *94*
Plata, M., 157, *162*
Plionis, E., 132, *135*
Plomin, R., 84, *94*
Polirstok, S. R., 20, *26*, 63, *73*
Popham, W. J., 88, *94*
Poresky, R. H., 125, *136*
Portner, J., 124, *136*
Preston, M. A., 147, *162*
Price, R. H., 157, *162*
Prieto, A. G., 58, *73*
Primavera, J., 68, *72*
Pugach, M. C., 106, 107, *113*, *114*
Pullis, M., 33, *53*
Purkey, S. C., 68, *73*
Putnam, M. L., 21, *26*, 69, *73*, 117, 118, 123, *136*

Q

Quay, H. C., 42, *53*, 124, *136*
Quinlan, D. M., 67, *73*
Quinn, R., 82, *94*

R

Ramsey, E., 61, *72*
Rankin, R., 43, *53*, 54, 60, *73*
Reid, J. B.124, *136*, 189, 191, *203*
Reppucci, N. D., 59, *73*, 188, 191, *204*
Reschly, D. J., 35, *53*
Reskin, B., 170, *184*
Reynolds, C. R., 19, *26*, 41, 42, *53*
Rhodes, J., 131, *135*
Rhodes, W. C., 16, 19, *26*, 35, *53*, 55, 58, *73*, 99, *114*, 209, *219*
Rickard, K. M., 35, *53*
Rio, A., 81, *94*
Roberts, G., 177, *184*
Robinson, E. A., 38, *53*
Robinson, E. L., 103, 108, *114*
Rodick, J. D., 190, *205*
Rodriguez, C., 171, *184*
Rogers, T., 35, *52*
Rojewski, J. W., 167, 175, *184*
Romig, D. A., 188, *205*
Romig, J., 188, *205*
Rosenberg, M. S., 59, *73*
Ross, A. W., 38, *53*
Rossman, G. B., 122, *135*
Rothman, R. A., 169, 170, 172, *184*
Rounds, J. B., 169, 172, *184*
Rowe, W., 171, *184*
Rowland, M. D., 192, *204*
Rubin, R., 31, 37, *53*
Rubinstein, R. A., 143, 150, 152, *162*
Rusch, F. R., 177, *184*
Rutherford, B., 117, *136*
Rutter, M., 33, *52*, 68, *73*
Ryan, C., 170, 174, 175, *184*

S

Sadowsky, G. R., 80, 81, *94*
Saenz, D. S., 83, *93*
Salem, D. A., 15, *26*
Salomone, P. R., 174, *182*

Sanford, J. P., 102, *113*
Santiseben, D., 81, *94*
Santos, A. B., 188, *205*
Sarason, S. B., 31, *53*, 151, *162*
Sattler, J. M., 32, *53*, 105, *114*
Savickas, M. L., 168, *184*
Scarr, S., 34, *53*
Schalock, R. L., 177, *183*
Scheel, M. J., 71, *72*
Schein, E. H., 168, *184*
Scherer, D. G., 191, 192, *205*
Schinke, S. P., 129, *134*, 191, *205*
Schmid, K. D., 69, *71*, 141, 145, 149, 150, 160, *162*, 209, 218, *219*
Schmid, R., 6, 17, 19, *26*
Schmitz, S., 147, *162*
Schneider, B., 10, *26*
Schoenwald, S. K., 9, *24*, *26*, 191, 192, 193, 203, *204*, *205*, 217, *218*, *219*
Schoggen, P., 6, 8, *23*
Schubert, M. A., 107, 109, 110, *114*
Schulenberg, J. E., 169, 170, *185*
Schuler, R. S., 37, *53*
Schulte, A. C., 107, *113*
Schunk, D. H., 79, *94*
Schwab, R. L., 37, 44, 52, *53*
Schwartz, H. S., 126, *134*
Schwartz, J. E., 189, *205*
Schwartzman, A. E., 190, *205*
Scott, M., 8, 17, 18, *23*, 70, *73*, 126, 127, *136*
Scripts-Bower, G. H., 82, *94*
Seitz, V., 190, *205*
Selvey, C. A., 132, *136*
Shane, H., 177, *184*
Shaw, D. G., 37, *53*
Sheridan, S. M., 124, *135*
Sherman, D., 86, 92, *93*
Shinn, M. R., 87, *94*
Shores, R. E., 4, 5, *24*
Siegel, D. J., 19, *26*
Simcha-Fagan, O., 189, *205*
Simek-Morgan, L., 119, *135*
Simon, H. A., 83, *93*
Sindelar, P. T., 106, *114*
Slaby, R. G.,191, *204*
Smead, V., 5, *26*
Smith, C. L., 167, 175, *184*
Smith, G. T., 188, *204*
Smith, L. A., 192, 203, *204*, 217, *218*
Smith, M. S., 68, 72, *73*
Smith, S. W., 106, *114*
Smolkowski, K., 189, *203*

Sobsey, D., 126, *136*
Spiegel-McGill, P., 13, 21, *24*
Stein, R., 192, *203*
Steinzor, R., 33, *53*
Stern, G. G., 13, 14, *26*
Steuart, G. W., 144, 159, *162*
Stevenson, H. C., 143, 148, *162*
Stockdill, S., 150, 152, 157, *162*
Stokols, D., 192, *205*
Straus, R. A., 131, *135*
Straus, L. K., 119, *135*
Stuart, F., 125, *136*
Stuart, R. B., 125, *136*
Sue, D. W., 119, *136*
Sue, D., 119, *136*
Super, D. E., 168, 169, 171, 173, *184*
Sutter, I. 39, *53*
Svendsen, R., 130, *136*
Swap, S. M., 58, *73*, 98, 99, 100, *114*
Swartz, J. L., 4, *25*, 86, *94*, 118, *135*, 172, *183*
Szapocznik, J., 79, 81, *94*
Szymanski, E. M., 18, *26*, 167, 169, 170, 171, 172, 174, 176, 177, 179, *184*

T

Tajfel, H., 81, *94*
Tams, A., 33, *51*
Taussig, C., 187, *205*
Tavormina, J. B., 124, *135*
Taylor, K. M., 175, *184*
Taylor, L., 141, 159, *160*
Terestman, N., 33, *53*
Terry, B., 66, *72*
Terry, D., 107, *113*
Thomas, A., 33, 34, 40, *51*, *53*, 55, *73*, 84, *94*, 98, 99, *113*
Thomas, C. R., 192, *205*
Thomas, M. B., 118, *136*
Thornberry, T. P., 187, *204*
Thousand, J. S., 110, *114*
Tobler, N. S., 132, *136*
Todd, D. M., 9, 10, *26*, 141, *162*, 217, *219*
Tolan, P., 217, *219*
Tollefson, N., 127, *135*
Toro, P. A., 15, *26*
Tracey, T. J., 169, 172, *184*
Trautlein, B., 157, *162*
Tremblay, R. E., 190, *205*
Trickett, E. J., 8, 9, 10, 15, 18, *23*, *26*, 66, 67, 69, 70, *71*, *73*, 104, 105, *114*, 140, 141, 145,

149, 150, 151, 152, 153, 154, 160, *161*, *162*, 209, 217, *219*
Trimble, J. E., 129, *134*
Trueba, H. T., 171, 177, *184*
Tseng, W. S., 119, *136*
Turner, T. J., 82, *94*

U

U.S. Indian Health Service, 129, *136*
Utley, C. A., 66, *72*

V

Van Hook, M. P., 144, *163*
Vass, M., 131, *135*
Vega, L. T., 81, *93*
Victor, J., 175, *184*
Villa, R. A., 110, *114*
Vincent, T. A., 9, 10, *26*, 141, 149, *162*, *163*, 209, 217, *219*
von Bertalanffy, L., 118, *137*
Vondracek, F. W., 169, 170, 171, 173, *184*, *185*
Vygotsky, L. S., 82, *94*

W

Wade, S. E., 107, *114*
Wadsworth, J. C., 8, 9, *26*
Walker, B. A., 32, 36, 44, *53*
Walker, D., 66, *72*
Walker, H. M., 43, 44, *53*, *54*, 60, *73*
Walker, L., 56, *72*, 125, *136*
Wall, D. A., 15, *26*
Wallace, K. M., 125, *135*
Walsh, W. B., 6, 8, *26*
Walter, B. R., 191, *205*
Wandersman, A., 8, 9, *26*
Watanabe, A. K., 106, *114*
Watson, T. S., 40, *54*
Watts, R. J., 9, 10, *26*
Weaver, C. L., 177, *185*
Webb, J., 153, *163*
Webster's Ninth Dictionary, 119, *137*
Wechsler, D., 88, *94*
Weiner, B., 79, 83, *94*
Weinrott, M. R., 191, *203*
Weinstein, R. S., 68, *72*
Weis, J. G., 190, *204*

Weiss, B., 191, *205*
Weisz, J. R., 191, *205*
Welch, M., 18, 19, 26, 105, 107, *114*, 120, 124, *137*
Wells, K. C., 35, *52*, *53*
West, J. F., 106, *114*
Wheeler, R., 35, *51*
Whelan, J. P., 192, *203*
White, H. R., 189, *204*
Whiteman, 37, *54*
Whitfield, E. A., 175, *183*
Whittaker, J. K., 191, *205*
Whorton, D., 81, *93*
Wicker, A. W., 6, 8, 27, 118, *137*
Will, M., 31, *54*
Willems, E., 192, *205*
Williams, R. A., 192, *203*
Wilson, B., 153, *163*
Wilson, L., 125, *136*
Witt, J. C., 19, 26, 40, *53*, 107, *113*
Wolfe, B., 170, 176, *183*
Woodcock, R. W., 87, *94*
Worsham, M. E., 102, *113*

Wrenn, C. G., 119, *137*
Wright, H. F., 6, 8, *23*, 126, *134*, *137*

Y

Yelin, E. H., 168, *185*
Young, C. C., 20, *27*, 120, *137*
Young, J. C., 37, *54*
Young, K. R., 66, *71*
Ysseldyke, J. E., 32, 40, *51*, *54*, 61, 70, *73*, 86, 87, *94*, 105, 111, *114*

Z

Zayas, L. H., 70, *72*
Zenk, C, 167, 168, 175, *182*
Zigler, E., 187, 188, 190, *205*
Zigmond, N., 38, *52*
Zimmerman. M. A., 155, *163*
Zou, Y., 171, *184*

Subject Index

A

Acculturation, 80–82, 85, 86
  cultural inversion, 81
Adaptation, 3, 12–13, 15, 16, 19, 22, 118,
  142–144, 146, 148, 150, *see also* Person–environment
Attribution theory, 79
Attributions, 79, 82–84

B

Barker, Roger
  behavior settings, 5, 8, 9, 18, 126–127, 143
    individual factors in, 8
  ecological psychology theory, 8, 126, 140
  view of behavior, 8
Becker Adjective Checklist, 124
Behavior
  definition of, 5–6, 32, 97, 118
  differences in perception of, 32, 35
  expectations, 16–19, 21, 34, 57, 79, 80, 84,
    87, 98, 120, 122
  goal of, 143
  intersetting, 5, 63, 198
  intrasetting, 8
  value of, 97–98
Bronfenbrenner, Urie,
  person-process-context-time model, 9, 11–13
    chronosystem, 13
  theory of human ecology, 9, 11–13, 77–79,
    118, 140, 192–193, 203
    ecological systems, 11–12, 96–97, 111
      exosystem, 12, 78, 79, 96, 97, 111
      macrosystem, 12, 78–80, 96, 97, 111,
        120, 215
      mesosystem, 12, 78, 79, 96, 97, 103,
        111
      microsystem, 12, 21, 77–79, 96, 111,
        120, 215
    and ecological transitions, 11, 12, 21

C

Career development, 169–178
Causal modeling, 188, 211
Child Behavior Checklist, 124, 134
Child study team, 44
Classroom Environment Scale, 18, 104
Classrooms, *see* Ecosystems; Ecological assessment, classroom environment; Ecological intervention, classroom
Collaboration, 61–62, 95, 97, 105–111, 139–146,
  148–154, 158–160, 197–198, 213,
  215–216, *see also* Ecological intervention
  assumptions of, 141
  benefits of, 107, 190, 214
  collaborative partnerships, 66, 139, 142
    child study team, 44
    parent involvement, 154
    school–community, 139–160, 215–216
    school–home, 20, 103, 111, 139, 154, 197
    school–home–community, 117, 128–129
    teacher support teams, 95, 96, 106,
      110–111
  community norms, effects of, 143
  consultant-teacher, 106, 108–111, 198
  consultation in, 96, 107–111, 213
  culture, influence of, 143
  defined, 107
  developing a collaborative intervention style,
    141–142
  and interdependence, 152
  necessary skills, 106–107
  process in, 149–154
  and succession, 153, 154
Collaborative consultation, *see* Collaboration;
  Consultation
Collateral learning, 83
Communication, bi-directional, 78
Community psychology, 10, 13, 209
Consultation, 51, 96, 97, 100–103, 106–111,
  197

consultant's role, 96, 97, 100–103, 106–108, 112
framework, 108–109
key informants, 122, 130
process, 96, 101, 108–109
plan implementation, 108–109
problem analysis, 108
problem evaluation, 109
problem identification, 108
Counseling psychology, 13
Cross-sectional studies, 190
Cultural and Contextual Guide, 86, 212
Culture, 15–16, 77, 79–82, 86, 119, 122, 128, 129, 131, 143, 144, 146–148, 150
and communication, 147
and community norms, 143–145
cultural differences, 156–157
cultural encapsulation, 119
cultural informants, 132
values, 34, 119

D

Developmental psychology, 13
Discordance, *see* Person–environment, goodness of fit; Ecological assessment, student variables
Disturbing Behavior Checklist, 42
Drug abuse prevention, 130, 132, 135

E

Ecobehavioral analysis, 126
Ecobehavioral Assessment Systems Software, 104
Ecological assessment, 14, 17–18, 22, 32–50, 60–61, 84–89, 103–105, 117–127, 133–134, 137, 197–198, 211, 212, 214, 216
assumptions of, 17
benefits of, 17
and career development factors, 169–173
and career development outcome factors, 172
and causal modeling, 189
characteristics of, 32, 104
child variables, *see* student variables
classroom environment, 18, 61, 77–93, 101, 103–105, 111, 197, 212–213
auxiliary personnel, 102, 110–111, 213
case example, 89–92
curriculum materials, 102, 108, 213

expectations, *see* Behavior, expectations; Expectations
instructional variables, 18, 102, 108, 197, 213
measurement of
Classroom Environment Scale, 18, 104
Ecobehavioral Assessment Systems Software, 104
Instructional Environment Scale, 40–41, 87, 105
physical setting, 18, 32–33, 197, 211, 213
social climate, 83
social variables, 82–84, 197
teacher management style, 102, 197, 213
teacher variables, 98, 101–102, 197, 213, *see also* expectations
community variables, 123, 125–126, 144–148
assessment of, 86, 144–145, 149, 159
community resources, 146
history of, 148
key informants (personnel), 122, 130
neighborhood and community assessment, 86
role of settings, 146
and culture, 77, 79–82, 86, 171, 119, 122, 128, 129, 131
Cultural and Contextual Guide, 86
cultural encapsulation, 119
cultural informants, 132
values, 34, 119
difficulties in, 129
environmental assessment, 86, 141, 142, 145, 147, 216
importance of, 142
factors to consider in, 32–38
family variables, 60–61, 85, 123–127, 131, 155–156, 195–197
home environment, 85
home–school interdependence, 155, 197, 213
measurement of
Family Adaptability and Cohesion Evaluation Scales, 124
Family Environment Scale, 124–125
Family Inventory of Life Events And Changes, 125
Family Life Space Ecological Model, 125–126
Family Pre-Counseling Inventory, 125
Family Satisfaction Scale, 125
Parent Belief Survey, 125
Parental Home Assessment Index, 125
Short Marital Adjustment Test, 125
Unrevealed Differences Questionnaire–Revised, 124

parent involvement, 156
roles of parents, 156
focus of, 122, 211–212
goal of, 17, 120
methods, 18, 49, 122–124, 133
    checklists, 104, 108, 111, 124
    chronologs, 126
    curriculum-based assessment, 87–88, 212
    developmental history, 85, 212
    dynamic assessment, 88–89
    ecobehavioral analysis, 126
    ecomap, 56–57, 122, 125, 214–215
    home visits, 86
    interviews, 45–47, 85, 104–105, 108,
        111, 127
    key informants (personnel) interviews,
        122, 130
    naturalistic research, 126–127
    objective assessment, 38–44, 88, 212
    observational data, 47, 104, 108, 111
    portfolio assessment, 88, 212
    rating scales, 48, 104, 108, 111, 124
    review of records, 45, 85
    specimen records, 126
    triangulation, 122, 130
models for assessment, 18, 122–123
multi-determined nature of behavior, 188
physical characteristics of the environment,
    32
school variables, 17–18, 37, 85–86, 117,
    120–123, 132, 155, 197–198
    case example, 129–133
social environment variables, 18, 38
social variables, 18, 32–35, 38
    peers, 38
    significant others, 34–35
stages of, 31, 215
student variables, 17, 34, 38–42, 60–61, 85,
    169–170, 196–197, 210–211, 216
    academic abilities, 85, 87–89, 197
    antisocial behavior factors, 189
    beliefs, 171–172
    case example, 44–50
    context, 85, 170–171, 216
    goodness of fit, 33–34, 44, 53, 211, *see
        also* Person–environment
    intellectual assessment, 88–89
    learning capacity, 85, 88–89
    measurement of
        Child Behavior Checklist, 124, 134
        Disturbing Behavior Checklist, 42–43
        Ecobehavioral Assessment Systems
            Software, 104
        Ecological Inventory, 126
        Eyberg Child Behavior Inventory,
            38–39

Kaufman Test of Educational
    Achievement, 87
McDevitt Behavioral Style Question-
    naire, 87
Revised Behavior Problem Checklist,
    124
Student Observation System, 41–42,
    47, 48
Sutter-Eyberg Student Behavior In-
    ventory, 39–40, 53
Temperament Assessment Battery For
    Children, 40, 87
WAIS–R, 88
WISC–III, 88
Woodcock-Johnson Tests of Educa-
    tional Achievement–Re-
    vised, 87
WPPSI–R, 88
physiological factors, 32, 211
prior knowledge, 82
temperament, 33, 34, 36, 40, 44, 48–51,
    83–85, 87, 93, 211
teacher variables, 17, 33–36, 48, 98,
    101–102, 155, 197, *see also* Ex-
    pectations
burnout, 36, 37
measurement of
    Disturbing Behavior Checklist, 42–43
    Instructional Environment Scale,
        40–41, 87, 104–105
    Maslach Burnout Inventory, 43–44, 54
    Student Observation System, 41–42,
        47, 48
    Teacher Social Behavior Standards
        and Expectations (SBS),
        43
teachability, perceptions of, 36
teacher management style, 102
tolerance levels, 37, 51
Ecological intervention, 4, 10, 18–23, 99–101,
    104–112, 114, 117–120, 123, 127, 128,
    130, 133, 190–198, 211, 213, *see also* Col-
    laboration; Consultation
assumptions, 57–58, 96–101
career development, 174–178, 216
    and disabilities, 176–177
    and minorities, 176–177
    planning, 175
    and poverty, 176–177
    support services in, 177–178
characteristics of, 19
classroom, 20, 66–67, 101–103, 107–111,
    197, 213, *see also* Ecosystems,
    classroom; Collaboration; Con-
    sultation
consultant's role in, 112

first order change, 99
focus of, 99–100
framework, 108–109
method selection, 100
objectives, 99–100
outcomes, 100
second order change, 99–100
stages of, 108–110
teacher support teams, 110–111
collaboration in, 20, 95, 97, 105–111, 117,
122, 130, 132, 197, 213; *see also*
Collaboration; Consultation
the Comer School Development Program,
157–159, 216
Comite De Padres Latinos, 158–159, 216
communities
collaborative interventions, 149–154
community-based teams, 68
resource conservation, 150
resource development 150–152
consultation, *see* Consultation
dimensions of change, 62–69
ecomap, 56–57, 122, 125, 214–215
family, 62–63, 117, 122, 130, 132, 154–157,
192–199
case example, 199–202
cross-sectional studies, 190
and empowerment, 194
and family therapy, 195
and longitudinal studies, 190
Multisystemic therapy, *see* Multisystemic
therapy
parent involvement in schools, 145,
154–157
the Comer School Development Program, 157–159, 216
Comite De Padres Latinos, 158–159,
216
Cooperative Communication Between Home and School
Program, 159
Parents-as-Teachers Model, 20
PUSH for Excellence Program, 190
parent roles, 64
parenting skills, 195–196
and peers, 196
and teachers, 198
focus of, 16, 20, 211–212
goals of, 16, 19, 58, 69, 99–100, 120
inhibiting forces, 60
intervention teams, 61
levels of, 59–60, 211
planning, 14–15, 17, 59–60
use of ecomap, 56–57, 122, 125, 214–215
PUSH for Excellence Program, 190
resources in, 60–61, 145–146, 150–152

schools, 18–20, 64–65, 67–68, 128, 197–199
case example, 129–133
focus of, 119, 213
goal of, 120
hidden curriculum, 65
parent involvement in, 145–146, 154–160
the Comer School Development Program, 157–159, 216
Comite De Padres Latinos, 158–159,
216
Cooperative Communication Between Home and School
Program, 159
Parents-as-Teachers Model, 20
PUSH for Excellence Program, 190
planning, 128, 133, 214
student assistance programs, 129–133
adult mentoring, 130–132
peer helper, 131, 132
SMART program, 190
serious behavior problems, 211
student system, 57–70, 213–215
cultural considerations, 65
disabilities, 65
strategies, 62, 213
academic, 62, 213
behavioral, 62, 213
resource, 62, 213
socio-emotional, 62, 213
strengths, use of, 60
supporting forces, 60
treatment plan, 63
teachers, *see* Ecological intervention, classroom; Consultation
Ecological Inventory, 126
Ecological metaphor, *see* Kelly, James
Ecological networks, *see* Ecosystems
Ecological psychology
assumptions, 4–6, 15, 96–97, 118
behavior, definition of, 32, 210
circular causality, 118
definition of, 3, 4, 118, 211
development of, 5–15
difficulties in, 3, 14, 210
ecosystemic approach, 95–96, 103, 105, 111,
112
focus of assessment, *see* Ecological assessment
focus of intervention, *see* Ecological intervention
goal of, 4, 16, 142, 209
history, 5
importance of, 3, 5, 16
influences outside of, 13
community psychology, 10, 13
counseling psychology, 13

developmental psychology, 13
  gestalt psychology, 7, 13
  personality psychology, 13
  person–environment psychology, 5
  need for validation, 191, 209–210
  philosophical underpinnings, 4
  and school community collaboration, 140
  unifying assumption, 15
Ecological systems, *see* Ecosystems
Ecological transitions, 11, 12, 20, 21, 23, 60,
    187–190, 216–217, *see also* Bronfenbren-
    ner, Urie
  and adolescent substance abuse, 188
  assessment in, 21
  career development, 167–169
  collaboration in, 21
  cultural appropriateness, 177
  intersetting relationship, 21
  and juvenile delinquency, 187
  planning for, 21
  PUSH for excellence program, 190
  school-to-work, 167, 216–217
  and serious emotional behavior, 188
  SMART program, 190
Ecomaps, 56–57, 122, 125, 214–215
Ecosystems, 3–5, 8, 9, 11–12, 16–19, 56–57,
    96–103, 120, 121, 134, 210, *see also* Bron-
    fenbrenner, Urie
  centralized, 147
  classroom, 17, 32–53, 95, 99–105, 111,
      212–213, *see also* Ecological as-
      sessment, classroom environment
    auxiliary personnel, 102, 110–111
    curriculum, 102, 108
    instructional materials, 102, 108
    physical setting variables, *see* Environ-
        ment, actual; Ecological as-
        sessment, classroom
        environment
    social climate, 83, 140
    social variables, 82–84
  community, 117, 118, 120, 123, 127–133, 214
    climate, 143
    norms, 143–144
    processes, 143
    resources, 145–146, 150–152
    structures, 143
    values, 144, 146
  decentralized, 147
  discordance, 5, 17, 19, 56, *see also* Per-
      son–environment fit
  educational, 139–140, 210, *see also* Ecosys-
      tems, classroom
    goals of, 139
    expectations, 16–19, 21
  family, 117, 118, 120, 122–127, 130, 132 155

interdependence, 58, 142, 147, 148, 152, 190
  and juvenile delinquency, 190
  roles in, 12, 16, 21
  school, 16–22, 117, 118, 120–124, 127–133,
      155, 213–215
    organizational characteristics, 140, 215
    parent involvement, 103
    subsystems, 120–121
  social ecosystem, 38, 120, 125, 130–132
Efficacy studies, 189, 190
  and juvenile delinquency, 188, 191
  and multisystemic therapy, *see* Multisystemic
      therapy
Empowerment, 142, 154, 155, 158
Environment, *see also* Ecosystems
  actual, 5–8, 10–13, 17, 86
  behavioral, 17, *see* perceived
  geographical, *see* actual
  objective, *see* actual
  perceived, 6, 9–13, 79
  psychological, 7, 13, *see also* perceived
  social, 9, 10, 17
Environmental assessment, 141, 142, 145, 147,
    see also Ecological assessment
Environmental psychology, 209
Expectations, 16–19, 21, 34, 120, 122
  community, 34, 117, *see also* Ecological as-
      sessment, community variables
  parental, 34, 117, 120, 122, *see also* Ecologi-
      cal assessment, family variables
  school, 34, *see also* Ecological assessment,
      school variables
  social, 34
  teacher, 34, *see also* Ecological assessment,
      teacher variables
Explanatory models
  group, 6, 8–11
  individual, 6–11, 13
Eyberg Child Behavior Inventory, 38, 39
Eye of the beholder perspective, 35

F

Family Adaptability and Cohesion Evaluation
    Scales, 124
Family Environment Scale, 124–125
Family Inventory of Life Events and Changes,
    125
Family Life Space Ecological Model, 125–126
Family Pre-Counseling Inventory, 125
Family Satisfaction Scale, 125

H

Holland, John, *see* Person–environment psychology
Homeostasis, *see* Person–environment

I

Instructional Environment Scale, 40–41, 87, 104–105
Interactionist framework, 5, *see also* Person–environment
Interdependence, *see* Ecosystems, interdependence; Kelly, James, ecological metaphor

J

Juvenile delinquency, 187, 191–192

K

Kaufman Test of Educational Achievement, 87
Kelly, James
    ecological metaphor, 10, 140–142, 149, 154, 158, 215–216
        adaptation, 10, 142, 215
        cycling of resources, 10, 142–145, 216
            community resources, 146
            latent, 145–146
            resourcefulness of people, 145
        interdependence, 10, 142, 147, 148, 152, 155, 216
        succession, 10, 142, 148–149, 216
        view of behavior, 10

L

Lewin, Kurt
    ecological psychology theory, 6–8
        life space, 7
        view of behavior, 8
    gestalt psychology, 7
Local ecology, 154, 156

M

Maslach Burnout Inventory, 43, 54

McDevitt Behavioral Style Questionnaire, 87
Moos, Rudolf, *see* Social ecological perspective
Multisystemic therapy, 188–195, 197, 212
    and adolescent substance abuse, 188
    case example, 199
    and causal modeling, 189
    and empowerment, 194
    and family preservation, 193
    and family therapy, 195
    interventions, 194
    and juvenile delinquency, 187
    and longitudinal studies, 190
    and peers, 196
    reconnecting schools and families, 197
    and serious emotional behavior, 188
    and teachers, 198
    therapy model, 193
    therapy principles, 194
Murray, Henry
    need/press model, 13

N

Neighborhood and community assessment, 86
New York Longitudinal Study, 33
Norms, 79, 80

P

Parents-as-Teachers Model, 20
Parent Belief Survey, 125
Parent involvement programs, 142, 155, 157
    Comer Program, 157–159, 216
    Comite De Padres Latinos, 158–159, 216
    Cooperative Communication Between Home and School Program, 159
    Parents-as-Teachers Model, 20
Parental Home Assessment Index, 125
Personality psychology, 13
Person–environment
    adaptation, 4, 5, 9, 15, 21
    goodness of fit, 4, 5, 9, 13–16, 18, 19, 22, 33–34, 44, 53, 58, 84, 98, 118, 211
    homeostasis, 9, 15, 118, *see also* adaptation
    interaction, 3–7, 11, 13, 15–17, 19, 22, 31, 83, 98–99, 209, 210
Person–environment psychology, 5, 172, 197, 209
    Holland, John, 14
    Parsons, Frank, 5
    theory of work adjustment, 14

Person-process-context-time model, *see* Bronfen-
　　brenner, Urie
Prior knowledge, 82
　　scaffolding, 82
　　schemata, 82
　　scripts, 82
Project ASSIST, 129–136
Psychosocial adaptation, 15, 16, 22, *see also* Per-
　　son–environment, adaptation
PUSH for Excellence program, 190

R

Racism, 143–144
Resources
　　classroom, 61
　　community, 146
　　latent, 145–146
　　manifest, 145
　　parental, 60–61
　　resource conservation, 150
　　resource development 150–152
　　resourcefulness of people, 145
　　student, 60
Revised Behavior Problem Checklist, 124

S

School–community relationship, 139–160,
　　215–216, *see also* Collaboration
School–home relationship, 20, 103, 111, 139,
　　154, 197, *see also* Collaboration
School–home–community relationship, 117,
　　128–129, *see also* Collaboration
School to work, *see* Ecological transitions
School-to-Work Opportunities Act, 167
Short Marital Adjustment Test, 125
SMART program, 190
Smith Hughes Act, 167
Social-cognitive development, 80
　　adaptation in, 80
　　teacher's role in, 84
Social ecological perspective, 9–10, 140
　　assumptions, 9–10
　　perceived environment, 10
　　social environment, 9, 10
　　view of behavior, 10
Social learning theory, 79
　　person–environment interaction, 79
　　self-efficacy, 79
Student assistance programs

adult mentoring, 131, 132
　　peer helper, 131, 132
Student Observation System, 41–42, 47–48
Sutter-Eyberg Student Behavior Inventory, 39, 40
Systems ecological perspective
　　focus of, 11
　　systems theory, 96
　　view of behavior, 11

T

Teacher Social Behavior Standards and Expecta-
　　tions, 43
Teacher support teams, 95, *see also* Collaboration
Teacher training programs, 120
Temperament, 34, 83–84, 87, 93, *see also* Eco-
　　logical assessment, student variables
　　ecological psychology, relationship to, 33
　　educational correlates, 33
　　goodness of fit, 33, 34
Temperament Assessment Battery for Children,
　　40, 87
Theory of human ecology, *see* Bronfenbrenner,
　　Urie
Traditional psychology,
　　assessment, 17, 31–32, 87
　　focus of, 1, 3
　　intervention, 16, 19, 95, 211
　　goal of, 95
　　limitations of, 32, 188, 210
Transition, *see* Ecological transitions

U

Unrevealed Differences Questionnaire–Revised,
　　124

V

Vocational psychology, 170

W

WAIS–R, 88
Wingspread conference, 31
WISC–III, 88
Woodcock-Johnson Tests of Educational
　　Achievement–Revised, 87
WPPSI–R, 88

DATE DUE